D1109679

WILLIAM DUNBAR

To
MY MOTHER

WILLIAM DUNBAR

A BIOGRAPHICAL STUDY

BY

J. W. BAXTER, Ph.D.

OLIVER AND BOYD
EDINBURGH: TWEEDDALE COURT
LONDON: 98 GREAT RUSSELL STREET, W.C.

Schir, ye have mony servitouris
And officiaris of dyvers curis . . .
Quhilk pleisand ar and honorable,
And to your hienes profitable,
And richt convenient for to be
With your hie regale majestie . . .
And thocht that I, amang the laif,
Unworthy be ane place to have,
Or in thair nummer to be tald,
Als lang in mynd my wark sall hald,
Als haill in everie circumstance,
In forme, in mater, and substance,
But wering, or consumptioun,
Roust, canker, or corruptioun,
As ony of thair werkis all,
Suppois that my rewarde be small.

Remonstrance to the King

FIRST PUBLISHED . 1952

PRINTED IN SCOTLAND BY
ROBERT CUNNINGHAM AND SONS LTD., ALVA
FOR OLIVER AND BOYD LTD., EDINBURGH

PREFACE

In recent years there has been a renewed interest in the old Scots poets, not least in William Dunbar. They have again won recognition as providing a rich national heritage of poetry.

Biographical memoirs have been written by the various editors of Dunbar's works, beginning with Laing, the fullest being that by Dr. Mackay in Vol. I of the Scottish Text Society edition. These memoirs have of necessity been short and intended mainly as introductions to the poems. Several detached biographical sketches have appeared also. But nowhere has Dunbar's career been discussed and documented on a scale adequate to its complexity and to the stature of the poet. Even the study by Professor Schipper of Vienna, which appeared in 1884, was designed chiefly as a framework for his translations of Dunbar's poems into modern German.

The chief evidence is contained in the poems themselves, which abound in historical and biographical material. Accordingly I have had to consider the texts carefully. But in addition I have tried to use to the full the evidence of contemporary records. My debt to the editors, moreover, is very great, and it is indicated continually throughout the work. Especially I must pay humble tribute to the learning and sound sense of David Laing. Continual reference is made to the admirably compact and readable edition by Dr. W. Mackay Mackenzie, since it alone is readily accessible to the general reader to-day.

My thanks are due to the staffs of the National Library of Scotland, H.M. General Register House, Cambridge University Library and Glasgow University Library, for their patience and helpfulness. For aid on particular points of detail I wish to record my thanks to the following: Mr. C. T. McInnes, Curator of Historical Records, H.M. General Register House; M. Malo, Musée Condé, Chantilly; M. van Moé, Bibliothèque Nationale; M. Thomas, Paris University Library, at the Sorbonne; Rev. P. Cuthbert, Assisi; Rev. P. Francis Blackwell, Fort Augustus Abbey; and Dr. A. G. Little, of the British Society of Franciscan Studies. For encouragement and guidance at an early stage I am indebted to Mr. H. Harvey Wood, and at the final stage to Professor Alexander of the University of Glasgow and to Professor Dickins of Corpus Christi College, Cambridge.

I gratefully acknowledge the support given me, in the form of a guarantee against loss in publication, by the Carnegie Trust for the Universities of Scotland.

J. W. BAXTER

Glasgow,
1952

CONTENTS

ABBREVIATIONS

B.	Bannatyne Manuscript.
CM.	Chapman and Millar Prints.
E.R.	Exchequer Rolls.
L.	Edition of the poems by D. Laing.
M.	Edition of the poems by Dr. W. Mackay Mackenzie.
MF.	Maitland Folio Manuscript.
R.	Reidpeth Manuscript.
S.	Prof. Schipper's *William Dunbar: Sein Leben und Seine Gedichte*.
S.ed.	Edition of the poems by Prof. Schipper.
S.T.S.	Edition of the poems by J. Small for the Scottish Text Society.
T.A.	Accounts of the Lord High Treasurer of Scotland.

CHAPTER I

'OF NOBILL STRYND'

WILLIAM DUNBAR was probably a connexion of the ancient family of the earls of Dunbar and March. In *The Flyting of Dunbar and Kennedie*, Kennedy attacks Dunbar with a scurrilous account of the history of that noble house, which had been suppressed in the reign of James I.

It has been objected that the very nature of *The Flyting* rules it out as evidence, for the statements of each poet about the other are not to be taken seriously and are only extravagant abuse. According to this view, Kennedy is taking advantage of a fortuitous correspondence of surname to associate Dunbar with treason. If Dunbar had in fact been connected with the former earls of March, it is said, he would have defended them instead of remaining silent on the whole subject.

But Dunbar had no opportunity to reply, as Kennedy's account is contained in the final extant section of *The Flyting*. Moreover, if Kennedy's attack was to be effective, Dunbar's connexion with the house of Dunbar and March could not have been wholly imaginary. Unless it was sufficiently known for the attack to be recognised as appropriate, little would have been gained by Kennedy in this lengthy passage. The precision with which he states that Dunbar is not descended from either of two collateral branches of the family, is a further indication that Kennedy has some regard for the facts. His reliability, too, in the other main charges which he makes against Dunbar in the same section of the poem is confirmed elsewhere: the report of Dunbar's misadventures when his ship almost foundered, is not at variance with Dunbar's own account in the preceding section of *The Flyting*,[1] and Kennedy's tale of his rival's begging exploits in the south is confirmed by Dunbar's own reminiscences in *How Dumbar wes Desyrd to be ane Freir*.

Kennedy would not have gained much advantage by inventing a relationship between the poet Dunbar and the earls of Dunbar and

[1] Cp. lines 89-96 and 377-384.

March. The downfall of that illustrious house had been due to one of the most arbitrary of Scottish kings, who wished to obtain revenge for offences long past. However black those offences seem now, the courtiers of the fifteenth century would regard them differently. Most noble houses must at one time or another, in the acquisitive struggles of feudal politics, have found themselves at enmity with the king and in league with his enemies. Far from inventing a fictitious descent of Dunbar from a great though unfortunate family, the probability is that Kennedy was replying to Dunbar's scorn of his own 'Ersch' ancestry, expressed in the previous section of the poem, by accumulating treasonous episodes from the history of the Anglophile family with which Dunbar himself was known to be connected.

Though Dunbar nowhere refers to the earls of Dunbar and March in the poems which have survived, his poems do indicate that he was of noble origin. He complains to the King that spurious additions have been made to a poem of his

> With rycht defamows speiche off lordis,
> Quhilk with my collouris all discordis.[1]

Complaints of his own composition were generally against upstarts of obscure origin. Appealing to the King to reward him for long and faithful service, Dunbar points to the wrongs suffered by nobles and by men of character and knowledge when James diverts his favour from them to 'churllis'. What must be the feelings of 'the lerit sone off erll or lord', who

> Is maister native borne
> And all his eldaris him beforne,

when he sees a prelacy bestowed on a man whose hands were intended to push a barrow and who, the higher he climbs, despises the more those of noble blood whom he helps to hold down?[2] Exasperated that detractors will misconstrue his demeanour at court, he writes

> Be I liberall, gentill, and kynd,
> Thocht I it tak of nobill strynd,
> Yit will thai say, baythe he and he,
> Yon man is lyke out of his mynd.[3]

[1] *To the King: Complaint against Mure*, lines 10-11.
[2] *To the King: Complane I Wald.*
[3] *How Sall I Governe Me?*, lines 16-20 in MF. and R. In B. the stanza is omitted.

He reminds the King that, while inferior birds fare sumptuously,

The gentill goishalk gois undynd.

James should cherish his lieges 'eftir thair degre'. When dandled on a nurse's knee Dunbar was already intended for a bishopric.[1]

Dunbar therefore appears to have been connected by birth with the house of Dunbar and March, and to have regarded himself as 'of nobill strynd'. Kennedy, in a preliminary extravaganza, draws 'Dunbar' from 'Dewlbeir' (devil-bear). But the Earls of Dunbar derived from Cospatrick, the Northumbrian earl who fled north with Edgar Atheling from the Conqueror and was granted by Malcolm Canmore the manor of Dunbar and other lands in Lothian.[2] His son became the first earl of Dunbar. The fifth earl married a natural daughter of William the Lion, with the result that Patrick, eighth earl of Dunbar and first of March, became one of the competitors for the Scottish crown on the death of the Maid of Norway. It may help in assessing the degree of weight to be given to Kennedy's statements in *The Flyting of Dunbar and Kennedie* if we compare his account of the family fortunes with historical tradition as recorded elsewhere.

Kennedy tells how Patrick—he keeps to the earlier form, 'Corspatrik'—brought Scotland to confusion by siding with Edward Longshanks. Kennedy states his authority to be 'the writ', the 'Cornicle', and his story agrees fairly closely with that of the *Wallace*, though the unknown author of that poetic chronicle is not so ungenerous.[3] Like the chronicler, Kennedy relates how the Earl betrayed Berwick to the English, causing the death of 7,000 Scots—7,050 in the chronicle.[4] He prevented certain Scottish lords, named in the *Wallace*, from leaving Dunbar Castle until after the disastrous Battle of Dunbar, which Kennedy calls 'Spottismuir'. The chronicle postpones the battle 'ner the Spotmur' to the struggle between the Earl of March and Wallace, but Kennedy's identification of this fight with the Battle of Dunbar is confirmed by the author of the *Scalacronica*.[5] Kennedy further blames Patrick for the removal to England of the coronation stone of Scone, 'the croce of Halyrudhous', and other jewels, for which offences 'he birnis in hell'.

[1] *To the King: Schir, yit remembir.*
[2] Macfarlane, II, p. 514; Sir A. H. Dunbar, p. 28.
[3] See Appendix V, No. 12.
[4] *Wallace*, I, 94.
[5] Sir H. Maxwell's translation, *Scottish Historical Review*, III, p. 19.

After Stirling Bridge, the Wallace of the chronicle called a council at Perth, at which a scornful message was received from the Earl of March, referring to Wallace as 'that King of Kyll'.[1] Kennedy tells of the same incident and of how the wrath of the 'king in Kyle' drove Patrick from the country. But treason will always linger, says Kennedy, among the stones of the castle of Dunbar. It does not suit his purpose to narrate, with the author of the *Wallace*, how Patrick's defiance of Wallace included a reminder that the Earl of March held as much land in England as in Scotland, and that he did not consider himself bound by the decisions of a Scots council. It is enough for Kennedy that the first Earl of March established an English footing in the land and 'Broght Inglese rumplis in'. Thus, the poet Dunbar having spoken proudly of the English speech of Lothian, the west-country Kennedy achieves a reference to the 'caudatus Anglicus', product of the scurrilous legend that Englishmen had tails ('rumplis').[2] Yet, in spite of his flyting, Kennedy's narrative of the first earl of March is seen to be in general accord with historical tradition.

By marrying into the family of the Regent Randolph, Earl of Moray, the younger brother of the tenth earl of Dunbar and March succeeded to the earldom of Moray.[3] Kennedy claims that the honourable qualities of the house of Dunbar passed to the younger branch. With the line of Moray, and especially with the Dunbars of Westfield, neither the poet Dunbar nor his associate the devil has connexion, according to Kennedy. Close ties bound the Westfield family with the south-west of Scotland, where the Kennedies were the leading house. Sir Alexander Dunbar of Westfield, in the parish of Spynie in Moray, was the illegitimate son of the fourth earl of Moray,[4] and died between the years 1497 and 1498.[5] He is mentioned in the public records in connexion with lands at Sanquhar.[6] His eldest son, Sir James Dunbar of Westfield, married Euphemia, eldest daughter of Patrick Dunbar of Cumnock, thus obtaining the barony of Cumnock in Kyle; and Sir Alexander's second son, Sir John Dunbar, married Euphemia's sister—who died in 1497—and acquired thereby the barony of Mochrum.[7] By excluding the Westfield branch from the family of 'Dewlbeir', Ken-

[1] *Wallace*, VIII, 21. [2] Barbé, p. 326. See also Ch. VI.
[3] Bain, IV, p. xxi.
[4] Innes, Carrick Pursuivant of Arms, in *Scottish Notes and Queries*, Third Series, IX, p. 148.
[5] E.R., XI, 83. [6] T.A., II, p. 181. [7] Macfarlane, II, p. 528.

nedy was sparing neighbours of his own family. There may even have been a family connexion between the poet Kennedy and the Westfields. A Mariota de Dunbar appears in the accounts of the Lord Treasurer, 1502-1504, as wife of Alexander Kennedy of Bargany.[1] The Westfields must have had considerable influence in the south-west.

On the other hand, disaster had overtaken the main line of the family of Dunbar. The tenth earl betrothed his daughter to the Duke of Rothesay, heir to King Robert III, but by the intrigues of the Regent Albany and the Earl of Douglas the engagement was broken, and Rothesay was married to a Douglas instead. The injured Earl of March withdrew to England in 1400 with his wife and family. His support was welcomed and rewarded by Henry IV, and the Earl aided Percy in defeating and capturing his rival, Douglas, at Homildon, forfeiting in consequence his Scottish domains.[2] But his enmity was too dangerous for the liking of Albany, who reversed the attainder in 1409. The Earl of March returned to Scotland and to the possession of the bulk of his former estates. James I, however, implacable towards the beneficiaries of Albany's administration, made use of the earlier forfeiture to arrest the eleventh Earl in 1434 and seize his castle of Dunbar. In Parliament at Perth he was deprived of his title and of all estates held directly of the crown, on the ground that Albany's reversal of the attainder had been beyond the powers of a regent and was therefore invalid. Only the barony of Kilconquhar in Fife appears to have been left to him, not being held directly.[3] The chronicles state that he was made Earl of Buchan and that he and his heir received an annual payment in compensation, but the Exchequer Rolls are silent on this point.[4] The sums there recorded as paid to him are few and irregular, and they ceased in 1454, though an annuity was paid to his daughter Euphemia in 1460.[5] His power was broken.

Walter Kennedy in *The Flyting* does not avail himself of these family misfortunes. Perhaps he was unwilling to draw upon himself the displeasure of some who smarted still from these penal measures and who would not lightly have excused the poet for such licence. The only reference by Kennedy to the Dunbars of the

[1] T.A., II, p. 173.
[2] Bain, IV, pp. 115, 124-126, 130-131.
[3] ib., p. xxiii.
[4] Major, p. 362. E.R., VI, p. cvi. E. W. M. B. Melville, p. 216.
[5] E.R., VI, p. 590.

fifteenth century is his account of the seizure of Hailes Castle, on the river Tyne in East Lothian, by Archibald Dunbar in 1446. The castle belonged to Adam Hepburn, who, with others among the enemies of the last Earl of March, had taken possession of Dunbar Castle in 1433.[1] According to Kennedy, the attack on Hailes Castle was an act of cruel retaliation by Archibald Dunbar, who threw Hepburn into a dungeon.[2] Pitscottie thus briefly disposes of the incident: 'Archebald Dunbar seigit the castell of Haillis in Lowtheane and at the first assault he wan the samin and slew them all that he fand thairin. He schortlie thairefter was beseigit be James Douglas in quhois will he put himself and the castell but ony farder debaitt.'[3]

In considering the question of the parentage of Dunbar the poet, it is necessary to bear in mind how widespread the family name was. The process by which it spread even to the remote north and south-west of the kingdom has already been indicated. In an earlier section of *The Flyting*, Dunbar may be interpreted as claiming connexion with Lothian:

> I tak on me ane pair of Lowthiane hippis
> Sall fairar Inglis mak, and mair parfyte,
> Than thow can blabber with thy Carrik lippis.[4]

But there must have been many of the name in Lothian, and there is no evidence that the poet belonged to any one particular branch. His parents may have been only remotely related to the main line. Further, it was a frequent practice for smaller families to place themselves by bands of 'manrent' under the protection of greater and to adopt the family surname.[5] The devotion of these affiliated members was no less than that of blood relations, and Kennedy's onslaught on the Dunbar family would not be ineffective even in these circumstances in damaging his rival's pride. But if we assume actual blood relationship the likeliest link would be with the Archibald Dunbar who attacked Hailes Castle. Alone among latter-day personages of the Dunbar name, he is mentioned with opprobium by Kennedy. But the identity of this Archibald is unknown. An Archibald Dunbar, son of the eleventh Earl, appears as a witness to a charter in 1423,[6] and in 1425-6 received from his father by

[1] *Scotichronicon*, II, p. 500. [2] *The Flyting*, lines 297-304. [3] Pitscottie, I, p. 56.
[4] *The Flyting*, lines 110-112. [5] Rait, pp. 95-101.
[6] Register House Charters, No. 260, cited by Sir J. Balfour Paul, *The Scots Peerage* (1906), III, p. 278.

charter the lands of Wester Spot near Dunbar.[1] An Archibald Dunbar, who may be the same, held the crown lands of Little Spot from 1452 to 1467.[2] Either of these may have been the assailant on Hailes Castle, which was quite near.

In trying to establish the poet's parentage, Laing turned his attention to the family of Sir Patrick Dunbar of Biel, in East Lothian, between Little Spot and Hailes. This knight took part in diplomatic negotiations between Scotland and England. At Homildon he fought with Douglas against the head of his own family, the tenth Earl of March,[3] and he has been identified with a 'Patricio de Dunbar, filio dicti comitis', appearing in an entry of 1416 and also in a charter of 1390.[4] He was a Scottish hostage for the return of James I to Scotland. There is mention of a son of his, also named Patrick de Dunbar de Bele, in 1452.[5] Laing, writing in 1834, states[6] that, according to information communicated to him by John Riddell, advocate, there was among the deeds contained in the charter chest of the Earl of Rosebery an obligation by George of Dunbar, Earl of March, to Robert Levingston, burgess of Linlithgow, dated 10th August 1440, in which George, Walter and William Dunbar are described as sons of Patrick of Dunbar of Bele. Laing adds that among these deeds was another, resigning the lands of Middle Binning in West Lothian, on 3rd July 1440, and that the same William Dunbar appears as a witness: 'Magistro Willielmo de Dunbar'. Laing concludes that this William, whose title shows him to have been a graduate of a university, was 'in all probability' the father or the uncle of the poet.[7] A search in the Rosebery archives, made on behalf of the present writer, failed to bring the two charters to light.[8]

In drawing his conclusion from these records, Laing was influenced on the one hand by the tendency to transmit the same Christian name through succeeding generations of a family, and on the other hand by the dearth of Williams in the extant records of Dunbars. But it is impossible to arrive at any firm conclusion from these general considerations. There is really no evidence for regarding Sir Patrick Dunbar of Biel as the grandfather or great-uncle of the poet. Kennedy's flyting provides no hint of it, pointing rather

[1] *The Book of Carlaverock*, Sir William Fraser, II, p. 428. Sir J. Balfour Paul, op. cit., III, 278.

[2] E.R., V, p. 581; VII, p. 495. [3] Major, p. 339.

[4] E.R., IV, 250; Bain, IV, p. 211. [5] *Great Seal Reg.*, II, 547. [6] L., I, p. 66.

[7] ib., I, p. 8. [8] The writer is indebted to Mr. Brebner for searching.

to a connexion with the Archibald Dunbar who attacked Hailes Castle. Laing's argument suggests only an interesting possibility. Yet a recent writer asserts that the poet 'was one of the younger sons of Sir Patrick Dunbar of Beil'.[1]

A statement is made by Smeaton that, 'from a chance reference in an old Latin deed' in the *Chart Book of the Priory of St. Andrews*, he was 'inclined to think' that the poet's father was also called William and held some lay office in connexion with the Franciscan house at Haddington.[2] It will be necessary in the course of this work to consider closely various other assertions by Smeaton which he advanced much more precisely and with more assurance than in this case, and for which the evidence claimed to exist is lacking. Here it is enough to point out that he regarded this reference, to which he alludes so vaguely, as being only such that he was 'inclined to think' that it warranted the inference. In view of Smeaton's other statements,[3] no weight at all can be given to so indirect a suggestion from him as to Dunbar's parentage.

As to the birthplace of Dunbar, his characteristic boast in *The Flyting*, already quoted, suggests that he was born in Lothian. Dr. Mackenzie has pointed out, however, that Dunbar's words are ambiguous ('I tak on me'=I undertake that), since they do not explicitly claim Lothian origin for Dunbar himself. Several writers have put forward what seemed to be more definite evidence. Kennedy had prophesied that his rival would yet come to the gallows:

Thou has a wedy teuch,
On Mount Falconn, about thy crag to rax.[4]

Misreading the first and fourth letters of Bannatyne's 'falcone'[5] Allan Ramsay arrived at 'saltone'.[6] Kennedy is suggesting to Dunbar that in Paris the gallows on Montfaucon will be conveniently near. But Hailes concluded that Dunbar was born at Salton in East Lothian,[7] though even if Ramsay's reading were correct it would still not show that Salton was Dunbar's birthplace. Sibbald, who was the first to point out Ramsay's mistake in transcription, attempted a new hypothesis.[8] Since the barony of Kilconquhar in Fife was a possession of the family of March, Sibbald thought that Dunbar

[1] Miss R. A. Taylor, p. 33. [2] Smeaton, p. 24.
[3] See especially Chapters II, III, IV and V, below.
[4] *The Flyting of Dunbar and Kennedie*, lines 367-368.
[5] CM. 'Falconn'; the reading of MF. has faded; R. 'falcon'.
[6] *The Evergreen*, II, p. 67. [7] Hailes, p. 227. [8] Sibbald, I, p. 358.

probably belonged to Fife, that the eastern of the Lomond Hills which overlooks Falkland in the same county might have been called 'Falkland Mount'—it is indeed called Falkland Hill to-day—and that a gallows might be expected to stand in proximity to a royal residence. A corruption of the words might then have led to 'Mont Falcone'. It was Laing who convincingly related the words to their context as referring to the celebrated gibbet of medieval Paris.[1]

Led by his view that Dunbar was probably descended from Sir Patrick Dunbar of Biel, Laing suggested that the poet was a native of Biel in East Lothian. Mackay followed on with the conjecture that Dunbar's vivid account of the voracious birds in *Ane Ballat of the Fenyeit Freir of Tungland* might be due to an early familiarity with the ways of sea-birds on the neighbouring Bass Rock.[2] Smeaton observed that Dunbar's mention of being already hailed as bishop while on his nurse's knee indicated that the poet was born near an ecclesiastical establishment, and therefore probably near Haddington.[3] A modern work on the poetry of William Dunbar states, without citing any evidence, that he was born at Roxburgh.[4]

Dunbar may have been born near Biel or Haddington, but there is no reason to favour any one particular place in Lothian. All we can say from the evidence is that he seems to imply that he was born in that province. Racially and historically it was the well of English in Scotland. Dunbar would therefore have local, as well as literary, warrant for his proud reference to 'oure Inglisch'.[5] Bishop Leslie writes that Lothian, of all the provinces of Scotland, 'indeid throuch the plentifulnes of the ground, decking and apparrelling of thair houses, and fairnes of thair biging, may weil be called cheif.'[6]

In fixing approximately the date of Dunbar's birth, importance attaches to the two entries of his name—if we assume that the name is his—in the records of St. Andrews University, in 1477 and 1479, though in neither case can any precise conclusion be drawn as to his age in that year. When he graduated as licentiate, in 1479, he may have been in his twentieth year, that being the statutory age required for licence[7], but he may have been older; he may, on the other hand, have been younger, for statutory provisions were not strictly interpreted, and dispensation was available. The baccalaureate attained in 1477 was followed by the normal two years

[1] *History of Paris* (London, 1825), III, p. 62, quoted by L., II, p. 432.
[2] S.T.S., I, p. xx. [3] Smeaton, p. 25. [4] Miss R. A. Taylor, p. 33.
[5] *The Goldyn Targe*, line 259. [6] Leslie, I, p. 22. [7] Hannay, *Statutes*, p. 35.

B

before licence. If the course leading to determination as bachelor were likewise of the normal duration, Dunbar would matriculate in the autumn of 1475, though it frequently happened at Paris University in the fifteenth century—and the practice of St. Andrews was based on that of Paris—that the bachelor's degree was obtained within a year of matriculation.[1] The ceremony of matriculating as a student of the University included the taking of an oath, and canon law required a juror to have reached the age of fourteen. But here again use and wont had led to exceptions. It was possible to be admitted to the University at a more tender age and delay the oath of incorporation until the required age was reached, or a parent or teacher might take the oath on the youth's behalf, to be confirmed by him at the age of fifteen.[2] But as the usual age for entering the University seems to have been fifteen, the date of Dunbar's birth approximates to the year 1460.

Because of certain poems written by Dunbar in the reign of James IV and apparently in old age, Laing was inclined to place the date of the poet's birth about the middle of the century and to regard 1460 as a lower limit of possibility.[3] Gregor, in his notes to the edition of the poems for the Scottish Text Society, sought to confirm the hypothesis of 1460 by independent evidence. He referred to a line in *The Flyting of Dunbar and Kennedie* in which Kennedy abusively says:

> Thou was consavit in the grete eclips.[4]

Gregor pointed out that on 18th July 1460, according to *L'Art de Vérifier les Dates*,[5] there was an eclipse of the sun that was visible from Europe.[6]

The statement in this line of *The Flyting* may be something more than a malicious fiction designed to suggest a monstrous birth. Astronomy was not only one of the subjects of scholarly study in the medieval world. In its astrological aspect it was a source of widespread interest and often of fear. In a quaint passage in *The Canterbury Tales*, Chaucer relates how the host of the Tabard Inn, 'though he were nat depe experte in loore', was able, by observing the position of the sun and the angle of its elevation, to conclude

[1] Rashdall, I, p. 462. [2] Anderson, p. xxiv.

[3] L., I, p. 8. [4] *The Flyting*, line 489.

[5] p. 78. This work was compiled by 'un religieux Bénédictin de la Congrégation de S. Maure' and published in Paris, 1783.

[6] S.T.S., III, p. 62.

that the day was the 18th of April and that it was ten o'clock. In the days of horoscopes, a pronounced eclipse in the year of one's birth might not escape notice, and there may be truth behind Kennedy's gibe. Unfortunately, however, consultation of the learned work of reference cited by Gregor shows that there were several major eclipses of the sun not far removed in time from the year 1460. Between 1445 and 1465, they occurred in 1448, 1450, 1453, 1460, 1462, 1464, and 1465. Gregor had no reason to single out 1460.

Laing wrote, after the lapse of many years, a supplement to his edition of Dunbar. He was sufficiently impressed by Gregor's argument to alter his own previous date of 1450 to 'about the year 1456', but still thought 1460 too late.[1] There are indeed difficulties in the adoption of the latter date. The poem *To the King: Petition of the Gray Horse, Old Dunbar*, earlier than Flodden, does not accord well with a view that would make the poet barely fifty years of age at the time when he wrote it. But perhaps the petitionary nature of the poem caused the poet to exaggerate his age. Moreover, men in those days aged more quickly than to-day, and Dunbar underwent at least one severe illness which may have contributed to a rapid decline.[2] The year 1460 may be taken as approximately Dunbar's date of birth.

[1] L., *Supplement*, p. 309. [2] *Lament: Quhen he wes Sek.*

CHAPTER II

ST. ANDREWS

LINES in one of Dunbar's petitionary poems have already been referred to:

> I wes in youthe, on nureice kne,
> Cald dandillie, bischop, dandillie.[1]

They show that the poet was in early infancy destined for the Church and that there was reason to expect for him speedy advancement in that calling, such advancement as would result from influential patronage.

But though in his tenderest years there were these hopes, it is clear from *How Dumbar wes Desyrd to be ane Freir* that he had a connexion with the Franciscan friars early in his life. It will be necessary later to consider this poem closely in order to try to determine how deeply he was committed to the Franciscans. Meanwhile it is sufficient that, so far as the poem has consistency, it means that as a young man he was at least a novice in the order. At what stage in his life did he undertake the novitiate? Was it before or after his graduation at St. Andrews University?

Laing states that Dunbar's novitiate may have been either before or after graduation.[2] To become in early boyhood a novice in a religious order would have been nothing new. According to John Major, Duns Scotus was no more than a boy when he was taken to Oxford by two Franciscans, in whose house there he lived and took the vows.[3] Complaints were common that mere children were inveigled into the religious orders.[4] But Dunbar's case must be viewed in relation to his graduation in arts at St. Andrews in 1479, at which date he was evidently not yet a friar.

The mendicant orders exercised a powerful influence on higher education. The Dominicans chose the university towns, where they might obtain recruits from among the students, for their 'studia

[1] *To the King: Schir, yit remembir*, lines 61-62.
[2] L., *Supplement*, p. 309. [3] Major, p. 206.
[4] Coulton, *Five Centuries*, II, pp. 181-188.

generalia'. But the regular clergy were permanently excluded from membership of the Faculty of Arts in Paris University,[1] and at Glasgow the regulars attended lectures but did not graduate.[2] The Dominicans were forbidden by their own Rule from graduating in arts. In the lists of matriculations at St. Andrews University, only thirteen names occur with the word 'Frater' affixed, and no names in the graduation lists are thus distinguished.[3] It is therefore reasonable to conclude that Dunbar, whose name in the graduation roll is prefixed by the usual 'Magister', was not at the time of his graduation a friar. It is possible that he may have already entered on his year's novitiate, though so recently as to be able to graduate before taking the vows, or that his novitiate was lengthened to enable him to graduate. But in the absence of any such evidence the probability is that he became a Franciscan novice after graduation in arts. Almost certainly he would still be little more than a boy.

Nothing is known about the early schooling of Dunbar. On account of his lineage and of his supposed prospects in the Church, he may have had private tuition from a parish priest, regular, or more highly placed cleric. In an ordinary parish school he would scarcely learn more from priest or sacristan than the elements of the Gregorian chant and of the Latin service-books. As choir-boy in the song-school of a cathedral or collegiate church, he would advance likewise along strictly practical lines only, just as he would if in the almonry school attached to a monastery or friary—and the extent to which facilities were available for external pupils at these establishments is very doubtful. Almonries and cathedral schools did, however, at times conduct instruction in Latin grammar, and gilds were active in the endowment of grammar schools in towns. In Edinburgh by 1500 there existed at least the Grammar School and the Canongate School.[4]

Teachers in the grammar schools were priests or at least laymen under ecclesiastical supervision and management, with undermasters to administer corporal punishment. The school day was long and arduous. There were few books, instruction being oral and in Latin. The use of the vernacular was banned. The curriculum consisted of the elements of Latin grammar, Latin reading, writing and chanting. The religious matter was drawn from 'grace-book' and

[1] Rashdall, I, p. 392.
[2] *Munimenta*, ed. Innes, II, p. 13. Hannay, *Statutes*, p. 24.
[3] Anderson, *Early Records*, p. xxix. [4] Kerr, p. 5.

'prymar', and Latin accidence from the fourth century *Ars Minor* of Aelius Donatus. From the 'donat' the master read, the pupils repeating his words in chorus and learning them by rote.[1] The indolent, negligent, or forgetful pupil was birched. Tale-bearing was an organised aid to class discipline.[2] Writing was practised on a waxed board with a stilus. Having clerical status, grammar-school boys wore the tonsure.[3]

But Dunbar's schooling may have been exceedingly slight before he began his studies at St. Andrews. The arrangement to-day by which a boy advances considerably in literary studies before proceeding to his university town is no criterion of practice in the fifteenth century. Boys usually arrived at Oxford at the early age of ten or twelve, not to continue but to commence their scholastic education.[4] They enrolled under a master of arts as guardian, in whose house they lived along with a number of other scholars. Not yet being students in the Faculty of Arts, they had no external lectures to attend, and received all their instruction within the establishment from a master or his assistants, not all the teaching being done by graduates.[5] At Merton there was provision within the college for such boys and for their instruction in grammar.[6] There were similar arrangements at Paris University.[7] At St. Andrews there was a grammar-school in 1464, under the charge of a regent of the University and supervised by the Dean of the Faculty of Arts.[8] At Oxford the grammar masters were responsible also for the moral and religious training of their boys. Besides the parsing required of the pupils, the master read various passages to them cursorily and taught the composition of verse and of letters, which later had to be repeated by rote before the master. Two or three years would usually be passed in this schooling.[9] The recreation of the boys at St. Andrews was supervised by a master; he went with them to the links (*ad campos*) and was to see that they spoke Latin and marched in order.[10] There was no test of fitness when the time came for them to enter the arts course, and some years later, in 1495, a qualifying examination had to be instituted, taking place before the Dean, four regents and the master of the school.[11]

There was no special matriculation roll at St. Andrews. So far

[1] Adamson, p. 14. [2] Coulton, *Scottish Abbeys and Social Life*, p. 26.
[3] ib., p. 178. [4] Anstey, p. lvii. [5] ib., p. lxii.
[6] Adamson, p. 47. [7] Rashdall, I, p. 518. [8] Hannay, *Statutes*, p. 35.
[9] Anstey, pp. lxix-lxxi.
[10] Hannay, p. 7. [11] ib., p. 35.

as a record of matriculation exists, it occurs in the manuscript *Acta Rectorum*, lists of names of matriculating students appearing from time to time among the records of administrative details and rectorial elections. The lists of these 'incorporations' begin in 1473, no previous list being extant. No names occur between 1474 and 1483. Dunbar's name appears in the records for the first time in 1477, when he was one of the 'determinants'. In the usual course he would matriculate in 1475.

The royal burgh of St. Andrews, where Dunbar spent several formative years, was dominated by the cathedral church near the cliffs. Beside it was the Augustinian Priory in its secluded grounds, and to the north, on the edge of the cliffs, was the Archbishop's castle. But the cathedral itself, with the neighbouring lofty tower of St. Rule, formed the most conspicuous features, seen from far or near. The three main streets, almost parallel, converged slightly towards the great church. The official centre of university life was in Southgate, where also stood the monastery of the Blackfriars and the parish church of the Holy Trinity. On the north stretched Marketgate, and beyond it Northgate with St. Salvator's College. Though the city was not walled, the western end of each street had its massive gateway. Along the cliffs towards the links ran the Castlegate (now the Scores), with crofts along its sides and extending beyond the Castlegate Port. The fashionable part of the burgh lay towards the east end of Southgate. The harbour was four miles away, at the mouth of the Eden.[1]

The statutes of the Faculty of Arts ordained an organisation of studies modelled on that of Paris, 'more Parisiensi'. Had Dunbar been eminently rich or noble, he might have had a private tutor to supplement public lectures and have lived apart. On the other hand, if very poor he might have lived a solitary life in a garret. But the normal arrangement was to live in one of the colleges or in one of the private halls kept by members of the teaching staff of the University. Of the colleges the older was the pedagogy in Southgate, attached to the chapel of St. John. Its endowments were not very substantial, but besides containing the official lecture-rooms of the University it had dormitories and kitchen.[2] The other college, St. Salvator's, was in Northgate and had been founded by Bishop Kennedy as lately as 1450, with a staff of masters and provision for six

[1] Anderson, *Scottish Historical Review*, VIII, p. 226.
[2] Kerr, p. 40.

poor scholars.[1] But such colleges provided for more than the indigent. At Paris and the other universities the colleges received as inmates 'commoners' who paid for their board and lodging and contributed towards the expenses of the institution[2] while sharing in the privileges of the foundationers and the amenities of the college. Laing[3] asserts that Dunbar was a student in St. Salvator's, but there is no firm evidence as to this. The poet does begin one of his poems by invoking St. Salvator:

Sanct Salvatour, send silver sorrow!

But it has been pointed out[4] that, even if this invocation could be regarded as proving the point in question, the name may have been chosen in this line for its alliterative effect only. Dunbar may not have lived in either college. Private 'halls' kept by members of the teaching staff of the University were still in existence in spite of the competition of the colleges. Having repeatedly failed to eliminate them, the Faculty had had to content itself with securing their obedience to the Dean, who, with the assistance of several masters, was supposed to pay them a weekly visit of inspection.[5] The head of such a house, and his staff of assistants, would privately tutor the students under their care, as the staffs of the colleges would tutor theirs—supplementing and expounding the public lectures which had to be taken in the Southgate by all students in arts, and also reading with their students more widely and cursorily. In addition, the hall or college offered to some extent the benefits of a common library, facilities for observing the rule that conversation was to be in Latin, provision for disputations, and, in general, the social advantages of collegiate life.[6] Indeed, instruction in the college or hall developed to such an extent that in Dunbar's time it was already overshadowing the formal lectures in the public schools in Southgate. These lectures were, however, still compulsory; they corresponded to the similar 'ordinary' lectures held in Paris in the Vicus Stramineus, and were therefore spoken of at St. Andrews as being held *in vico*.[7]

Under the normal procedure, Dunbar's studies in the Faculty of Arts would begin in October 1475. He would follow up his previous introduction to the rudiments of Latin with a study of the

[1] Rashdall, II, p. 308. [2] ib., I, p. 515. [3] L., I, p. 9.
[4] M., p. xx. [5] Hannay, *Statutes*, p. 16.
[6] Rashdall, I, p. 515. [7] Hannay, p. 26.

more advanced formal grammar of Villedieu's *Doctrinale*, which was written in hexameters as an aid to memorisation. It dealt with etymology, accidence and syntax, quantity, prosody and rhetorical figures.[1] It remained the standard work until the scholars of the Renaissance attacked it with their ridicule. There was no attempt to make contact with the poets, orators, and prose writers of ancient Rome. Dunbar would speedily pass from this work to the core of university education at this stage—the venerated works of Aristotelian logic. As an introduction to them he would be taken as usual through the *Summulae* of Petrus Hispanus. He would then proceed to take down at dictation speed, as read by his master, the Aristotelian texts in Latin translation, with full commentaries. Porphyry's *Introduction* led to the main body of the 'old logic' (*vetus ars*)—the *De Interpretatione* and *Praedicamenta* of Aristotle, and the *Divisiones* and *Topics* of Boethius[2]—followed by the *Analytics* and *Elenchi*.[3] The work in rhetoric was very slight, being by this time a matter mainly of legal correspondence more appropriate to a faculty of law.[4] The students' transcriptions of the texts in logic were to be regularly inspected by the master.

Transcription appears at first sight to provide little scope for the student's initiative. But, though the texts were authoritative, the glosses of the teacher were disputable and offered material for active disputation. Studies in logic had thus a practical outcome, and the student's proficiency in building up similar arguments was of importance to him in securing his degree as 'determinant' or bachelor. Before Christmas, 1476, Dunbar would take steps to 'determine'. He would be required to pay the fee of ten shillings, give caution that he would proceed to the bachelor's degree next Lent, and promise to give obedience to the Dean and Faculty and to keep the secrets of the Faculty. 'Responsions' would be a first test, in which Dunbar would dispute in grammar and logic with a master. Successful, he would go before a board of examiners and satisfy them that he had duly performed his classwork and that he knew his texts. The ceremony of donning the bachelor's *cappa* would follow, and festivities.[5] These were on so considerable a scale that the expenditure of each 'determinant' was officially limited to forty shillings as a maximum. It was customary to present gloves to the

[1] Adamson, p. 69. [2] Rashdall, I, p. 442.
[3] Hannay, p. 11. [4] Abelson, p. 60.
[5] Rashdall, I, p. 452.

guests; and in 1467 it had been found necessary to lay down that the gloves must be of good quality. For purposes of these festivities, determinants were required to associate with themselves any of their fellows who were too poor to be able to meet the expenses.[1] The final stage was reached in the following Lent, 1476-7, when, before the masters and his fellow-students, assembled in the pedagogy under the chairmanship of a master, Dunbar would dispute with a less advanced student and, at the conclusion of the proceedings, would sum up.

Dunbar's name appears in the manuscript records of the Faculty of Arts as a determinant in 1477.[2] (There is nothing, however, to warrant the statement[3] that he appears as a determinant in St. Salvator's College.) There are eighteen graduates, divided into four 'acts', each act having a due proportion of poor students who were unable to pay the dues though they would no doubt give their oath, or caution, to pay later. Dunbar's name is in the second act, which has three names in all:

Willelmus Dunbar—*solvit*.
Georgius Jhonstown—*solvit*.
Donaldus Gray—*pauper*.

The payments referred to included, besides the ten shillings already paid in December to the treasurer of the Faculty, a payment to the common chest (*bursa*).[4]

Though the number of students in the University was small, a keen-minded young cleric must have found his surroundings stimulating. A hundred and fifty or two hundred students formed a community of very modest proportions in comparison with the thousands who frequented the University of Paris. But opportunities for social intercourse and mental development vary by no means in direct proportion with the mere size of such a community. Though there could be few foreigners at St. Andrews, the constitution of the student-body into the nations of Fife, Angus, Lothian, and Britain (the rest), preserved a cosmopolitan outlook and combated the tendencies towards parochialism. The students in arts, the predominant faculty, were generally very young, but there was a leaven of older students who formed the faculties of theology, civil law, and canon law. There must have been intimate relations

[1] Hannay, p. 37. [2] MS. *Acta Fac. Artium*, p. 76.
[3] L., I, p. 9. [4] Anderson, *Early Records*, p. xxxii.

with the teaching staff. The members of the University, being under the civil jurisdiction of the rector, held a position of independence and privilege, but the influence of the Church was all-pervasive. Students and masters wore clerical garb. The masters were mainly holders of benefices in the country at large, who had appointed vicars to their charges. The Chancellor of the University was the Archbishop himself, and the cathedral chapter consisted of the Augustinian Canons-Regular of the Priory, one of the wealthiest and most illustrious religious houses in the land. In St. Andrews there were also small communities of the Franciscans and Dominicans, whose members, though they did not graduate, were in contact with the University. There was much religious ceremonial, notably on the eve of the feast of St. John the Evangelist, which was celebrated annually by the Faculty of Arts with full pomp. Yet the community was far from being lulled in an ecclesiastical calm. A few years before, when St. Salvator's College had advanced claims prejudicial to the University, feeling ran so high that the St. Salvator's supporters attacked, with bows and arrows, their opponents and even the Dean of the Faculty.[1] While Dunbar himself was a student, the whole University must have been stirred by the strange case of its Archbishop, Patrick Graham, who was deprived of his see on many grave charges and who died miserably. That the community was not idyllic is shown by the foundation bull of St. Salvator's College, which directs the inmates to avoid *publicas concubinas*, and not to become night-walkers, thieves, or criminals of any other kind.[2] The Faculty of Arts found it necessary repeatedly to make and enforce regulations as to the conduct of students. At various times the students were forbidden to engage in rough and dangerous games, especially football,[3] to spend more than two or three days on cock-fighting, or to wear secular costumes when engaged in hawking.[4] The processions and masquerades of 'bringing in the May' were denounced, and the students were enjoined, if they wanted to go to the links and take the air, to go respectably dressed and to hear a mass on their return to town.[5]

Dunbar, now a bachelor of arts, passed on to the course for licence, consisting of psychology, natural and moral philosophy, and metaphysics. The dominating influence was that of Aristotle

[1] Hannay, p. 30. [2] Lyon, II, p. 239.
[3] Herkless and Hannay, p. 19.
[4] Kerr, p. 48. [5] Mill, p. 17.

and his school. The influence of Plato was great but only indirect, descending through the medium of Aristotle, Augustine, Boethius, and the Arabic writers who had absorbed neo-Platonism. The practical significance of these studies appeared immense. On the question of the reality of universals there seemed to hang the very existence of the individual soul. Was humanity the reality and did the individual belong merely to the world of appearances? There was matter in all this for strenuous and subtle disputation.[1] As in their earlier studies, the students had to copy out to dictation the main works as they were read and expounded *in vico*, on the mornings of 'legible' days, by masters authorised by the Faculty. These 'ordinary' books were[2] the *Physics*, *De Generatione et Corruptione*, *De Caelo et Mundo*, *De Sensu et Sensato*, *De Somno et Vigilia*, *De Memoria et Reminiscentia*, *De Anima*, the *Meteorics* and the *Metaphysics*. In the afternoons and in the vacations, some at least of the 'extraordinary' books, taken in hall or college by tutors, were covered cursorily, without having to be written out. These appear to have been selected from the *De Sphaera*, the *Ethics*, *De Perspectiva*, *Algorismus*, *Principles of Geometry*, *Politics*, *Economics*, *Rhetoric*, and perhaps the *De Musica*.[3]

In Lent, 1479, Dunbar would go before the Chancellor, Archbishop Schevez (or his deputy), and a panel of masters from the Faculty. Sitting 'upon the blak stane', he would be examined generally as to his eligibility for graduation as a master of arts.[4] In May or June, the Chancellor not being present, he would be tested by the examiners of the Faculty independently, and proceed with other candidates to the graduation ceremony, at which some of the candidates at least would be called upon to give lectures ('collations') in the classroom manner.[5] In full ceremonial dress, kneeling, he would receive from the Chancellor the licence to teach (*jus ubique docendi*). The list of licentiates of 1479 contains ten names, of which Dunbar's is the fourth—'M. Wilelmus Dunbar'[6]—followed by that of 'M. Georgius Jonston', who had accompanied him to the bachelor's degree in 1477. Graduation was a serious expense to candidates, for, besides presents to the examiners and to the guests, festivities were again expected and had to be paid for.

What trace is there, in the extant poems of Dunbar, of these

[1] Rashdall, I, pp. 38-44. [2] Hannay, p. 11.
[3] ib., p. 12. Rashdall, I, p. 447. [4] Hannay, p. 48.
[5] Rashdall, I, p. 457. [6] MS. *Acta Fac. Artium*, p. 79.

years devoted to study at a university? There is none. His university course was, as it was intended to be, strictly vocational, designed to train the mind to logical disputation and exposition in the service of the Church. It was conceived in the main as a mental discipline. It could not fail to influence his ability in later years with tongue and pen. It would whet his mind for what diplomatic errands he was to be entrusted with in later years, and for the exigencies of court life, in an indirect fashion, given the native shrewdness and quick wits which would, however, have been sufficient without the aid of a scholastic training. His studies certainly failed conspicuously to turn his interests from the ways of the world. As to literary pursuits, the metrical facility which he shows in his poems is proof of a wide acquaintance with poems of similar nature, but they can have had no contact officially with his studies at St. Andrews. He makes a few references to popular medieval poems, and to poetic romances, but anyone interested in poetry could have picked up as much. His life as a priest is enough to account for his religious poems. Above all, his professed discipleship to Chaucer, Gower, and Lydgate, is adequate to explain the acquaintance which he has with personages of classical mythology; those he mentions are the stock-in-trade of the medieval poet—Flora, Vulcan, Phoebus, Aeolus, Aurora, and the like. And even these he handles at times ineptly. In *The Goldyn Targe*, a hundred goddesses land from the ship and disport themselves in the meadow, and only later and in sharp contrast a throng of gods is introduced; and yet, in spite of this emphatic segregation, there appears as one of the goddesses Apollo. This might, as Laing suggested, be an oversight, though the early print and both the manuscripts agree in their readings. But what are we to think when, a few lines later, the same unanimity includes among the ladies both 'Pallas and prudent Minerva'? It is clear that Dunbar's poetic apparatus came to him through medieval literature. The truth is that his poems are prompted usually not by literary interests at all but by piquant incidents or situations or personalities, generally in his social circle at court, and he deals with them with his own sharp mother-wit. To call him a mere Chaucerian or Lydgatian is the result of confining one's attention to a few of his poems. And so far as his poetry is concerned, Dunbar might just as well never have been at a university, except for the social stimulus he found there.

There is no reason to suppose that he passed from arts to study in one of the higher faculties at St. Andrews. The records for the Faculty of Theology are in any case missing. The only entries in the University records that relate to Dunbar are those of 1477 and 1479. Leith, in his list of masters of arts from 1500 to 1560, includes '1513. M. Dunbar, William, St. Andrews'.[1] He states that his material is 'taken chiefly from official papers and partly from Catholic sources'. In this instance there is no support for his statements in the manuscript records of the University. In any case, this could not have been Dunbar the poet.

It has been suggested[2] that Dunbar studied later at Oxford, for the poem on Oxford University is followed in one of the two versions in the Maitland folio manuscript by the words *Quod Dumbar at oxinfurde*. Lists of matriculating students and of graduates at Oxford for this period are not extant.[3] Dunbar was certainly in England in later life—he was there in 1501, when he was already a dependant at the court of James IV—and the colophon of the Maitland manuscript is insufficient evidence that the poet attended Oxford University in his student days. It is clear from the context of the poem, however, that the University town is being spoken of and not merely Oxenford in Midlothian. The poem may have been written during a visit to Oxford in 1501 or even later. Laing and Schipper[4] rightly state that the poet's tone is not such as a student would use of his teachers but accords more with later years and experience of teaching others. Dunbar praises the learning of Oxford but insists that studies are perilous unless they issue in good living. The subtleties of logic, eloquence, natural philosophy, divinity, and poetry must alike be brought to this practical test. The scholar must be a lamp in our darkness. Schipper conjectures that the poem may have been prompted by a conversation at Oxford as to the mode of life of its professors.

Paris University was much more likely for a Scots student in the fifteenth century than Oxford. Scots students were numerous at Paris. It was Laing who first suggested that Dunbar might have studied there after leaving St. Andrews, and Laing has left on record[5] that he tried more than once, but in vain, to discover whether Dunbar did go on to Paris University. Michel states definitely that Dunbar was a student there, the evidence given being a line of *The*

[1] Leith, p. 112. [2] Ellis, I, p. 373.
[3] Boase, I, p. v. [4] L., II, p. 347. S., p. 306.
[5] L., I, p. 10.

Freiris of Berwik[1] where Dunbar is said to speak of Paris as a town with which he is familiar. This evidence is completely unsatisfactory. It is Friar Robert, not Dunbar, who says that in Paris he has learnt 'mony sindry practikis', but this would scarcely prove even that Friar Robert (if he were not a fictitious character) had studied at Paris University; and there is no reason to suppose that *The Freiris of Berwik* was written by Dunbar.

We come to what seems like evidence in Smeaton's *William Dunbar*, published in 1898. After declaring his opinion that Dunbar studied at Oxford, Smeaton proceeds as follows: 'Furthermore with regard to his studying at the University of Paris, although to Laing belongs the credit of having thrown out the tentative suggestion that the poet studied at Paris, no definite settlement of the question could be arrived at until, after careful inspection of the registers of the old University of Paris, the name of "Gul Donbere" was discovered, which I have little doubt refers to the poet. This fact would seem to indicate that Dunbar resided in Paris in 1480-1, or during parts thereof.'[2] Smeaton's statements of newly discovered 'facts' are often startling. On this occasion, though he gives no precise source, there is at least a reference to the registers of Paris University and to a definite date. It seemed to the writer that Smeaton's statement should be followed up, in order not only to establish, if possible, the facts alleged, but also to afford some criterion by which Smeaton's other statements with vaguer reference might be tested. The writer accordingly in 1937 made a search of the manuscript records of Paris University.

In 1480 there were four 'nations' in the Faculty of Arts at Paris. Scotsmen belonged to the German (formerly known as the English) nation which, in turn, had three provinces—High German, Low German, and Scots.[3] From the records, it is clear that students from Scots dioceses, predominantly from the diocese of St. Andrews, formed a large proportion of the graduates of the 'nation', though it is certainly an exaggeration to say that[4] every Scots student, however poor, completed his education in Paris. Scotsmen at Paris University were to the fore in debate and in the student assemblies; they were especially watchful of the good name of their compatriots, and inclined to overdo their *esprit de corps*.[5] No lists of matriculated

[1] Line 302. See Appen. IV, No. 7. [2] Smeaton, p. 33.
[3] Samaran and Moé, III, p. xi.
[4] Miss R. A. Taylor, p. 12. [5] Coissac, p. 76.

students remain, but lists of graduates (bachelors, licentiates, and *incipientes*) in arts are to be found as they were written down by the procurators of the 'nation' in the manuscript *Conclusions de la Nation d'Allemagne*, 1477-1492,[1] in the Sorbonne. The lists appear from time to time among the various items of Faculty business recorded by the procurators or their scribes. There is no mention of a 'Gul Donbere' in 1480-1, nor in any other year dealt with. A second manuscript record, of graduates in the years 1461-1493, is available in the Bibliothèque Nationale in the form of the *Livres des Receveurs*[2] which were compiled by the annually elected *receptores* of the 'nation', but the name of Dunbar does not appear. There was one tantalising uncertainty in the Sorbonne list for 1480-1,[3] which is inserted between other records dated 31st March and 5th April respectively: the licentiates named are six in number (of whom four are from Scottish dioceses, three of them from St. Andrews) and reappear on the next sheet as *incipientes*, but at the foot of the list of licentiates is a seventh name that has been erased, long ago, and probably by a contemporary hand, though the tops and tails of some of the letters escaped the eraser.[4] The uncertainty was ended, however, by consulting the corresponding list in the Bibliothèque Nationale where, in the *Livres des Receveurs*, a seventh name appears which corresponds exactly with the remains of the letters in the Sorbonne entry and which reads 'Dns georgius tyme dyoc. bomburgensis'.[5] No doubt therefore remained: Dunbar's name had not been in the list. Nor does he appear in the lists of the Picardy 'nation' which are extant for the years 1476-1484.[6] The records of the other two nations, Normandy and France, have not survived. Opportunity was taken to search the various cartons containing miscellaneous records of the period, without positive result. The records of licentiates and doctors in theology[7] were also searched in vain; there is no matriculation list in theology.

Smeaton's account implies, but does not assert explicitly, that Dunbar was a student of Paris University. He writes of 'careful inspection of the registers of the old University'. By whom were

[1] Paris Univ. Archives, No. 8 (MS. Register No. 10, First Series, 2nd Divison).

[2] Bib. Nat., MS. Archives, H 2588.

[3] Univ. Archives, No. 8, f. 53.

[4] M. van Moé, in the printed *Auctarium*, III, p. 470, writes, 'Postea sequitur una linea cancellata ex qua nihil nunc legi potest'.

[5] Bib. Nat. Archives, MS. H 2588, f. 80.

[6] MS. Univ. Archives, No. 9. [7] Bib. Nat. Archives, MS. 5657A.

they inspected? Were they inspected by Smeaton himself? If not, why does he not state his authority? Where exactly was the name of 'Gul Donbere' found? Was it found in the records of 1480-1? If so, why does it merely 'seem to indicate that Dunbar resided in Paris' at that time? No reliance can be placed on statements so vague and so ill-supported, when precision would have been easy. This is not the last time when it will be necessary to reject Smeaton's assertions of fact. There is no evidence at all that Dunbar attended Paris University.

CHAPTER III

'MONY WRINK AND WYLE'

As a licentiate in arts, Dunbar would in the normal course be expected to take his place on the teaching staff. The mere licence to teach would thus be converted into full membership of the St. Andrews corporation of masters. In the ceremony of admission (*inceptio*), the new member ascended to the master's chair in front of the assembled masters and the procurators of the 'nations'. A banquet was afterwards provided by the *incipientes* for the distinguished company, among whom the provost and bailies of the city were sometimes numbered. But the teaching obligations that were assumed in these proceedings, and the considerable expense, made some of the licentiates avoid inception. In 1419 one third of their number seem to have defaulted, and in 1448 six out of thirteen.[1] The early stipulation for licence, that the licentiate must undertake to assume his teaching responsibilities by means of inception within eighty days, was made more stringent in 1476 by reducing the eighty to forty, but without much effect.[2] The licence itself was becoming to an increasing extent the termination of the course in arts. And, like the obligation to go forward to inception, the requirement that the graduate should teach for at least two years in the University had also lapsed. It had been abolished in Paris in 1452,[3] and dispensation from it was easy at St. Andrews.[4] Failure to pay even the fine for default had become a matter of course.[5]

We do not know how long Dunbar taught after graduating as master of arts in 1479, nor whether he did teach, nor again whether he incepted at all. Between the 1479 entry in the graduation roll and the grant of a pension from King James IV in 1500, there is a complete gap in the external evidence as to Dunbar. But one of his poems shows that many years before the date of its composition he wandered far abroad in Franciscan dress. He was not a Franciscan

[1] Hannay, *Statutes*, p. 8. [2] ib., p. 38.
[3] Rashdall, I, p. 464. [4] Hannay, p. 33. [5] ib., p. 21.

in 1500. His connexion with the friars must now be considered, and the hypotheses to which it has given rise.

For this purpose we are thrown back entirely upon internal evidence in one of the poems, *How Dumbar wes Desyrd to be ane Freir*. The poet relates how he was visited during the previous night by (as he thought) St. Francis, carrying the habit of one of his Order. Addressing Dunbar in tones of authority, the visitant told him to put on the dress and turn from the world, for he must be a friar. But the poet took fright at both the speaker and the clothes he carried, as at a ghost. When the supposed saint threw the dress over him, Dunbar at once leapt to the floor, shunning the dress, and would never come near it. The saint tries next to soothe him, though insisting still that Dunbar, who has for long taught the laws of Venus, must now become a friar and preach in the proffered garb. St. Francis' brethren have often pleaded with Dunbar in letters, sermons, and 'relationis', to take the habit, but he always[1] postponed. Now he must put aside all circumstance and excuse. The poet replies mildly, thanking the seeming saint for his goodwill and for the kind offer of the clothes, but denying that it ever entered his mind to wear them.[2] In sacred legends he has heard it stated that, among the saints, bishops have been sevenfold more numerous than friars, and that very few friars have been saints. Therefore he tells St. Francis to fetch him a bishop's robes if he wishes Dunbar's soul to reach heaven. If ever his fortune was to be a friar, the date thereof 'is past full mony a yeir', for in every pleasant town of England from Berwick to Calais he has made good cheer in Franciscan garb. In friar's dress he has flattered adroitly. He has entered the pulpit in it and has preached in 'Derntoun kirk and eik in Canterberry'. In it he passed at Dover over the ferry and through Picardy, where he taught the people. As long as he bore the style of a friar, there was many a trick and wile in him, and falsehood with which to flatter everybody, which could be absolved by no holy water. He was always ready to beguile.[3] The final stanza ends the dream abruptly. This friar that had the appearance of St. Francis was a fiend in likeness of a friar. He vanished with stink and fiery smoke, seeming to the poet to take with him all the house-end, and Dunbar awoke in bewilderment.

[1] The 'ay' is in MF. and R., but not in B. See the note on the sources of this poem, in Chapter X.

[2] This stanza, lines 21-25, is omitted by B. and R.

[3] MF. 'to bakbyte'.

On this poem different conclusions have been based. Some writers take Dunbar to have been at one time a friar. Others, the greater number, conclude that he had been a novice but had avoided taking the final vows. And also the view has been put forward that there is no convincing reason to believe that Dunbar was ever even a novice.

Laing, considering that without becoming a full friar Dunbar could not legitimately have preached, takes the poem to mean that he had indeed been a friar.[1] But the medieval church had an enduring problem in the vagabondage of the members of regular orders,[2] and a quick-witted novice trained in his rule and willing to dissemble would not easily be detected in distant parts. In later life Dunbar was clearly not a friar. He might no doubt have obtained papal dispensation to leave the Order, but dispensation was not easy to obtain unless warranted by circumstances outwith the applicant's control. Mere disinclination was not a sufficient ground. The chief difficulty, however, in the view that Dunbar had been a friar is to harmonise it with this poem, for the poem would have to mean that the temptation presented to Dunbar was to become a friar for the second time in his life.

> Gif evir my fortoun wes to be a freir,
> The dait thairof is past full mony a yeir.

There is ambiguity in the first of these lines. Does it mean, 'If at any time (at one time) there lay in store for me the life of a friar'? Or, 'If at one time I was a friar'? There remains, even with the second interpretation, a playful hint of a doubt. We cannot feel that the line is accurately read as meaning plainly 'Though at one time I was a friar'. The point will be returned to in a moment. Meantime it is noteworthy that in no other line of the poem is it suggested that the poet had already been a friar. He is told,

> Reffus the warld, for thow mon be a freir.

'Thow . . . Sall now be freir.' The Franciscan brethren have urged him, not to resume the habit, but 'to tak the abyte'.

On the other hand Dr. Mackenzie questions whether Dunbar's

[1] L., I, pp. 10-11. Haliburton, p. 218, misquotes the line 'Gif evir my fortoun wes to be a freir' by omitting the first two words. Shairp, p. 207, says that, having become a friar, Dunbar soon became ashamed 'of wandering about preaching and living on the alms of the poor'. This is to mistake the whole tone of the poem.

[2] Coulton, *Five Centuries*, II, pp. 328-330.

previous connexion with the Franciscans went the length even of a novitiate.[1] He refers to Dunbar's answer when he was offered the Franciscan clothes:

Bot thame to weir it nevir come in my mynd.

But this answer is comic when related to the many adventures which he almost immediately after admits to have had while actually wearing the garb. Nor, in view of the 'mony wrink and wyle' to which Dunbar pleads guilty, can Dr. Mackenzie's further objection be accepted that a novice was not entitled to wear the full Franciscan dress. Again, the same editor states that refusal by Dunbar, after becoming a novice, to enter the Order would have made him an apostate. But until the final vows were taken a novice was not bound by the Rule and could draw back. There is, moreover, one reason for believing that if Dunbar was not a friar he was almost certainly a novice, or had been a novice, at the time of his preachings and wanderings as a Franciscan. Without some intensive training in the traditions and ways of the Order, it is almost incredible that he could have posed as a friar both in public and in private without detection.

In these circumstances Mackay and Schipper were justified in concluding that, though not a friar, Dunbar had been a novice of the Franciscan order.[2] When he wandered through England and Picardy in the dress of a friar, Dunbar was therefore pretending to be what he was not. In later life he was himself to narrate fancifully in *Ane Ballat of the Fenyeit Freir of Tungland* how John Damian, having slain a friar, clad himself in the habit and conducted himself as a friar until his pretence became known.

Viewed thus, the poem, *How Dumbar wes Desyrd to be ane Freir*, acquires added point. When the supposed St. Francis instructs his 'servand' to put on the Franciscan dress, he means of course that Dunbar is to become a friar. But the poet takes comic fright not only at the vision of the saint but also at 'his abbeit',

With him and with his abbeit bayth I skarrit,

for the dress reminds him of his frauds in youth. He is, as he himself says, like a man confronted by a ghost—the French *revenant* would express the exact shade of meaning. When the dress is thrown upon his bed, he leaps to the floor at once, and St. Francis

[1] M., p. xxi. [2] S.T.S., I. p. xxiii. S. ed., p. 238.

asks, 'Quhy skarris thow with this holy weid?' The Franciscan brethren would be more likely to supplicate him elaborately

Be epistillis, sermonis, and relationis,

if he had already at some previous time been a novice; and in the next line,

To tak the abyte, bot thow did postpone,

the word 'postpone' is exactly applicable. The continual references in the rest of the poem to 'freiris weid' and 'the freiris style' are likewise appropriate and, finally, so is the comic ambiguity already discussed, in the line

Gif evir my fortoun wes to be a freir.

We do not know in what year Dunbar became a Franciscan novice. He may have entered a friary after a short period of teaching at St. Andrews, following upon his graduation in arts, so that his year's novitiate was perhaps over by 1481. The mention of Picardy in *How Dumbar wes Desyrd to be ane Freir* allows him to be assigned to the reformed or Observant branch of the Franciscan order, a branch which, reaching Scotland in 1447, was already eclipsing in importance the older Conventual fraternity which it later absorbed. Dunbar's account of having travelled to Picardy and of having taught the people there, would have little significance in relation to the Conventuals, but Picardy was the centre of the Observant movement in Northern Europe, and from the friary at Mirabelle in Picardy the Observants had spread their influence far and wide.[1] The difficulty suggests itself that if masquerading as an Observant friar Dunbar would rather have kept well away from headquarters in Picardy. But there were no doubt ways of avoiding suspicion: the cowled cloak of the friar could on occasion be laid aside, the company of a friar accomplice ready to vouch for him might tide him over awkward moments, or in certain areas he need not risk overstepping legitimate limits.

In Lothian, the Franciscan houses at Haddington and Inverkeithing were Conventual. The Observant fraternity at Stirling was not established until 1494, but that at Edinburgh was of unusual importance. Here Dunbar would probably receive the main part of his Franciscan training. But novices of the Order were sometimes

[1] Bryce, p. 52.

given a preliminary course at the Observant house in St. Andrews, and Dunbar's first close contact with the friars may therefore have been in his own university town, where the Franciscans had been appointed by the Archbishop to be the confessors of the students.[1]

The Edinburgh friary was situated on the south side of the Grassmarket and looked north to the rough slope, intersected by winding paths, that rose to Castle Hill. It was outside the city walls, which at that time, after coming across Castle Hill, struck east at the West Bow behind the houses of the High Street. The valley of the Cowgate, in which the friary stood, was still rural, its southern slopes dotted with the houses of religious communities such as the Franciscans. Near the friary, on the east, ran the Loaning, the main roadway from Edinburgh to the south, descending from the West Bow and climbing the southern slope.[2] The Edinburgh friary was the chief house of the Observants in Scotland, and the residence of the vicar of the Scottish 'province'. In it was the provincial seminary of philosophy and theology.[3] The community received annually an allowance from the crown, paid through the 'custumars' of Edinburgh,[4] and as mendicants they would obtain supplementary donations. The glebe was used for grazing cattle. The friars worked among the poor of the city, and were the recognised agents of the priests of the collegiate church of St. Giles in the distribution of certain charities.[5] They were thus fulfilling the precepts of their founder, whose interests lay not in study nor in manual labour but in the poor. The domestic work of the friary, the care of the vegetable garden and orchard, would lie mainly with lay brothers, though one can imagine that the services of a novice might be called on. The friars themselves were the auxiliaries of the parish priests, under whom they were meant to work as confessors and preachers. Indeed, so close were the friars to the people that they were regarded by the secular clergy with some uneasiness, for where the confessor was dependent on the public for his upkeep there was risk of too great indulgence at confession, in addition to the danger that the work of the friar would undercut that of the parish priest. As a novice, Dunbar would not be allowed to confess or to preach, but he would be employed in a more humble capacity in the general social ministrations undertaken by the friars. Though not entitled to wear the friar's cowl, he would wear the coarse brown cloak,

[1] Bryce, p. 140. [2] ib., p. 265. [3] ib., p. 277.
[4] ib., p. 272. [5] ib., p. 279.

breeches under it, the cord, and the hood reaching to the waist; he would normally be barefoot, though the Rule permitted the wearing of shoes in wintry weather. His studies would be mainly vocational. The scholastic qualifications demanded of a friar were probably extremely slight. But that is not to say that facilities and encouragement were not given for very much more. In England the Franciscan educational system was highly developed; most of their houses had a lecturer to conduct instruction and disputation, there was a more advanced central school of theology for each of the 'custodies' or districts, and a supply of university-trained teachers was carefully maintained.[1] As centre of the Scottish Observant 'province', the Edinburgh house may be assumed to have provided similarly advanced instruction for those of their novices or friars who were capable of benefiting. Dunbar's course in arts at St. Andrews had already taken him some way in philosophy, and a youth of his acumen would not fail to grasp whatever was offered him in theology. The preaching traditions of his Order would provide him too with experience and models of which he was shortly to make extensive use in his own itinerant preaching.

In connexion with the friary at Edinburgh, it is necessary to refer to another of Smeaton's alleged discoveries. He writes, 'In the school of the Observantines there was one peerless Latinist, John Leyrva, a Lombard, whose personality has been but a shadowy one until recent discoveries have proved that the supposed coterie of great Franciscan scholars in the Edinburgh of the fifteenth century was in reality but the different designations of this one brilliant genius. That Dunbar was one of Leyrva's pupils is more than probable, particularly as the latter, when he returned to Italy, mentioned in one of his sonnets a Gulielmus Donbar as being "*carissimus discipulusque amicus*".'[2]

For all this information, no source is stated at all. In his preface Smeaton writes, 'Being a popular sketch, therefore, in a popular series, I have purposely avoided, as far as possible, the discussion of recondite controversial topics, and the introduction of dry disquisitions on obscure points of diction or on matters which possess an interest merely antiquarian.' But if this foreword is intended to explain why no source is indicated for information so novel as that just quoted, it is insufficient. There was no need here for controversy. The discoveries were recent, and they were precise. Even

[1] Little, p. 163. [2] Smeaton, p. 27.

the source of the sonnet quoted would have given a clue to be followed up. There are footnotes on many matters in Smeaton's book, but this new material, so illuminating and suggestive, receives no support, no further comment.

What writings of this 'peerless Latinist' are extant? Where is there any shadowy reference to him, contemporary with him or not, previous to that by Smeaton? Who made the recent discoveries, and where are they? When were they made? Where can the record of the supposed coterie of scholars be found? And other questions suggest themselves with particular reference to Dunbar. Where are the sonnets? When did Leyrva return to Italy? What are the other reasons hinted at that make it 'more than probable' that Dunbar was one of Leyrva's pupils? What else was said about Dunbar in the sonnet? What was the rest of the sonnet? When the whole account is so unsupported, what reliance can be placed on these statements of Smeaton, especially when viewed in connexion with others of his which are unreliable?

The writer has completely failed to trace a mention of John Leyrva in any available work other than that of Smeaton.[1] In addition he has consulted several living authorities on the Franciscans, but they know nothing of Leyrva.[2] He is also unknown at the present friary in Edinburgh.[3] Smeaton died in 1914, and all his papers were destroyed after his death.

As to the general reliability of Smeaton's information, his statement that Dunbar's name occurs in the registers of Paris University in a specified year has already been discussed. Actual investigation

[1] He has not been able to consult the Brockie MS. at Blairs College, Aberdeen, as the MS. has been on loan elsewhere for a protracted period. It is described in a letter to him from Dr. Cronin, Rector of the College, as 'a Monasticon Scoticum of three volumes, collected by Father Marianus Brockie, a monk of the Benedictine monastery of St. James, Ratisbon, of which he was prior. In his preface he says it contains all discoverable information from the most ancient codices, civil and ecclesiastical instruments, and the most trustworthy authorities, concerning the abbeys, priories, cells, churches, and houses of all the religious orders in Scotland, from the introduction of Christianity to the dissolution of the monasteries. Tome III deals with the various orders of friars.'

[2] Among those consulted was Dr. A. G. Little, chairman of the British Society of Franciscan Studies and an authority on the Franciscans who lived in England and Scotland. The Rev. P. Blackwell of Fort Augustus Abbey kindly directed the writer to the Rev. P. Cuthbert at Assisi, formerly head of the Franciscan house at Oxford; Leyrva was unknown to him, and also to an authority on Franciscan writers, whom he was so good as to consult on the writer's behalf.

[3] Information communicated by Mr. F. Harvey, who obliged the writer by consulting the Guardian of the Friary in Lothian Street.

of the Paris records by the writer has shown these statements to be unfounded in fact. In the present case there is no clue to follow. It will be shown later that Smeaton's production of an equally surprising mention of Dunbar in a supposed letter from Archbishop Blackadder to the Bishop of Beauvais is not justified when the matter is investigated.

Smeaton wrote also a book on Allan Ramsay, in the same series as that for which he wrote on Dunbar.[1] Mr. Andrew Gibson, in a more recent work on Allan Ramsay,[2] remarks, 'The "we learn" information presented by Mr. Smeaton is, however, very different from anything on the subject that is stated by any other writer known to us.'[3] His character of Ramsay's stepfather, Mr. Gibson describes as 'most largely imaginary'.[4] Where Smeaton, having set down a dialogue *verbatim*, refers to it as 'the brief dialogue recorded above—for the authenticity of which there is abundant evidence', Mr. Gibson comments as follows: 'We do not believe that there is, or ever was, "abundant evidence", or any evidence, of any weight whatever, for the "authenticity" of the "brief dialogue" that is "recorded" by Mr. Smeaton.'[5] Again, Smeaton having quoted a statement which he said was made by Dr. Ruddiman in a letter to a friend, Mr. Gibson remarks as to this letter, 'We characterise it as a bogus production', and he proceeds to show that it contains misstatements of fact which could not have been made by Ruddiman.[6] Of a letter 'hitherto unpublished' which is quoted extensively *verbatim* by Smeaton, Mr. Gibson suggests that if extant it should be produced and should be examined by an expert in handwritings, and Mr. Gibson adds that the letter may be one of the many documents forged by Alexander Howland Smith.[7]

This mention of Smith is worth dwelling upon for a moment. 'Antique' Smith was sentenced to twelve months' imprisonment for fraud, at Edinburgh High Court of Justiciary, on the 27th June 1893,[8] five years before the publication of Smeaton's book on Dunbar. Smith's offence was that he had pawned and sold, as genuine, spurious manuscripts. Some of those pawned were sold in 1890 in batches of two or three, by one of the pawnbrokers concerned, the sale book being later destroyed. At one particular sale Mr.

[1] *Allan Ramsay*, 'Famous Scots' Series, Edin., 1896.

[2] *New Light on Allan Ramsay*, Andrew Gibson, Edin., 1927.

[3] ib., p. 12. [4] ib., p. 13.

[5] ib., p. 30. [6] ib., p. 44. [7] ib., p. 18.

[8] *Reports of the High Court of Justiciary in Scotland*, Edin., 1895, I, p. 6.

George Traquhair Thin, the bookseller, bought some of the manuscripts but, examining them next day and finding them to be forgeries, he passed them to the procurator fiscal. But not all the forgeries of Smith that reached the public were dealt with so sensibly. Hundreds were disposed of at various times, and opinions differed as to their genuineness. Only some of the forgeries were produced in court, among them letters purporting to be written by Scott, Burns, Hogg, James Watt and Lord Macaulay.

In the Edinburgh of the nineties many forged manuscripts were therefore circulating. Smeaton, who was a friend of at least one member of the firm of Messrs. Thin, booksellers,[1] and who had returned to this country from Australia in 1893, must have heard of particular letters and may even have seen some of them. The possibility is there, though it is scarcely probable, that some of the forged letters were claimed to be written by William Dunbar. It is improbable, for it would be much more difficult to forge with any degree of verisimilitude a letter of the fifteenth century than a letter of so recent a period as that of Scott or Burns.

Before leaving 'John Leyrva' and his 'sonnets', reference must be made to a review of Smeaton's book on Dunbar and to a significant occurrence a few years later. The review, which was unsigned, appeared in October 1898 in *The Scottish Antiquary*.[2] Picking out and listing the 'discoveries' set down by Smeaton, the reviewer expresses regret that no authorities are cited for these, and writes, 'Did we not know from Mr. Smeaton himself that many of his "facts" have been obtained by "a sort of hypothetical literary synthesis, resulting from the comparison of probabilities", we might readily have suspected that so much new information as the book affords about Henryson and Kennedy, to name only two of the *dramatis personae*, had been courteously and specially communicated by some "dusk undeveloped spirit" from Elysium.' The present writer has failed to trace any reply by Smeaton to this review. But in his *Story of Edinburgh*, 1905, Smeaton returns to 'John Leyrva': 'The schools of the Greyfriars were in great repute; and tradition asserts that William Dunbar, the poet, was educated there under the great Latinist, John Leyrva, a Lombard.'[3] So far from taking the opportunity of giving some proof of his earlier assertions,

[1] Mr. James Thin, senior, informed the writer that he knew Smeaton well.
[2] *The Scottish Antiquary, or Northern Notes and Queries*, XIII, p. 97, Oct. 1898.
[3] Smeaton, *Story of Edinburgh*, p. 335.

Smeaton has now abandoned the 'recent discoveries' and 'sonnets' of which he wrote in 1898, and has substituted merely that 'tradition asserts'. We have no further hesitation in rejecting the whole story.

It would be fruitless to attempt to determine how Dunbar came to leave his Franciscan house—at Edinburgh or elsewhere—for the life of the open road. But had he been a *bona fide* friar, there was nothing illegitimate for him in this life. The Franciscan rule enjoined[1] that a friar should avoid settling in a fixed residence lest his poverty might become modified in comfortable and secure surroundings. The injunction had long been passed over in practice, but it was still true that the friar, as a pilgrim and stranger, should live on the alms of his fellow-men. It was his part to mingle with the motley throngs of wayfarers, peasants, wandering artisans, pedlars, thieves, beggars, messengers, students, felons, pardoners, minstrels, quacks, tumblers and others. He would normally be on foot, staff in hand, but it was not infrequent for a friar to travel on horseback.[2] There were plenty of roads of a sort, the main ones dating from Roman times. Their upkeep was a duty of landed proprietors, and it was also a pious duty of every Christian to contribute, in order that pilgrims might be spared undue hardship and danger. Yet in fact the roads were in disrepair and would vanish often in the quags; the bridges, neglected, would become dangerous. Dangerous, too, would be the outlaws and broken men that hid in the innumerable forests. The peasants used crude two-wheeled carts, and well-to-do ladies used horse-litters, but the speediest and safest mode of travel would in general be on horseback. Even a friar's robe might hide a dagger for self-protection in need. Hospitality for the night could be sought in the guest-house of a monastery or on the rush-strewn floor of a castle hall. The common inns, sleeping several men in each bed, and flea-infested, would usually be too expensive.[3] At crossroads stood the ale-houses, with projecting pole and bush, many of them places of ill repute. Shelter might often be found with some 'hermit' of dubious character, who kept a cottage on a busy highway and lived on the alms of his guests.[4]

In *How Dumbar wes Desyrd to be ane Freir*, the poet makes much of his misadventures as a preacher. The main duty of preaching

[1] Bryce, p. 479. [2] ib., p. 18.
[3] Jusserand, p. 125. [4] ib., p. 143.

lay with bishops and parish priests, who had the cure of souls, and the friars were supposed to be only helpers. But, in practice, preaching had become mainly a matter for the friars, as the parish priests had so many other duties, whereas the friar was a specialist preacher. Indeed, only a few sermons a year were expected of the parish priest, except during Lent when there were to be daily sermons.[1] To preach, a friar had to be nominated by the provincial minister of his Order. Dunbar not being a friar, we may assume that no nomination was made in his case. But he may have started his Franciscan travels in the company of an authorised friar-preacher and, once at large and far from his home establishment, may have begun to usurp the function of preacher. The right to preach within any particular diocese depended upon the licence of the bishop.[2] But the medieval discrepancy between theory and practice no doubt operated here as in other fields. Enforcement of the system, and verification of the identity of the friar authorised, would be very difficult because of the state of communications. The invitation of the parish priest to preach in his church would be sufficient,[3] and for open-air preaching no invitation would be needed or asked. Nor was the confessional any more a monopoly of the secular clergy than preaching; but a Franciscan novice was entitled neither to hear confession nor to preach, and if Dunbar had to do with the confessional this would be another of the misdeeds which, he says, 'mycht be flemit with na haly watter'.

The ordinary church sermon, at mass, was brief, only a few minutes before or after the offertory. The great preachings were on the Sunday afternoons and might last two hours.[4] The friars preached always in the vernacular, whether in church or in the open air. Even at the indoor preachings the crowd was disorderly, especially in the large naves of friary churches.[5] Out of doors, in the churchyard or at one of the preaching crosses, the friar had to compete with all the tumult of business and amusement. His preaching tended to be spectacular in the extreme. His jests would provoke roars of laughter. His denunciations of worldliness, including the worldliness of the clergy, would invoke the terrors of hell-fire. All his stores of striking anecdote, his experiences of wayfaring, his knowledge of foreign parts, would be drawn upon.[6] Metrical effects appeared in some sermons, 'macaronic' verse sometimes interlard-

[1] Owst, p. 146. [2] Bryce, p. 404. [3] Little, p. 114.
[4] Owst, p. 156. [5] ib., p. 157. [6] ib., p. 82.

ing English and Latin, as in some of Dunbar's poems written later. John Wycliffe had complained of the rhyming sermons of the friars.[1]

In these circumstances there were many charlatans. Some of the friars preachers were suspected of having no preaching licence from the superiors of their Orders.[2] Mere boys are stated to have been sent out preaching and begging.[3] Many Scottish friars passed through England, going to and from Rome, and would be able to fill their pockets without difficulty. The frequent regulations by the Church for the stern treatment of apostates and vagabond friars is an indication that the problem was of considerable magnitude.[4]

Dunbar tells how in Franciscan attire he made good cheer in

> every lusty toun and place
> Off all Yngland, frome Berwick to Kalice.

If this means that he made a crossing of England from north to south, from Berwick to Dover, he would pass through or near five of the seven great educational centres of the English Franciscans, Newcastle, York, Stamford, Norwich, and London. He says he preached from the pulpit

> In Derntoun kirk, and eik in Canterberry.

Derntoun has been variously identified, as Darlington, Dearn in south Yorkshire,[5] and Dirrington near Greenlaw in Berwickshire; but Professor Bruce Dickins refers to early forms of the word which amply support the identification with Darlington.[6] Dunbar would, no doubt, be at least a visitor to St. Paul's churchyard in London, the most famous scene of outdoor preachings, and he would cross the Thames by old London Bridge, lined on each parapet with lofty dwelling-houses, some of which collapsed in 1481.[7] From Southwark onwards he would be on the great highway to the Continent. At Canterbury the body of St. Thomas lay behind the altar of Trinity Chapel.[8] He would require a passport at Dover, as in the case of 'all manner of people, as well clerks as other'.[9] The crossing from Dover was indeed a ferry, as Dunbar calls it, for Calais was also under English rule. There was a noted *Maison Dieu* or hospital

[1] Owst, p. 276. [2] ib., p. 76. [3] ib., p. 84.

[4] Bryce, p. 104. Coulton, *Five Centuries*, II, p. 330.

[5] S.T.S., III, p. 213, note by Gregor.

[6] Prof. Bruce Dickins, *Modern Language Review*, Oct. 1933, p. 507. He cites Dr. Mawer's *The Place-Names of Northumberland and Durham*.

[7] Jusserand, p. 47. [8] ib., p. 349. [9] ib., p. 370.

at Calais for the relief of pilgrims.[1] Once in France, he would soon be at Amiens, and so

> Throw Piccardy, and thair the peple teichit.

In Picardy, as has already been said, was Mirabelle, the friary from which the Franciscan Observants had spread wide their community.[2] Beyond lay Paris, from which, some years before, another master of arts, Villon, had fled to a life of vagabondage. The escapades of Dunbar recall those of the French poet, though Dunbar's may have involved nothing so serious as manslaughter or the robbing of the College of Navarre.

A passage in *The Flyting of Dunbar and Kennedie* probably refers to this period of travel in Dunbar's life. The most likely date for *The Flyting*, as will be shown in a later chapter, is the latter part of the year 1500.[3] Dunbar being then about to set out for the Continent, Kennedy taunts him with the disreputable life he has led as a vagrant pardoner.[4] One cannot feel entirely satisfied about an interpretation which stretches reminiscence over a long period of years, but a few lines later[5] Kennedy narrates the tale of the disastrous voyage of Dunbar in the *Katryne* twenty years before. It is reasonable, therefore, to regard the pardoner expedition also as belonging to a period many years before *The Flyting*, and therefore to the days when Dunbar wore the dress of a Franciscan, or at least to an extension of that period. Kennedy says that Dunbar went with his pardons into all the churches from Ettrick Forest to Dumfries, and by his sales was able to provide himself with collops, curds, meal, groats, pigs (*grisis*), and geese, and under cover of night he stole stags and stirks. How far is this information reliable? Not very far, probably, in view of the traditional devices of flyting poets, the exigencies of alliterative verse, and the fact that this is a reply to Dunbar's abusive account of Kennedy's thefts of poultry in the west country. But there is, no doubt, a substratum of truth, or the arrow would have no target. The campaign with pardons would fit readily into the life of the wandering preacher and mendicant. The pardoner was not always scrupulous about having an episcopal licence, and so much lucre was attached that the life was often undertaken as a private venture, in which the whole of the

[1] Jusserand, p. 371. [2] Bryce, p. 52. [3] Chapter VI.
[4] *The Flyting*, lines 425 onwards.
[5] ib., lines 449 onwards.

proceeds would be the reward of enterprise.[1] The wandering pardoner would occupy a pulpit as special preacher, the collection being frequently on these occasions in aid of a hospital; and the sacred relics, donated in former times to hospitals for curative purposes, would be carried by the pardoner on tour in order to reinforce, with the indulgences he had to offer, his appeal to the generosity of the pious and charitable.[2]

[1] Jusserand, p. 316. [2] Owst, pp. 100-104.

CHAPTER IV

'IN REALMES BY'

IT is the generally accepted view that even before 1500 Dunbar was employed by the King on diplomatic missions abroad.

We have no reason to suppose that all or even most of his poems are extant, but not much that is definite can be gathered from references in the poems that have survived. The poems themselves are of doubtful dates. He writes to the King of his long and faithful service,[1] but was this service abroad or at court? His supposed allusions to his travels are somewhat ambiguous. In one case it is not clear whether he himself is heard tell of 'throw all regiones', or only his poems.[2] In another case,[3] when he has lamented in general terms how, in this unstable world, rewards are not commensurate with services rendered, he adds,

> Nocht I say all be this cuntre,
> France, Ingland, Ireland, Almanie,
> Bot als be Italie and Spane;
>   Quhilk to considder is ane pane.

These lines have been interpreted, unconvincingly, as relating to his own travels.[4] Elsewhere there is slightly firmer evidence. He writes,

> Quhen I was young and into ply,
> And wald cast gammaldis to the sky,
> I had beine bocht in realmes by,
> Had I consentit to be sauld,[5]

and he criticises Edinburgh houses for their stairs which project into the street and make the houses dark

> Lyk na cuntray bot heir at hame.[6]

[1] *To the King: Complane I Wald*, lines 69-71. *To the King: Schir, yit Remembir*, lines 1-3. *To the King: Petition of the Gray Horse, Old Dunbar*, lines 68-70. *To the King: On the World's Instability*, lines 3, 13-16.

[2] *To the King: Complane I Wald*, lines 71-73.

[3] *To the King: On the World's Instability*, lines 17-20.

[4] L., I, p. 12. Miss R. A. Taylor, p. 34. S.T.S., p. 390.

[5] *To the King: Petition of the Gray Horse*, lines 7-10.

[6] *To the Merchants of Edinburgh*, lines 17-18.

Yet there is surprisingly little mention of his experiences in foreign lands, in the poems extant. There is enough, especially in *The Flyting of Dunbar and Kennedie* which will be considered in a later chapter, to show that he did travel abroad. On the other hand, it is only a doubtful inference that his travels before 1500 were in the royal service.

James IV kept up a continual exchange of diplomatic missions with the leading powers of the Continent. The military predominance of France was a source of uneasiness to her neighbours even before she launched her fateful expedition into Italy in 1494. From that year, other powers of Europe worked to build up an effective counterpoise and a common understanding to oppose her aggressive policy. In these circumstances the position of Scotland, the traditional ally of France, at the rear of England gave James a European importance of which he availed himself to the full. The record of diplomatic activity is complex, and shows that there must have been plenty of scope for men of intelligence, education, and some knowledge of other lands. It may well be that Dunbar played a minor role in some of these missions.

Since the days of Laing it has been customary to associate Dunbar's name, without good reason, with that embassy in particular which left Scotland for France in July 1491. In May of that year, Parliament recorded that the King had entrusted to Blackadder, Bishop of Glasgow, and to Patrick Hepburn, Earl of Bothwell, the charge of an embassy which was to pass to France, Spain and other countries, to seek a suitable match for James in marriage.[1] On 16th July, in the Accounts of the Lord Treasurer, a payment occurs 'to my Lord Boythwell, quhilk the King gart him gif to the schipmen of the Katryn, besyd Northberwic, quhen the Imbassatouris past in Franss.'[2] At the same time, 'Item, til a prest that wrayt the instrumentis and oderis letteris, that past with the Imbassitouris in France, xxxvi s.'[3] This entry is followed in the manuscript accounts by a deleted one 'to my lord boythwell quhen he lay at north berwic with the schippis'.[4] The embassy returned to Scotland in November 1491, payment being recorded on the 29th November, of eighteen shillings 'quhen the King com fra Sanct

[1] *Acts*, II, p. 224.

[2] T.A., I, p. 179. L., misled by an accompanying entry, assumed Lord Monypenny to be one of the ambassadors (see Michel, p. 301).

[3] ib., I, p. 180.

[4] MS. *Compot. Thesaur.*, 1488-92, f. 88.

Johnstoun to Edinburgh, quhen the Erle Boythwell com hame, til a boyt he com owr the water in'[1]; and again on the same date, £9 'quhen the King com fra Pertht, quhen my Lord Boythwel com hame to the King efter none, in the Abay, to the cartis'.[2] On the 20th February following, the Lords of the Articles agreed that the business of the embassy had been efficiently conducted.[3]

Laing writes that 'it is more than probable' that Dunbar was with this embassy,[4] since Laing considers Dunbar to have been in Paris when the last passage of *The Flyting of Dunbar and Kennedie*, with its reference to the ship *Katryne*, was written. It will be shown in a later chapter[5] that Dunbar could not have been in Paris when the passage referred to was written, and Laing only maintained that Dunbar was by abandoning as incoherent the poem as it is extant. It is by no means incoherent. As for the mention of the ship *Katryne* in Kennedy's account of Dunbar's seasickness, and, again, in the Treasurer's Accounts in connexion with the 1491 embassy, there is no justification for placing the two together and inferring that Dunbar sailed with the embassy in 1491 in the *Katryne*. If *The Flyting* is dated correctly at 1500, and traces of Dunbar's discomfort remained on the ship 'this twenty yere', 1491 would be too late for the poet's misadventure. But there is no reason to suppose that the *Katryne* made only this one voyage recorded in the accounts of 1491. She may have plied on the seas for many years, in any one of which she may have been sailed in by Dunbar on the occasion referred to by Kennedy; and the name was used for more than one ship, for a *Katerine* of Edinburgh is recorded in 1410.[6] It is impossible to accept Mackay's statement,[7] in his memoir prefaced to the edition of Dunbar for the Scottish Text Society, that Dunbar accompanied the embassy. Indeed, Gregor in his notes in that edition points out that the 'prest that wrayt the instrumentis and oderis letteris, that past with the Imbassitouris in Franss', may not himself have gone to France, but only the 'instrumentis and oderis letteris' which he wrote.[8] The sentence is ambiguous. And Gregor adds that in *The Flyting* Dunbar is represented as having been so ill when in the *Katryne* that the skipper ordered him to be landed at the Bass, so that even on Laing's supposition Dunbar would probably not have proceeded to France on that occasion.

[1] T.A., I, p. 183. [2] ib., I, p. 172. [3] *Acts*, II, p. 230.
[4] L., I, p. 16. [5] Chapter VI. [6] Bain, IV, p. 161.
[7] S.T.S., I, p. cxiii. He has been followed in a recent work: Conway, p. 37.
[8] S.T.S., III, p. 390.

That Dunbar once sailed on the *Katryne*, that a ship of that name carried ambassadors to France in 1491, that a priest engrossed the documents of the embassy, that Dunbar travelled abroad, that he might at times have been employed on diplomatic missions—these do not form sufficient evidence to justify the conclusion that Dunbar was the priest who sailed (if the priest did sail) with the 1491 embassy. Even if it could be shown that Bishop Blackadder, leader of the embassy, was at the time a patron of Dunbar, there would still be a vast gap to fill in the story. Ten years later, during the winter of 1501-2, Blackadder, now Archbishop, was in England as ambassador in connexion with the betrothal of King James and Princess Margaret, and Dunbar was certainly in England that same winter as is shown by the accounts of the Lord Treasurer;[1] but surely this is far too slender a thread on which to hang a supposition that Blackadder was, ten years earlier, a patron of Dunbar, and there is no further evidence of such connexion.

Here Smeaton introduces, once again, new material at once extraordinary and unsubstantiated. As to James IV's power of 'knowing by a sort of intuitive divination whom he could trust', he writes: 'The same instinct led him to select William Dunbar as his confidential "King's Messenger". Why the fact never occurred to David Laing or Dr. Schipper, when compiling their exhaustive Lives of the poet, is a circumstance which to me is inexplicable.'[2]

Smeaton goes on to tell, with much circumstantial detail, how Dunbar was brought to the King's notice by Blackadder. This part of his story is better reserved for the next chapter. But it is convenient to note cursorily at this point Smeaton's further account of Dunbar's diplomatic work, based on the supposed association with Blackadder. He claims that the poet was the King's confidential agent, useful in the process by which, Smeaton says, James threw off the control of his Council of State. He adds that Dunbar 'was undoubtedly' the clerk in an embassy to Denmark arranged in 1490, the evidence being the references in *The Flyting of Dunbar and Kennedie* to 'Holland, Zealand, Zetland, and Norway coast' [*sic*]. 'Again and again Dunbar refers to Zealand or Denmark, exhibiting an intimate acquaintance with the country only to be attained by a personal visit to it. Had I space I would cite the references.'[3] It would be interesting to have this evidence. The only indication Smeaton gives is 'Vide also *Calendar of State Papers* and *The Flyting*, lines

[1] T.A., II, p. 95. [2] Smeaton, p. 45. [3] ib., p. 52.

377-384', but these references do not confirm his statements. 'The next mission of State wherein, from the internal evidence of his poems, it is almost certain he was employed, was to Rome', with certain Scots ambassadors who arrived in Venice in June 1495. 'That Dunbar visited Venice is proved by his references to the city in his poems, and I think this chain of evidence is sufficient to create at least the very strongest presumption, if we cannot go the length of affirming the absolute certainty of it, that Dunbar was a member of the embassy.'[1] Dunbar's references to Venice are imaginary, and equally baseless is the further statement that Dunbar testifies in *The Flyting* that he was absent from Scotland in 1493-4. 'From 1491, therefore, until the close of 1495, William Dunbar was ceaselessly travelling abroad in the service of his master. That fact is beyond doubt, whether he was a member of the embassy or alone.'[2] Dunbar is placed next in Spain, 'probably' just when the news of Columbus's discovery was being spread. 'That Dunbar had been deeply impressed with what he saw and heard is evident from his reference to the New World in his poem on *The World's Instability*, the date of the composition of which cannot be later than 1496.'[3] Dunbar complains in this poem that the benefice he seeks

> micht have cuming in schortar quhyll
> Fra Calyecot and the new fund Yle.

This scarcely shows a deep impression. And 'the new fund Yle' is very likely to be Newfoundland, discovered by Cabot for Henry VII in the voyage of 1497.[4] In any case, the mention of 'king' and 'quene'[5] places the poem presumably after the marriage of 1503. From Spain, Smeaton takes Dunbar to Italy: 'His poems teem with references to that Italian exuberance of beauty', and so on, and Dunbar returns homewards 'a changed man'. 'His poems before and after this memorable epoch of travel are quite distinct in tone from each other.'[6] Smeaton brings him home in the autumn of 1496, 'Dunbar having been absent considerably over four years from his native land.'[7] It can only be said that this is romancing.

[1] Smeaton, pp. 53-54. [2] ib., p. 54. [3] ib., p. 55.

[4] L., II, p. 351, quotes from *The Privy Purse Expenses of Henry VII*: 10th Aug. 1497, 'To him that found the New Isle', and 25th Aug. 1505, 'To Clays going to Richmount with wylde catts and popyngays of the New-found Island'.

[5] *To the King: On the World's Instability*, line 56.

[6] Smeaton, p. 56. [7] ib., p. 57.

CHAPTER V

'BALLATTIS UNDER THE BYRKIS'

As already stated, between the entry of Dunbar's name in the list of masters of arts graduating at St. Andrews University in 1479 and the record of his award of a pension in 1500, there is a gap in the external evidence. The considerations which suggest that his voyage in the *Katryne* and its continuation to France—if it extended to France—were shortly after 1479, will be given in the next chapter. The poems themselves, skilfully arranged, served Schipper as a tentative record of Dunbar's life during this period and in later periods. Mackay based his arrangement of the poems closely on that of Schipper, which was chronological.

The poems thus form a sequence corresponding to a supposed inner development and harmony of the poet's life. To the years before the King's marriage in 1503 are assigned those poems that seem appropriate to the court circle of a youthful monarch free from the ties and responsibilities of married life, and, on the other hand, the poems which, by their care-free air, bawdry, and satire against women, are regarded as being productions appropriate to a poet comparatively young and not yet under the supposed necessity of avoiding outrage to the delicacy of a queen. But it must remain doubtful how far there was in fact such a moral development, in King or Queen or poet, as this arrangement of the poems requires. From 1503 onwards, some of the court poems can be confidently assigned to definite dates and, around these, other poems were grouped by Schipper and Mackay according to their similarity of tone or treatment. Further, it was assumed that Dunbar's reflective and religious poems were later than the calamity of Flodden and therefore written in years when Scotland was in dire straits and when the poet would be advanced in years. This hypothesis is also unsafe. The medieval literary tradition saw nothing incongruous in an alternation of the religious and the licentious. There is no need to suppose that Dunbar's poetry on the Virgin was later than *The Tretis of the Tua Mariit Wemen and the Wedo* or *A Brash of*

Wooing. Mariolatry was the counterpart of the representation of women as the daughters of Eve, and traditionally the poet and the cleric found each of absorbing interest.

It cannot be claimed that the usual chronological groupings of Dunbar's poems have any very considerable degree of validity either in general or with reference to particular poems. But the poems do provide a mine of interesting material relating to the poet's life, and must form the principal sources for the biographer of Dunbar. Provided that what is tentative is recognised as such, the evidence of the poems is highly significant, and it is surprising with what verisimilitude, at least, the undated poems can be related to poems fixed in time and to the known circumstances of the poet and of the Scottish court. We follow generally, though with many alterations, the suggestive arrangements of Schipper and Mackay.

The pension of 1500, and the promise of a well endowed church living to which the grant was stated to be preliminary, were clearly not bestowed before, but after, services rendered to the King. What these services were is unknown. They may have been in what would now be called the diplomatic service, although, as has been shown above, the evidence for this view is very slight. It seems much more likely, from what is known of Dunbar's later position at court, that the favour shown in 1500 was the result of previous services as court poet, We are thus brought to the group of Dunbar's poems usually associated with the period before 1500, and, whatever the nature of Dunbar's early services to King James, it can scarcely be doubted that he had already at that date been much at court.

At this point it is once again necessary to refer to surprising information put forward by Smeaton. He writes: 'Who the good Samaritan was that brought Dunbar directly under the notice of his young King we have only traditionary hints whereon to base our hypothesis. Let us give them for what they are worth. Robert Blackadder, Bishop of Glasgow, . . . had always been a firm friend to Dunbar. He knew and valued the genius of the young priest, and there is a strong presumption in favour of the theory that he was the individual to whom we are indebted for introducing Dunbar to the Court of King James. . . . The Bishop, for he was not yet Archbishop, observing how easily the youthful monarch was led astray by immoral companions, is reported to have thrown Dunbar into the society of the King designedly, in the hope that he might exercise a restraining influence on the youthful ruler's headlong sensuality. There is extant in the private collection of the late Duc d'Aumale at Chantilly—by the will of the latter now the property of the French Academy—a letter of Blackadder's to the Bishop of Beauvais, wherein, after describing the excellences of the young King, he expresses regret over his glaring sensuality, but adds that he had placed a young man, a secular priest, among the royal attendants, from whose influence he expected much. The name of the young man was "Gulielmus Dunbar, a scholar, and also an excellent poet". Such then was the means whereby Dunbar was brought into contact with the monarch. From collateral evidence we glean the fact that the introduction must have taken place about January 1490. Previously to that date our poet must have made that lengthened sojourn in the Bishop's house of which the latter speaks on many occasions—a sojourn which enabled the keen-witted prelate to gauge the calibre of the man in whom he was interesting himself, and to appraise him as "without his marrow in our aige".'[1]

Smeaton cites several sources for all this. For the statement that the d'Aumale collection at Chantilly had become in terms of the Duke's will the property of the French Academy, he refers to an article by Pierre de Coubertin, *Royalists and Republicans*, in the *Century Magazine* of September 1897. For the alleged letter of Blackadder to the Bishop of Beauvais, its drift, and the quotation from it, Smeaton cites only the 'd'Aumale Collection'. For the 'collateral evidence' Smeaton gives no reference at all, nor for the repeated statements by the Bishop, whom he quotes again.

We are thus faced with a situation such as has already been analysed in connexion with Smeaton's account of 'John Leyrva'. As in the former case, Smeaton is himself inconsistent. He states first that, as to Dunbar's introduction to the King, 'we have only traditional hints whereon to base our hypothesis', and Smeaton sets out to give them 'for what they are worth'. But he next affirms that a letter is extant at Chantilly which he describes and from which he quotes. If it were extant and in the terms described and quoted, there would be no need for 'traditionary hints' on which to base a hypothesis, nor would any hypothesis be required. Smeaton himself proceeds in his next sentence to regard the evidence as definite. What then are we to make of the further 'collateral evidence' unspecified, from which emerges the 'fact' that Dunbar was introduced to King James about January 1490? In what documents

[1] Smeaton, pp. 46-48.

is it that Bishop Blackadder 'speaks on many occasions' of Dunbar's 'lengthened sojourn' in his house? Are they also the d'Aumale letters? If so, why are they only 'collateral evidence'?

The present writer visited Chantilly in 1937 in order to investigate. The collection of manuscripts there is intact as when in the possession of the Duc d'Aumale except for a number of documents of personal and family interest only, which were removed in 1897 to Belgium in accordance with the wishes of the Duc de Guise. (Smeaton's book appeared in 1898.) The manuscript letters, which are scrupulously indexed and annotated, under the names of both sender and receiver, including the letters in the family archives, do not date back so far as the fifteenth century. Smeaton's words, 'There is extant . . . a letter', must surely refer to a manuscript. There are many thousands of printed volumes. Books printed before the middle of the sixteenth century are separately indexed and annotated with great care. Nothing could be found answering to Smeaton's account.

His remarks about Blackadder's alleged letter and about Blackadder's statements were noticed by the reviewer in *The Scottish Antiquary* of October 1898, along with Smeaton's other allegations of fact about Dunbar.[1] 'We confess we should like to see the authority for these statements; and, had Mr. Smeaton printed them either in his text or in an appendix, his book unquestionably would have possessed more value than it has at present.' There is no authority for them, and Smeaton's whole story must be rejected. We can only regard the whole narrative of Dunbar's close relations with Blackadder, whether derived from 'traditionary hints', 'collateral evidence', or the supposed letter at Chantilly, as fiction. There is no evidence that Dunbar was introduced to the Scottish court by Blackadder.

The court of James IV was highly developed, the multiplicity of the officers of the household being apparent from the public records. It was well attended by the nobility and by ecclesiastics; and the lords were entitled to bring with them a number of their own followers who likewise had their meals in the palace. The burden of expense must have been heavy in so poor a realm.[2] The towns privileged by visits of the court, which followed the restless King, were small, and must at these visits have been dominated by

[1] See Chapter III.

[2] Letter of Ayala to Ferdinand and Isabella, 25th July 1498. Bergenroth, I, p. 210.

it. In Edinburgh the royal apartments in the Castle were still occupied, but were too restricted to accommodate the court. The Abbey of Holyrood had been used for centuries for this purpose. In its picturesque setting, with the Hunter's Bog and Arthur's Seat behind, it was a favourite resort of King James, who loved hunting and hawking. A few years later he was to undertake, in preparation for his marriage, the construction of a palace near by.[1] Linlithgow Palace was favoured with the royal occupation in most years at Christmas. The King visited Stirling often with his court, was a patron and a frequent guest of the Stirling Franciscans, and in 1496 began the building of a house there, 'a palice verie honorable, maist magnificent. Thairfra it is a fair and plesand sycht to the feildes, to the River, to the Parke, and to the nerrest mountanis.'[2] Another residence was the Palace of Falkland, under Lomond Hill,—a royal burgh where many of the barons provided themselves with quarters; from its gates a great hunting forest stretched over the Howe of Fife. But James did not stay long in any one place. Ayala, the Spanish ambassador, states that the King's frequent progresses through the land were partly due to his continual vigilance in matters of administration, and partly in order to consume the rents in kind which were due to him throughout the country.[3] Wherever he went, amusements and festivities accompanied him; Curry, the court fool, was on occasion sent on ahead to await his coming.[4]

The chief court festivity was at Yule, which lasted over New Year to Twelfth Night (Uphaliday). At Yule it was the custom of the King's heralds to shower largesse in public, the money being provided from the purse of the Lord Treasurer. Handsome gifts went to members of the household. On New Year's morning the Treasurer waited upon the King when he was still in bed, to supply the sums destined for the royal bounty. The King's servants were admitted with their gifts, no person being accounted too humble to have this privilege; and the King's 'rewards' to the givers were not niggardly, but probably of greater value than their gifts. It has been pointed out that the minstrels and other recipients who figure in the Yule accounts may in many cases not have been regular attendants at the court but may have gathered there only at these seasons of largesse.[5]

Perhaps one of Dunbar's earliest extant productions is the *New*

[1] T.A., II, p. 269, etc. [2] Leslie, I, p. 28. [3] Bergenroth, I, p. 210.
[4] Dickson, T.A., I, p. clxiii. [5] ib., I, p. ccxlii.

Year's Gift to the King.[1] The carefree pleasures which Dunbar wishes for his 'Prince' would be appropriate to James in comparative youth. Dunbar addresses him in confidential terms, and counsels him to persevere throughout his reign in good government. Characteristically, the poet ends in less serious vein. There are no gloomy fears yet as to his own security. All he asks at this stage is that God may send James many a French crown, and that the King may loosen his purse-strings for the benefit of his dependants at the festive season. It would be incumbent on a poet to present an ode of greeting, for on Hansel-Monday the King was lavish with his gifts, and little harm could result from anticipation.

A poem which it is also perhaps natural to assign to the early years of James IV's reign on account of its theme is *The Wowing of the King quhen he wes in Dumfermeling*.[2] Dunbar professes to report what he has heard in Dunfermline the previous night. The story is told as a fable, and no more fitting literary form could have been chosen for an incident which occurred in the town of Robert Henryson. But there is no moral attached to Dunbar's fable. It is the tale of how a fox seduced a lamb, and narrowly escaped from the wolf that suddenly beset the house. The lamb was one of the ladies of Dunfermline, and the fox, if we are to believe Bannatyne's title, was the King himself. But in the body of the poem there is no indication of the royal status of the fox, and the other manuscripts give no title. This is not the only place where Bannatyne has implicated King James without the confirmation of internal evidence, and his titles are not always even probable. The fox was red-haired and by no means lean; according to the portrait of James by Mytens,[3] the King's hair was brown, and his hands at least were slender. Still, there is Bannatyne's title. James was doubtless *incognito*. It is useless to try to date the poem by referring[4] to visits paid by James to Dunfermline, for the Treasurers' accounts show that visits occurred throughout the reign. But in *The Thistle and the Rose* Dunbar urged the King to be true to his Rose. That was in 1503, and the incident narrated in *The Wowing* is, one would like to believe, of earlier date.

In his refrain Dunbar affects to marvel at the ineffective resis-

[1] 'My Prince, in God gif the guid grace.' R., f. 2b. L. supplied the title.

[2] 'This hindir nycht in Dunfermeling.' B., f. 116; MF., p. 335; R., f 58. R. breaks off after the second stanza, without colophon. M. follows B. except in line 36, where without warning he gives the version of MF. Ramsay headed the poem *The Tod and the Lamb*.

[3] Description by J. M. Gray, quoted by Sir J. B. Paul, T.A., IV, p. lxxxvi.

[4] Mackay, S.T.S., I, p. clviii.

tance offered by the lamb, and her compliance is rather more emphatic in Maitland's version. Finally, when the wolf thunders at the door, and the old ewes within are speechless with fear, the fox avoids detection in much the same manner as Byron's Don Juan in the house of Doña Julia. It is not necessary to assume[1] any direct literary influence from the French *fablaux*. Henryson's fables must have been well known and deservedly admired. There is no evidence that Dunbar came in contact personally with Henryson, though the latter was, according to the 1571 manuscript copy of his fables, 'scholmaister of Dunfermling'.[2] Henryson was dead before Dunbar wrote his *Lament: quhen he wes Sek*, but how long before is unknown.

In another poem, using the conventional opening of the *chanson d'aventure* which occurs elsewhere in his poems, Dunbar affects to be eavesdropping, on this occasion at a keyhole. *A Brash of Wooing*[3] is attributed to Dunbar by two of the three manuscripts. The third manuscript, Bannatyne's, assigns the poem to Clark, but the attribution is in a different handwriting, which is shaky and more faded, or perhaps the ink was dried when still fresh. The poem is in the same verse-form as *The Wowing of the King quhen he wes in Dunfermeling*. The poet listened at his keyhole, or feigns that he listened, on the previous night. It has been suggested[4] that the man concerned may have been employed in the royal kitchens, as his beard is spattered with droppings of kail. The ballad may have been intended for the amusement of the household, the identity of the man being hinted at in this way. The tittering woman has the dominant will, and yields only when presented with a pretty stone. The inventive faculty which the two, but especially the contemptuous woman, display in their terms of affection, results in what Dr. Mackenzie has called a sort of baby language, passing continually into the obscene so far as it has any established sense. After translating the first stanza, Schipper deemed it best to go no further.

Dunbar reverts to women as his theme in his longest work, *The Tretis of the Tua Mariit Wemen and the Wedo*.[5] Again in the tradition

[1] S., p. 119. [2] ed. Mr. H. Harvey Wood (Edin., 1933).

[3] 'In secreit place this hyndir nycht.' B., f 103b; MF., p. 308; R., f 34b. Ramsay named the poem *A Brash of Wouing*. [4] S., p. 123.

[5] 'Apon the midsummer evin'. CM., p. 177; MF., p. 81. The title is from MF. The CM. version is a fragment beginning at line 104 at the top of a page and continuing to the end of the poem, the earlier pages being missing; three blank pages precede p. 177. For the missing lines, M. follows the frequently illegible MF., except that he omits the Latin rubrics.

of the *chanson d'aventure*, he overhears the libidinous confidences of three ladies in a garden. The three have been well described as 'of the type for whom harlotry is a hobby rather than a profession, but skilled amateurs who make a good thing out of it. And they discuss their methods as they might their service at tennis, completely satisfied with their own outlook as a natural and adequate view of life.'[1] The same critic describes these revelations as 'ghastly', but there is no sign that Dunbar himself regarded them in that light. To him also, as well as to his ladies, their reminiscences present themselves as 'a natural and adequate view of life'. Thus the satire, if it can be called satire, involves the poet no less than the women he creates—or reports—and the age in which he lived. But to strain the word 'satire' in this way would not be justified, as the poet is indifferent to the moral aspects. It is a distortion of the poem to claim[2] that Dunbar represents the ladies as objects of infamy. Several writers have tried to set the poet right in his readers' opinions. Pinkerton[3] excuses his interest in the poem by quoting the dictum, *Sanctum est vetus omne poema*.

The poem opens and closes with some of the finest natural description to be found in Scots medieval literature. It is past midnight on Midsummer Eve. After his revels, the poet wanders alone into a quiet garden, gay with flowers and hedged to a great height with hawthorn. He listens to the call of a bird, and is soothed by the scent of the flowers and by the stillness of night. But the quietness of his retreat is broken by feminine voices, the accents of which indicate their owners to be of no mean social status. His curiosity getting the better of him, he takes cover as usual and peers through the foliage. There, in an arbour among the greenery, are three ladies, their blonde hair garlanded with flowers, their kerchiefs of the finest lawn, their mantles green as their surroundings. The ladies are known to the poet; two of them are married to lords, and the other he knows to be a widow of lively disposition. Breathless, he is near enough to observe their carefully tended countenances, soft, and meek, and fair as the lily. A table is before them, covered, and set with winecups from which they drink deeply, their tongues becoming the looser, until at length the widow propounds the subject of marriage. What do her young companions think of it and of their husbands, and would they in the light of experience choose differently if the chance could be

[1] Dr. A. M. Mackenzie, p. 86. [2] Irvine, I, p. 415. [3] Pinkerton, I, p. x.

offered them? As one after another relates her experiences, the reader is reminded of Chaucer's Prologue to the Wife of Bath's Tale, in which the Wife of Bath tells of her various husbands. Several passages in Dunbar's poem strongly recall Chaucer.[1] On the other hand it is to be borne in mind that the *chanson de la mal mariée* was an established pattern in French poetry.[2]

The first wife finds her chains irksome. If she might only emulate the birds, and enjoy change with each round of the seasons, her husband might be cast off blithely; she would then be free to haunt fairs and plays, preachings and places of pilgrimage, choosing a mate where she wished. But she is bound to an aged man who combines senility with jealousy. Only his purse is some compensation, and she sells her favours dear.

Her companions greet these confidences with loud laughter, the cup circulates with its heady wine, and then the second wife addresses herself to her own case. Her husband, by contrast, is young and swaggers with bonnet on side of head, a gallant in the eyes of the world. She alone knows him to be worse than an old man, for he is a cheat. She mourns her lot at midnight, though she must dissemble by day.

The cup goes round once more, and when the gay, swan-white ladies have rallied one another again, the widow settles down to her tale, lengthy and circumstantial, with a prayer that she may have the inspiration of God in her speech. She has profitably disposed of two husbands. The first was an aged huckster with a hacking cough, whom she made much of to his face—though she found consolation elsewhere—and she obtained by her wiles a settlement of his chief property on her son (hers, but not his). The widow does not mention his fate, but the cough that shook him no doubt cut his days short. The second husband was a wealthy merchant, whose inferiority of birth offered her a convenient stick with which to beat him into submission until she had secured his property also for her child. Thenceforth she knew no curb but the undesirability of public rumour. She set him to a woman's tasks, bought costly adornments to be displayed when he was not by, and dressed her own children like barons' sons while she made fools of his children by a former wife. Now that she is rid of him, she preserves an air

[1] Cp. lines 409-412, 555-559, 587-592 of the Wife of Bath's Prologue with lines 137-138, 68-74, and 436-444 of *The Tretis*. Also cp. lines 94-96 of *The Tretis* with lines 1823-1827 of the Merchant's Tale. Smith, p. 40.

of respectability. Seated in church in mourning clothes, she spreads her illuminated service-book broad on her knee, draws close her cloak, and peeps slyly on knights, clerics, and courtiers. To impress the friends of her late husband, she carries, hidden in her cloak, a sponge to wet her cheeks as if with tears, and is accounted a pious woman. Like the widow of Chaucer's tale, she loves pilgrimages and the press of people. Many visitors enter her house and do not lack encouragement, but she plays one off against another.

The two married women acclaim the widow's exposition, and swear to profit by her instruction. And so they apply themselves again to the sweet wine, and the night drives on with carousal and dancing, till the dawn comes and the song of the mavis trills out as the mist rises from the fragrant meadows. The richly clad ladies go home to rest, while Dunbar steals to a pleasant arbour where with his pen he sets down the whole incident. He ends with a question to the distinguished gathering to whom he recites the work. Which of these three ladies would they choose as wife?

It is unfortunate that the poem cannot be dated precisely. The only external evidence is the issue of the poem in 1508, or a year or two later, from the press of Chapman and Millar. It has been generally assumed to be an early work of the poet, on not very convincing grounds. It is written in the ancient alliterative measure used in *Piers Plowman* and already archaic in the days of James IV, but the contention that the alliterative measure shows the poem to have been written before Dunbar came to prefer romantic strophes is a doubtful one. The mature handling of character and circumstance might equally suggest a rather later date. Certainly the argument[1] that the poet's concluding statement presupposes an early date in his life is unsound. The line in question,[2] alluding to 'this uncouth aventur quhilk airly me happinnit', far from indicating an early period in Dunbar's life would, as Schipper points out, mean that even if the incident occurred in his early years the poetic narrative itself would have to be very much later. The line may just as well be interpreted[3] as meaning that the adventure was 'airly' not in the poet's life but in the hours of the day, 'neir as midnicht wes past'.[4]

[1] S.T.S., I, lxxxvi. [2] Line 528.
[3] S. ed., p. 46. [4] Line 2.

The poem named by Pinkerton *The Twa Cummers*[1] is an indoor counterpart of *The Tretis of the Tua Mariit Wemen and the Wedo*. The two gossips of whom Dunbar treats in similarly objective fashion seem, however, a good deal more advanced in years; lasciviousness has passed into love of drinking. It is early on Ash Wednesday, and Lent has barely begun, but our two gossips beside the fire drink deep. Then, spreading her bulk over the couch, one of them complains with tipsy irony that the long term of Lent makes her woefully lean. Her companion finds excuses for her on the score of heredity, for had not her mother disdained to drink anything but the best Malmsey in Lent? And in any case the 'lean' one's husband will have to foot the bill. This thought is welcome, and there is some mirth on the subject of his senility. By the time a couple of quarts have disappeared, both women are on the way to some measure of confidence that they will survive the rigours of the fast.

In *The Fair Solicitors*[2] Dunbar turns to the ladies who frequent the lawcourts to obtain favours from the bench. In a swiftly moving *versus caudatus*, ingeniously rhymed, he thinly veils the precise nature of the ladies' efforts. In three days they will prevail more than their goodmen could in ten, such are the skill and secrecy with which the fair supplicants urge their plea; and the cost to their husbands, if any, is not apparent. A laird who wishes to prevail in a lawsuit has only to send his ladies, gaily dressed, in his stead. These ladies are, the poet says in conclusion, greatly to be prized.

It has been held[3] that the poem is probably earlier than 1503, when an effort was made to remedy some of the abuses of the lawcourts. The argument is unconvincing, nor is there justification

[1] 'Rycht airlie on Ask Weddinsday.' B., f. 137; MF., p. 37; R., f. 19b; Aberdeen *Minute Book of Seisins*, II. The Aberdeen text, which was printed by L., corresponds generally with B. The refrain of B. is unvaried, marching lamely in the context of several of the stanzas, but that of MF. has the requisite flexibility. M., however, follows B. almost entirely, though he has borrowed the refrain of MF. for the last stanza. He wrongly states that the refrain of MF. in stanzas 2, 3, 4 and 5 is 'That lentrune sall (3, suld) nocht mak us lene', for 'us' is displaced in stanza 3 by 'hir' and in stanza 4 by 'yow'. The strongly alliterative tendency is obscured in B. in lines 4 and 16, and the 'migernes' of MF. in line 12 is more appropriate. M.'s arrangement of inverted commas is also unsatisfactory; stanzas 3 and 4 would more fittingly be given to the second speaker, and the following stanza to the first speaker.

[2] 'Thir ladyis fair.' B., f. 261a; MF., p. 324; R., f. 38b. M. follows B. mainly, and gives the poem L.'s ambiguous title, *Of the Ladyis Solistaris at Court*, as does the S.T.S. editor, who says that the similarity with the title *Aganis the Solistaris in Court* suggests that the two poems may be about the same date. There is, however, no title in any of the MSS.

[3] S., p. 147.

for the further speculation[1] that the reforms of 1503-4 may have been effected partly by Dunbar's satire.

Dunbar writes so scathingly of women that, when he treats of them in more complimentary vein, doubts have been cast upon his authorship. Pinkerton declared *In Prays of Women*[2] to be a paltry piece and probably not by Dunbar, but the Bannatyne and Maitland manuscripts agree in ascribing the poem to him. It is a eulogy of women. In the poet's view they should be honoured by men above all else in the world, and he who disparages them by word or deed brings dishonour on himself. It ill befits the fruit to belittle the tree. They conceive us, and bear us with pain, nurse us, and are our comfort through life. The father of Christ was more than man, and the son of the Virgin reigns with majesty in heaven and earth.

One editor speaks of the dullness of the poem. But Dunbar's was the spirit of the fifteenth century, not of the nineteenth. As already stated, to the medieval mind woman was symbolised in a dual fashion—on the one hand as Eve and on the other as the mother of God. In the former case she provided matter for ribaldry, in the latter for reverence. *The Tretis of the Tua Mariit Wemen and the Wedo* and *In Prays of Women* are examples of the two modes. It is unnecessary to regard[3] the latter poem as making amends. As Schipper himself adds, amends by Dunbar would probably have taken a much slyer form. Dunbar is unmistakably the child of his age when he writes *In Prays of Women*.

We pass from the general to the particular in that most sententious of love-poems, *To a Lady: Quhone he List to Feyne.*[4] The poet appeals to the 'man slayar' to have mercy and not to cause his death, lest she should be put to shame in the eyes of the world. His spirits are so low that he often swoons, and on his knees he begs to be spared the intolerable pain which no balm can assuage. Let her have pity on his tears and pallor, for pity is the grace of womanhood. He will not cease to plead for mercy till death. Such poems were fashionable exercises, and Dunbar was writing in the current manner, either on his own behalf or perhaps to further the

[1] S. ed., p. 74.

[2] 'Now of wemen this I say for me.' B., f. 278b; MF., p. 294. The colophon, 'quod Dumbar in prays of women' occurs in MF. but not, as L. supposed, in B., which ends with only 'q Dumbar'.

[3] S., p. 150.

[4] 'My hartis tresure, and swete assured fo.' MF., p. 322, with colophon 'Quod Dumbar quhone he list to feyne'. A syllable is lacking in line 10, but there is no gap in the MS.

suit of a friend. In this sense Maitland's description of the poem can be understood, but scarcely the view of one editor[1] that the poem is in the spirit of self-mockery. Pinkerton remarks, 'This is a ballad by Dunbar, but worth nothing.'[2]

These poems would find their way into court circles. Dunbar writes more directly of court life in his *Dirige to the King, Bydand Ouir Lang in Stirling*.[3] The King went sometimes to the seclusion of the Franciscan house at Stirling, as if his spirit sought a period of quiet. Perhaps he was prompted by recurring fits of penitence for his part in the melancholy incidents of 1488 which led to his father's death. On this particular occasion he seems to have lingered longer than usual, and Dunbar tries to draw him back to the glitter of the court by an accomplished piece of travesty. The poet casually identifies himself with an apostle[4] in heaven, and in his own name and that of his fellow revellers in Edinburgh addresses to the King a 'dirige'. It is no dirge in the modern sense of the word, but a parody of parts of the Office for the Dead (*Dirige, Domine, gressus meos*). The profane choir laments the austerities of Franciscan life, and intercedes with God and St. Giles to deliver James from the purgatory of Stirling and restore him to Edinburgh. Certain aspects of Franciscan asceticism would not suggest frugal living to-day. The King supplied the Gray Friars with many a barrel of good ale, Malvoisie, and Hamburg beer. But to Dunbar their drink is 'thyn and small'.

There is no direct reference to the King in this poem, but the colophon of each of the three manuscripts states that the lines were addressed to him, and this unanimity cannot be opposed, though to exalt the joys of Edinburgh in the King's absence may be considered lacking in tact. But it is necessary to reject Bannatyne's identification with King James V in the title 'The dregy of dunbar, maid to King James the fyift, being in Striuilling'. James V would be most unlikely, on account of his very tender years, to be addressed thus until a considerable number of years after the last date at which there is any evidence that Dunbar was alive, and the poem is surely not the work of a poet in extreme old age. Despite

[1] S., p. 187; S. ed., p. 118. [2] Pinkerton, II, p. 464.

[3] 'We that ar heir in hevins glory.' B., f. 102a; MF., p. 290; R., f. 55b. The original table of contents of the Asloan MS. shows that the poem was on p. 67. in a portion of that collection that is now missing. The title is from the colophon of MF. M. follows B. and indicates deviations except the reading from MF. at line 102.

[4] The version of MF., in line 8, adopted by M., obscures this pose.

the precision of Bannatyne's title, the person addressed is James IV. The invitation to join in the play, song, dance, and general good cheer of Edinburgh, might well have been sent to James IV at any time of his reign, even in the last years before Flodden, but would be most fitting in the days of his youth. On the other hand, the convent of the Observant Gray Friars of Stirling was not founded until 1494, and the humorous reference to the hermits and anchorites of Stirling, and the penance endured at their tables, is fairly clearly directed against the house of Franciscans.

He writes with the assurance of an associate of James, and plans to visit the King in his retreat, descending upon him in purgatory like the angel Gabriel, with good tidings, so that James may leave his penance and return to Edinburgh before the beginning of Yuletide,

> To eit swan, cran, pertrik, and plever,
> And every fische that swymis in rever;
> To drynk with us the new fresche wyne,
> That grew upoun the rever of Ryne,
> Fresche fragrant clairettis out of France,
> Of Angers and of Orliance,
> With mony ane cours of grit dyntie.

The mock 'dirige' proceeds with all the paraphernalia of the liturgy—lections, responses, and prayers of strange import. The easy movement of the couplets breaks out at the responses into the ingenious involutions of the French triolet, the repetitive harmonies of which are suggestive, it has been said,[1] of peals of bells. The final Latin requiem parodies in detail the sacred words: may the poet and his friends be led not into the testing trials of Stirling but be delivered from its evil, so that God may grant that the peace of Edinburgh may shine upon them, and that they may taste the wines of Edinburgh in the city of those who are truly living. Thus Edinburgh may be satisfied and, adds the poet oddly, hinting perhaps that the King's stay may be inconvenient to the staid friars, thus Stirling also may be at peace. Hailes omitted the poem because of its irreverence.

Dunbar appears to have believed that his own future was secure, and that royal patronage would bestow unasked what it might withhold from the importunate. But how far, when he states his confidence in favours to come, is Dunbar really certain, and how far

[1] Dr. A. M. Mackenzie, p. 95.

is he trying to exert the force of suggestion, or perhaps of auto-suggestion? A poem which looks serenely to his own future is that entitled, *Aganis the Solistaris in Court.*[1] There is no more politic method of securing the ear and heart of a patron than to remind him of the self-seekers by whom he is beset, and Dunbar sketches in a few lines the motley throng whose business it is to solicit favour at court. Though some of these adventurers try to advance themselves by loyal service, others, less active, merely stay at court, always at hand as long as their material resources last. Pale loiterers almost swoon for eagerness, or bear themselves as on the verge of madness. Others make a gayer show, prominent with tales or songs or the morris-dance, and ready with superficial flattery. Sometimes the exigencies of their situation betray them into clumsy folly, or they whisper their plans in corners to potential helpers. And there are others whose advocates urge their suit in the inner circles of privilege and in ways which reflect no glamour on those who prompt such advocacy: the allusion becomes clearer from a reading of *The Fair Solicitors.* Still another class of self-seekers are more concerned at mass with the impression they create than with the devotional content of the service. But for his simple self, he concludes, he knows of no avenue to satisfaction other than waiting humbly on the King's grace, which for him is riches sufficient.

The opening line of *To the King: Sanct Salvatour Send Silver Sorrow*[2] may be prompted by associations with St. Salvator's College, in St. Andrews University, but it has already been said that the poet may have been guided only by the desire for alliterative effect. Money, he says, is the root of his troubles both day and night, making him void of charity and gladness of mind, so grievously his purse troubles him. Such a complaint would be most appropriate before 1500, in which year he was awarded a pension.[3] Though he would gladly write poems, languor assails him, and he is sustained only by hope. When he sets himself to sing, dance, or be otherwise blithe, the thought of penury troubles him, and when men with full purses pass to regale themselves of a morning he must heavily refuse to

[1] 'Be divers wyis and operatiounes.' MF. has two versions, on p. 8 and p. 316, of which M. follows the first; but his title is from the colophon of the second, not of the first. R., f. 10, reads as MF. 1.

[2] B., f. 113b, concluding with the words 'q dumbar to the King'.

[3] Schipper's assertion is not justified, that the poem recalls 'the somewhat frivolous intimacy which prevailed between the poet and the king in their younger years' (S. ed., p. 232).

join them, saying he means to fast till noon. There is perhaps a hint of gaming habits when he deplores his inability to keep money in his purse whoever may win and whoever may lose. If he could find some enchanter who would make his purse remain always full, his mind would be freed from the devil that troubles it. Having made enquiries in many quarters, he finds everyone agreed that the best remedy is in the King's hands.

If these poems were written shortly before 1500, his hopes were not in vain. The year 1500 is an important date in Dunbar's life, for his name then appears for the first time in the extant public records. The Privy Seal registers have, however, not survived for dates previous to the 16th April 1499, though some earlier writs that were then still awaiting registration are recorded.[1] Gifts of pensions from the King, and presentations to many benefices, were made by letters bearing the royal sign manual (*per signaturam*) and addressed to the Keeper of the Privy Seal, who at that time and until the end of the reign was Bishop Elphinstone of Aberdeen. The Keeper or his clerk thereupon issued a writ, with the seal affixed, and the issue was duly recorded in the Register of the Privy Seal. The grant to Dunbar reads as follows: 'A lettre maid to maister William Dunbar of the gift of ten lib. of pensioun to be pait to him of soverane lordis cofferis be the thesaurair for al the dais of his life or quhil he be promouit be oure soverane lord to a benefice of xl lib. or abone etc. de data xvth Augusti Et Regni regis xiii. Per signaturam.'[2] The thirteenth year of the reign began on 11th June 1500.[3] Beside the entry is written the word 'gratis', indicating that the sealed writ was given to Dunbar without charging him the usual fee for registration, but it is impossible to know whether in any such particular case the concession was due to special favour or to poverty.[4]

Apparently at a single step, Dunbar was thus, on 15th August 1500, placed in an assured position, with the very considerable annuity of £10 for life or until his presentation to a benefice of not less than £40 a year.

[1] Livingstone, p. v. [2] MS. *Reg. Secreti Sigilli*, II, f. 9b. Livingstone, I, p.80.
[3] Sir A. H. Dunbar, p. 222. [4] Livingstone, I, p. viii.

CHAPTER VI

'THE FLYTING OF DUNBAR AND KENNEDIE'

From his activities in later years as court poet, it is reasonable to infer that the 1500 pension granted to Dunbar under the Privy Seal was largely on account of services already rendered in that capacity. But a similar line of argument would suggest that to some extent the grant was a reward for work done as an envoy to foreign lands, as there is reason to believe that he was in northern European waters in the later part of 1500, and that he made a separate expedition to England and France towards the close of the same year; there is definite evidence that late in the following year he was again in England. It is one of the main purposes of this chapter to show that *The Flyting of Dunbar and Kennedie*, in conjunction with the entries in the public accounts, affords a probability that the poet was abroad twice in 1500.

Some remarks must first be made on the identity of Dunbar's antagonist and of the two seconds in the wrangle. Walter Kennedy is ranked by Gavin Douglas[1] and by Sir David Lindsay[2] high among the poets of the time. He was a younger brother of John, second Lord Kennedy of Dunure in Ayrshire,[3] was a nephew of the celebrated Bishop Kennedy, and was descended from a daughter of King Robert III.[4] 'I am the kingis blude,' he claims in *The Flyting*.[5] In the manuscript records of Glasgow University there is mention of him as 'nobilis viri'; probably because of his blood he heads the list of bachelors of arts in 1476, and of masters in 1478, 'Magister Walterus Kennedy'; in 1481 he was nominated one of the examiners for the Faculty.[6] His graduation as master of arts at Glasgow was therefore one year earlier than that of Dunbar at St. Andrews.

[1] *The Palice of Honour* (ed. Small, I, p. 36).

[2] Prologue to *The Testament and Complaynt of the Papyngo*, lines 15-16.

[3] *Great Seal Reg.*, II, No. 2457.

[4] Pitcairn, p. 80. The anonymous MS. *Historical and Genealogical Account of the Principal Families of the Name of Kennedy*, of the early seventeenth century, was edited for the Bannatyne Club in 1830 by R. Pitcairn. [5] Line 417.

[6] MS. *Annales Univ. Glasg.*, 1451-1558, I, p. 51; II, *Annales Collegii Fac. Art.*, pp. 50, 60, 69.

The Kennedy family had the patronage of the collegiate church of Maybole,[1] to which Laing therefore concludes, but without any good evidence, that Walter was appointed provost.[2] In *The Flyting*, Kennedy states that his trust is in the King,

> to have of his magnificence
> Guerdoun, reward, and benefice bedene.[3]

In the same poem, however, he declares himself to be a man of substance and landed property.[4] The Kennedies of Dunure were hereditary bailies of Carrick, and the poet appears to have acted as deputy for Lord Kennedy on occasion, for in 1491 an action was successfully raised, before the Lords of Council, against Master Walter Kennedy, 'pretendit bailye depute of carrik', for wrongful and inordinate proceedings.[5] Kennedy may, as Laing suggests, refer to his official connexion when he describes himself in *The Flyting* as the King's 'trew speciall clerk'.[6] It is clear that the poet Kennedy belonged to a family of rising importance in the land, just as that of Dunbar had fallen into comparative decay. The contrast of fortunes is present to the minds of both parties in *The Flyting*.[7]

The identity of John Ross, 'Schir Johine the Ros', Dunbar's second, is unknown, though several persons have been put forward of that name.[8] He was dead by 1505-6, for he is mourned in Dunbar's *Lament*. Kennedy's 'commissar', or second in the flyting, was Quintene, who was to be at loggerheads with Dunbar again in later years with reference to Sir Thomas Norny.[9] Quintene seems to have been himself a poet,[10] no doubt the one whom Gavin Douglas quaintly celebrates, in company with Dunbar and Kennedy, in his poem of 1501, *Palice of Honour*, as 'Quintene with ane huttock on

[1] *Great Seal Reg.*, II, 416.

[2] The *Account* edited by Pitcairn stated that it was the second Lord Kennedy's brother Gilbert who was the provost of Maybole. But, as Wood's *Peerage* did not mention a brother called Gilbert, L. concluded that it was very probably Walter who was the provost (L., II, p. 440). Laing appears to have been led to this conclusion partly by his knowledge that another Walter Kennedy, who matriculated as an arts student at Glasgow University in 1511, when he was already rector of Douglas (MS. Vol. I, *Annales Univ. Glasg.*, 1451-1588, p. 90), was later provost of the collegiate church of Maybole (ib., p. 105). Paterson, without citing any authority, describes the poet as 'parson of Douglas', and the second Walter Kennedy as rector of Douglas, provost of Maybole, and son of the poet (*History of the County of Ayr*, 1847, p. 280).

[3] Lines 421-422. [4] Lines 361-368.

[5] *Acts of Lords of Council*, I, p. 212. [6] Line 417.

[7] Mackay, S.T.S., I, p. xix. [8] Appen. V, 20.

[9] Chapter X. [10] *The Flyting*, lines 1-3.

his heid'.[1] In 1530 Sir David Lindsay refers to him among other poets as deceased though his 'libells bene leuand'.[2] Quintene has been regarded as identical with the other poet, Quintyne Schaw, whose death was recorded in 1505-6 by Dunbar, in the *Lament*, as having occurred shortly before. The more one considers this supposed identity, the more unnecessary and unconvincing does the supposition appear. That Quintyne Schaw might, in *The Flyting*, where the poets concerned were on intimate terms, have been referred to by his Christian name, would be credible, though it would still be strange that the other poets were not named in similar fashion. But no reason at all has been advanced why the poet named in 1501 by Douglas, and over a quarter of a century later by Lindsay, as 'Quintene', should be Quintyne Schaw.[3] The attempted identification is therefore rejected. No poems of Quintene have survived, nor are the public records enlightening about him.[4] His connexion with the Kennedy family is shown, however, by Walter Kennedy's description of him as 'My cousing Quintene'.[5]

Kennedy refers again to his 'commissar' in the final portion of *The Flyting*,[6] but not by name, and bids Dunbar, in asking pardon, to seek the services of Stobo. This perhaps implies that Stobo, not Quintene, is now Kennedy's second, but Stobo may be only an additional personage introduced for a special reason. Such a reason is not far to seek. John Rede, known as Stobo, had been one of the King's secretaries in three reigns, and could be relied upon in the engrossing of legal documents. Later, he was mourned along with other fellow-poets in Dunbar's *Lament*. In the records he is mentioned on 6th and 27th May 1505 as lying sick, and he was dead in July.[7]

The value of *The Flyting of Dunbar and Kennedie*[8] in the biographical study of Dunbar has been discussed at the beginning of this work. Much of the effect of the flyting is due to exaggeration rather than to a sober regard for the truth. Where the flyters indulge in general abuse, it may be discounted. But where detrac-

[1] Small's ed. of Douglas, I, p. 36.

[2] Prologue to *The Testament and Complaynt of the Papyngo*, ed. S.T.S., I, p. 56.

[3] See Appendix V, No. 22.

[4] In 1497 the Treasurer's Accounts record a payment of bridle-silver 'to Quentin, the Lord Hammiltounis man', and, in August 1505, 'to Quentin to pas to rais his breves' (T.A., I, p. 356; II, p. 158).

[5] Line 34. [6] Line 329.

[7] Appendix V, No. 21. [8] 'Schir Johine the Ros . . .'.

tion takes the form of statements as to the past and present activities of the antagonists, in matters of fact which would be known to the audience or easily verifiable by them, more reliance can be placed upon the poems, especially if the truth of the statements is not denied or is even admitted in part.

Laing was right to give careful consideration to the series of *Flyting* poems in his prefatory memoir. He tried to reconcile many apparent inconsistencies, especially as to the geographical whereabouts and movements of Dunbar at the time of the last reply of Kennedy. This question particularly interested Laing for two reasons: in the first place, Kennedy's last reply contains a phrase to which Laing thought that Dunbar had already given an answer in an earlier section; secondly, at the time of Kennedy's last reply Dunbar seemed to Laing to be at the same moment in Scotland and in Paris.[1] Laing was therefore led to suspect that at least lines 497-512 had been misplaced and should have been in an earlier section of the poem, Kennedy's first reply. The view that there were inconsistencies was further elaborated by Schipper. He did not possess the key which has since been provided by Sir William Craigie to the misplacing of the leaves of the Maitland manuscript. He therefore misapprehended the sequence of stanzas as they were actually transcribed by Maitland, wrongly assumed that Maitland and Reidpeth transcribed the stanzas in the same sequence, and wrongly claimed that his objections applied in the same way to the Bannatyne version as to the versions of the other two manuscripts.[2] Schipper in consequence recast the whole series of poems to form not four, but six sections. The result, however, besides being open to the charge of arbitrary ingenuity, and besides being contrary to the versions of all three manuscripts and of the early print, betrays clearly that it is not the original form of the poem. The difficulties of the authentic text, which is wisely adopted by Dr. Mackenzie, are not insurmountable. The problems of the texts are discussed more fully in an appendix.[3]

Dunbar and Kennedy were writing in the tradition of the Provençal and French 'tenson',[4] and therefore we need not suppose any real enmity between them. The technique of initiating a flyting is scarcely less elaborate than that by which Touchstone conducts the 'duello'. The first poem of the series is written by Dunbar to

[1] Lines 500 and 97; and lines 437 and 504. [2] S. ed., p. 146.
[3] Appendix VI, A. [4] Smith, p. 54.

his 'commissar' or second, John Ross. It consists of three stanzas in which he invites Kennedy to the fray. The opening lines show that there had been a previous production, now lost, by Kennedy and his second, Quintene. According to Dunbar, his rivals had shown a pride ominously comparable to that of Lucifer, praising themselves above the stars, without, however, descending to any indictable disparagement of others. Had they done so, earth and hell would have quaked to hear what Dunbar, if provoked to anger, would have written. He would take up his pen unwillingly, since flyting was more suited to a common bard, but let Kennedy and Quintene once raise the devil in him and he would denounce them far and wide.

We do not know how far the lost poem referred to was intended to call forth Dunbar's threats, nor how far he was deliberately or unintentionally misconstruing it. We therefore do not know who was the aggressor, though Dunbar's own account would suggest that he himself was. But John Ross was clearly intended to convey the menacing epistle to Kennedy. In his reply, consisting also of three stanzas, Kennedy looses a torrent of vituperation on Dunbar's head, and threatens worse still if Dunbar dares to make a stand against Kennedy's laureate powers. None can take seriously the scholastic qualifications of Dunbar, who, of diminutive stature and in threadbare gown, has been branded thrice for his rascality. Quintene seems to have taken a hand in still another lost poem, for Kennedy says that Dunbar has refused to obey Quintene. Both John Ross and Dunbar shall be made to skirl unless they make amends to Quintene and accept chastisement from him.

This preliminary sparring over, each of the two principals proceeds, in a lengthy poem, to inflict as much discomfort as possible upon his opponent. 'Iuge in the nixt,' says Bannatyne, 'quha gat the war.'

In power of abuse, Dunbar does not lag behind. He begins by stamping Kennedy as one of the Irishry. He returns to this theme again, continually reflecting upon Kennedy's racial origin and characteristics, which are unfavourably contrasted with those of the English stock of Lothian to which Dunbar appears to claim proudly that he belongs. This, coupled with Kennedy's equally fierce vindication of the Gael, is a feature of the poem which gives it some width of significance in our national literature. In recent centuries there has been a 'Highland line'. In the days of Dunbar and

Kennedy the 'Inglis' area was very much more restricted, so that Dunbar's gibe applied—and was willingly accepted by Kennedy as applying—no less to Ayrshire and the west country in general than to the Highlands. Flyting was appropriate, says Dunbar, for a mere Erse bard, who thus revealed his Highland strain. But Kennedy's powers were slight in English eloquence. A man of Lothian could by less polite means produce fairer English

> Than thow can blabbar with thy Carrik lippis.[1]

In physical build Kennedy was gaunt, and withered in aspect. There is a consistency in Dunbar's jests in this respect, just as Kennedy continually finds matter for mirth in the smallness of Dunbar's stature. Kennedy's forbidding appearance prompts many unsavoury images, among others the comparison with the dried bodies of Danish criminals exposed on the executioner's wheel. His mental qualities are represented as equally repellent, and more fit for a scurvy beggar, club in hand, than for a scholar. Had not Kennedy planned to poison the King[2] in Paisley, as Dunbar was prepared to prove in court? And Kennedy had added the personal affront of disparaging Dunbar's friends with his pen. Here again, we are led to assume that a poem of Kennedy's is missing from the series. Therefore, when Dunbar a few lines later rejects Kennedy's claim to distinction in letters,

> Thow callis the rethory with thy goldin lippis,[3]

it is impossible to conclude, with Laing, that this line refers to a line in Kennedy's later reply,

> Rymis thou of me, of Rethory the Rose?[4]

and that the poems require to be arranged in reconstructed sequence. Dunbar may be referring to a boast of Kennedy's in a previous poem now lost.[5]

[1] Lines 49-56, 105-112.

[2] Lines 77-78. B., 'our Lordis cheif'; MF. and R., 'the lord thy cheif'. The imputation of treason in line 73, and Kennedy's denial in line 418 of ever having conceived injury to the King, justify the view that the King is meant. Dr. Mackenzie (p. 199) points out that the S.T.S. editor's explanation of 'poysone' as mere rebellion (supported by Schipper in his edition of Kennedy's poems, p. 4) is unsatisfactory. So also is the view that 'poysone' is used only to alliterate with 'Paislay'. The historical allusion awaits elucidation, but a fit of indisposition on the King's part while on a visit to Paisley may have prompted the malicious accusation.

[3] Line 97. [4] Line 500.

[5] References to lost poems of the series are in lines 1, 33, and 85.

This is an instance of how easy it is for a reader of *The Flyting* to lose his bearings. So far, if we leave out of account lost poems of the series, Dunbar and Kennedy have had one innings each, and there has been no question of the whereabouts of either poet. But now, as Dunbar proceeds with his second piece, it becomes apparent that he has been abroad since he wrote before. Kennedy, he says, took care to delay his reply till he saw Dunbar's ship hoist sail for foreign parts. We shall have to consider later the facts he narrates about this voyage. It was an ill-fated one for Dunbar,

> Yit come I hame, fals baird, to lay thy boist.[1]

This line has been interpreted needlessly[2] as meaning that Dunbar was abroad when he wrote this poem, and that he was about to come home or was on his way home. But there is no more evidence that he was abroad then than when he wrote his first poem of the series. The line may equally well have been written after his return. We therefore interpret the line as meaning that Dunbar is at home again and can now reply to Kennedy.

How far is the indigence ascribed to Kennedy, in the stanzas that follow, due only to Dunbar's inventive malice? Kennedy may have been in temporary straits which Dunbar seizes upon and exaggerates to suit his purpose, but in part Dunbar seems to be drawing upon the townsman's belief that country life must be primitive. Kennedy is described as a hungry vagrant living in filth and disreputable disease, indecently clad, fain to beg a handful of corn and rub it at the ingle of some compassionate countrywoman. Now, in winter, his importunities become intolerable to housewives and beggars alike. Dunbar with his own eyes has seen Kennedy's wretchedness in his Galloway home. If, as is not unlikely, Dunbar at one time had gone in the King's train on one of the frequent pilgrimages to Whithorn, returning by way of Bargany Castle and the Kennedy country, and, meeting Walter Kennedy in landsman's dress, had rallied him for his uncouth appearance, the allusions would be the more appropriate. Lousy and with long nails, Kennedy begged meal or stole hens, says Dunbar, in company with a woman of thrawn temper whom Dunbar refers to as 'ane sowtaris wyfe'—a repulsive description if we bear in mind the habits attributed by Dunbar elsewhere to soutars. Together they lived in a desolate glen in a foul abode that had been the haunt of lepers. The

[1] Line 96. [2] S.T.S., I, p. xxvii. S., p. 66.

very look of his face would scare the sheep. Even Quintene, it is suggested, spoke of Kennedy with immeasurable contempt.

The lines that describe how the boys of the burgh baited Kennedy, the clodhopper, in the streets of Edinburgh, before he took refuge in his native wilds, form a vivid and forceful passage of the poem. Dunbar writes that Kennedy had long frequented Edinburgh, clad in sweaty clothes and borrowed gown,[1] and ridiculed by boys in the streets with sounds imitative of the bleating of sheep. He passed along the street on foot, bringing the clay of Carrick to Edinburgh Cross on his boots of hard leather, from which the wisps of straw hung out. Should he ever venture there again, the citizens will release the school-children to stone him up the causeway, and Dunbar anticipates the scene. The boys emerge like bees from a hive, crying gleefully, 'Heir cumis our awin queir Clerk!' Kennedy takes to flight, like an owl chased by crows, while all the bitches of Edinburgh bark at his heels. At sight of him, old women warn one another to take in their linen from the lines on which it hangs. Lacking a shirt, he may snatch one in passing. On he runs, with the clamour of boys behind him, and the town tykes with their teeth at his heels. Horses bolt with their carts, and the hacks of chapmen cast off, in their fright, their creels and coals, as the boots of hapless Kennedy rattle past, the angry fishwives throwing down their baskets and pelting him with clods.

On top of this climax come Dunbar's two final stanzas, the metrical fireworks of which have received frequent comment. In addition to the normal end-rhymes, each line contains a triple internal rhyme, so that each of these eight-lined stanzas has no fewer than thirty-two rhyming words, not to speak of a considerable number of irregular alliterative effects. With cumulative resonance, abuse falls on the head of Kennedy. The passage has been described as 'a miracle of literary Billingsgate'.[2]

Kennedy replies boldly in the poem which ends the series so far as it is extant. He begins with—and returns to—the charge that such a scoundrel as Dunbar is not fit to aspire to priestly office.

[1] Line 201, 'Thow held the burch lang with ane borrowit goun'. Baildon, in a note on this line, suggests that the 'burch' of B. means 'birch', not 'burgh', and that Kennedy had been a schoolmaster of the town. He has, however, misread the word, for B. uses precisely the same contracted form in line 217 in the word 'Edinburch', and MF. and R. both read 'burgh' in line 201 itself.

[2] Baildon, p. 259. Miss Taylor (p. 81) says that the most hardened reader will slip 'scunnered' in this mire.

Kennedy likens the pretensions of Dunbar in this direction to the similar ambitions of the Biblical Dathan and Abiron.[1] He next attacks his antagonist as a connexion of the house of March. This part of *The Flyting* has already been dealt with. Now the dead earls rise from their tombs against the descendant who has brought upon them Kennedy's anger. Let him fall on his knees at the cross,[2] acknowledging Kennedy's superiority. He must humble himself before Kennedy's 'commissar', obtain the help of Stobo—a well known writer of legal documents—in saving his life, renounce rhyming, and burn his poem. If he will not, Dunbar shall be burnt on Arthur's Seat or on a higher hill.

Kennedy rejects Dunbar's ridicule of the Gaels and of their literature. Had not Kennedy scaled Parnassus and drunk from the fountain of eloquence when it flowed cold and clear? Dunbar had gone at a less propitious season, and drunk the frog-spawn. His style offended the ear. Dunbar had proclaimed his dislike of Erse, but Erse should be every true Scot's study. It had been the language of old and had made Scotland prosper, until a Corspatrick of Dunbar treasonously brought in the tailed Englishmen.[3] And Kennedy adds that Dunbar with his English sympathies would emulate his ancestor's treason if he might succeed to the earldom.

The proof of Dunbar's ignorant folly might be seen in his jest that Kennedy looked like the dried victims to be seen exposed on the wheel in Denmark. Danes were akin to the King (apparently because the wife of James III had been a princess of Denmark), who was therefore indirectly attacked by Dunbar's tactlessness. It was untrue that Kennedy had been reduced to theft as a means of livelihood. In contrast with the penniless and landless condition of Dunbar, his state was affluent. He owned lands and properties, and Dunbar would gladly gnaw with his gums the bones under Kennedy's table.

Now comes Kennedy's first mention of Dunbar in relation to foreign parts. All Dunbar might claim as his was a stout halter on 'Mount Falcoun', in which he would hang by the neck. And yet,

[1] Numbers, xvi.

[2] Line 325. By writing 'croce' with an initial capital, M. seems to imply that Edinburgh Cross is meant, but there is no confirmation in the sources.

[3] Line 351. See Chapter I. The tails were said to be a punishment for the use made by the English of fish-tails to torture St. Augustine. Dunbar had invited this taunt by his gibe (line 125) that 'he that dang Sanct Augustine with ane rumple' had just such a face as Kennedy's.

on second thoughts, Mont Faucon, the great gallows-hill of Paris, would be too grand a scaffold for him.

> Cum hame, and hyng on oure gallowis of Aire.[1]

The influence of Kennedy in his county town would save Dunbar's dead body from the dogs and ravens—except that his tongue must go to the ravens in punishment for its malice.

Laing regarded this passage as evidence that, at the time when Kennedy wrote it, Dunbar was abroad and probably in Paris.[2] It has already been pointed out that, on account of a somewhat similar line,[3] Dunbar's previous poem—to which this is Kennedy's answer—has been thought to have been written while Dunbar was abroad, although the assumption is unnecessary. Applied to the passage at present under consideration, such a view is not merely unnecessary but unjustifiable unless, with Schipper, we submit the whole series of flyting poems to a radical and arbitrary reconstruction. Dunbar cannot have been abroad when this, the last poem of *The Flyting*, was written. As we shall see, in the course of it Kennedy urges Dunbar to set off through England on foot, since no ship will accept him as passenger. He threatens to bundle Dunbar out of Scotland, and hounds him off over the fells on foot, on his way to France.

Yet Kennedy says,

> Cum hame, and hyng on oure gallowis of Aire.

All that is required to resolve the apparent inconsistency is to assume that Dunbar, who has been abroad and has returned, is still in Scotland though he intends to leave shortly for Paris. In this way, Kennedy's suggestion as to what is due to Dunbar on Mont Faucon becomes intelligible, like his subsequent emendation, quoted above, that Ayr would be a more suitable place of punishment when Dunbar comes home.

The remainder of Kennedy's poem is taken up chiefly with reminiscences of Dunbar's past—no doubt distorted for purposes of ridicule—and gleeful anticipations of misfortunes to come when he is on the proposed journey. In preparation for his recent voyage, Dunbar had had to beg small sums of his friends, only to lose them in the storm.[4] His efforts to salvage his property had been vain,

[1] Line 371. [2] L., II, p. 452. [3] Line 96.

[4] Line 378, 'To stanch the storm wyth haly muldis thou loste', is obscure in meaning, but seems to refer to the jettisoning of the contents of the ship to lighten it in a heavy sea. Do the 'haly muldis' (ashes of the dead, according to Dr. Mackenzie) refer to sacred relics which it was Dunbar's supposed intention to peddle?

and it lay on the coast of Zealand. Dunbar while abroad had therefore had to subsist on cold fare or remain supperless, barefooted and in rags, begging at doors for charity. He merited the penalties Kennedy would now mete out. He would deprive Dunbar of his academic dignities, set a fool's cap on his head, and have him hanged for the traitor he was by nature and heredity, or exiled to England, to which his family had been attached. For himself, Kennedy repudiates the suggestion that he had practised against the King, and recalls that he is of the blood royal and the King's 'trew, speciall clerk'. In return for the constancy of his allegiance and service, he trusts to have reward and a benefice soon, when Dunbar's body lies on the wheel of which he presumed to write.

Dunbar, says Kennedy, had begged his way as a vagabond from church to church with his pardons, from Ettrick Forest to Dumfries, and had thieved by night. This appears to be a reference to Dunbar's youthful escapades in Franciscan dress. But it should be borne in mind that the Provençal flyters were fond of accusing their adversaries of stealing cattle and fowls,[1] just as Dunbar had already accused Kennedy of stealing hens. Now that Scotland was weary of Dunbar's importunities, it was his intention[2] to wander through France with a pilgrim's scallop-shells and staff. But beyond France his way would be blocked by the snow blizzards and wild beasts of the Alps—'Mount Barnard . . . Mount Scarpre . . . Mount Nycholas . . . Mount Godart'. Let him therefore settle in Paris. A suitable lodging would be with the hangman, whom Dunbar might serve as apprentice until Dunbar should himself mount the gallows. In Scotland he certainly might not stay. Having drunk his property and pawned his clothes, he could find no employment in the service of any lord. Implying a hope that on the coming journey Dunbar might be driven by the elements even further beyond Scottish ken than Zealand, Kennedy ironically promises him, when he reaches Danzig, that he will receive as a bounty on Kennedy's account—not a sum of money this time but (perhaps to avoid the laws against export of currency) a pack of flea-skins, and if that does not avail Dunbar, may the devil take him.

Kennedy reminds him how, twenty years before,[3] Dunbar had sailed in the 'Katryne' for foreign parts, and soon after leaving port

[1] Smith, p. 55.

[2] Line 430. CM., 'Thow scapis in France to be a knycht of the felde'. B. reads 'schaipis', and MF. and R. read 'schapis'. [3] Line 452.

had lost his sea-legs completely. This voyage in the 'Katryne' has been discussed in an earlier chapter. He had so befouled the ship that her tackle was not clean yet. The combined efforts of fifteen mariners at the pumps had been insufficient to keep pace with his misfortunes, and in desperation the skipper had ordered him to be disembarked at the Bass. No ship would receive him now as passenger.

The sea-route was therefore denied to Dunbar. Kennedy must have been aware that, after Dunbar's recent privations at sea, he had good reason to prefer the route through England. Moreover, this route may already have been decided upon for him by others.

Probably Kennedy was elaborating this malodorous extravaganza from some long past misfortune of Dunbar at sea, to account maliciously for the choice of the land route. Dunbar must go through England[1] on foot, and Kennedy recommends, for some obscure reason or none, the disguise of a horse-groom. There was nothing to fear: if it should happen that Dunbar were hanged in Northumberland, his kinsmen would be well quit of him, and in any case that fate must befall him some day.

A little earlier Kennedy had ventured to catch the ear of the King. He now boldly addresses James directly. This sinful sot Dunbar must not be permitted to pass to foreign lands and there do shame to the name of Scot. Banish him instead to some desolate place beyond civilisation, suitable for a monster whose very birth —in the darkness of an eclipse—had foreshadowed his detestable career. This fool, with little capacity in poetry or prose, had insolently turned his rhymings against Kennedy, 'me, of Rethory the Rose'.[2] Let him loose his hose, or Kennedy will throw him out of Scotland. Who would give such a beast a benefice, unless as a carnival mockery? Let Dunbar—and here again Kennedy seems to have in mind Dunbar's wanderings in former days—use his skill with fiddle, flute, and 'geste'. He is ordained for nothing else. With patched cloak, cross, and scallop-shells, let him fare on into France[3] and never return. The devil speed him over the fells!

In his peroration, Kennedy passes to more general terms, ransacking the Bible, ancient history, and martyrology, to pile a load of opprobrium upon Dunbar.[4] In his last stanza, not in the last

[1] Line 473. [2] Line 500. [3] Line 510.

[4] Since Dr. Mackenzie's edition was published, Professor Bruce Dickins, whose interpretation of 'Throp', line 540 (*Times Literary Supplement*, 10th July 1924), is

two as in Dunbar's poem, he adds a metrical *tour de force* imitative of his rival's. 'Iuge ye now heir quha gat the war,' concludes Bannatyne.

The date of composition of this remarkable series must now be considered. It is evident that a considerable period of time elapsed between the first and last poems. The first and third poems are by Dunbar, the second and fourth by Kennedy. The second, we are told by Dunbar,[1] was written after Dunbar had set out on his voyage, and between this poem and the third is a gap represented by that voyage and Dunbar's privations overseas, which would take months rather than weeks. Yet it is unlikely that *The Flyting* spread itself over years. The first two extant poems are short and introductory, and the only long interval of time which is necessary is between the second and third. It has been shown that Dunbar was not abroad when the fourth poem was written. It seems likely, therefore, that the whole series extended over a period of several months.

To what year or years is *The Flyting of Dunbar and Kennedie* to be assigned?

It has been suggested[2] that, when Kennedy contrasts the kin of his antagonist with the kin of 'Dunbar of Westfelde knyght',[3] he refers to Sir James Dunbar of Westfield who died in 1505. But Kennedy's statement does not refer to any particular member of the Westfield family and might apply to Sir James's father or son.[4] Moreover, the allusion need not be to a knight still alive. Again, it has been stated[5] that the abusive term 'carrybald'[6] means 'Carib'. This would imply a date for the poem much later than the discoveries of Columbus in the Indies. But Schipper cites Jamieson's *Dictionary* where the word is associated with the French *charavel* (beetle).

One most promising line of circumstantial evidence proves to be unsatisfactory when investigated. In the introduction to his edition

mentioned in that edition, has solved also the puzzling 'Puttidew' of line 541. He finds that, in an insertion in B.M. Additional MSS. 31042 which follows verse 1520 of *The Northern Passion* (ed. A. Foster, I, pp. 174 and 176), the Wandering Jew, who 'putt Ihesu with his hande' (pushed roughly) on the way to Calvary, is called 'Iohn putte dieu' (*Times Literary Supplement*, 14th December 1935). Professor Dickins showed also that the 'grete Egeas' of line 537 was the persecutor of St. Andrew (ib., 21st February 1924).

[1] Lines 89-90. [2] S.T.S., I, p. ccl. [3] Line 388.

[4] Elsewhere (S.T.S., I, p. ccxix) Mackay confuses this Sir James with his father Sir Alexander who died in 1497-8 (E.R., XI, pp. 13, 83).

[5] M., p. 199. [6] Line 184.

of Dunbar's poems, Laing records his debt to James Chalmers, nephew of George Chalmers the author of *Caledonia*, for communicating both a transcript of the Reidpeth manuscript made by Ritson and 'copious notes illustrative of several of Dunbar's poems, the result of his own extensive, accurate, and unwearied research'.[1] When Schipper in turn edited the poems and came to consider the problems presented by *The Flyting*, he laid stress on two lines of one of the poems, in trying to discover the date of the work. When Dunbar ridicules the supposedly primitive conditions of Kennedy's life in the west, he writes:

> In till ane glen thow hes, owt of repair,
> Ane laithly luge that wes the lippir menis.[2]

On these lines Schipper bases his view that the poem was written after 8th December 1504, for, according to Schipper,[3] Laing said[4] that James Chalmers mentioned this as the date when Kennedy acquired the house of Glentig—in the valley of the Stinchar, which reaches the sea at Ballantrae—and Schipper identifies Glentig with the 'laithly luge'. He has, however, another source for this information in addition to Chalmers. In his biographical and critical study of Dunbar, Schipper states[5] another source for this acquisition of Glentig by Walter Kennedy at the date specified—the statement made by Paterson, in his *The Life and Poems of William Dunbar*,[6] that Walter Kennedy acquired Glentig from John Wallace and had a charter of the lands, dated 8th December 1504. Mackay, in his introductory memoir to the edition of Dunbar for the Scottish Text Society, says[7] that in Schipper's view *The Flyting* must have been written after that date, when Kennedy acquired a house called Glentig in Carrick which had been a leper house.

If the property in Glentig had indeed been a leper house, there could be no reasonable doubt that the lines quoted above referred to Glentig. But it will be observed that Mackay, though citing Schipper as his authority, goes far beyond Schipper's own statement, which, while implying that the 'laithly luge' was to be identified with Glentig, made no claim that Glentig had in actual fact been shown to be a leper house, whereas Mackay states this as known. Further, Schipper claims to derive his information from two sources—Chalmers, through Laing, and Paterson. Reference to Laing at the page cited by Schipper shows, however, no mention

[1] L., I, xiii. [2] Lines 153-154. [3] S. ed., p. 142.
[4] S. cites L., II, p. 437. [5] S., p. 82. [6] p. 24. [7] S.T.S., I, p. cxiii.

of Glentig at all (nor is there any mention of it elsewhere in Laing's edition), Chalmers's dating of *The Flyting* on that page being based on quite other considerations. We are thus forced back upon Paterson, only to find that though he relates Dunbar's two lines to Glentig he gives no indication of external evidence that Glentig had been a leper house. It becomes clear that Mackay's statement is not backed by his authorities.

In these circumstances it is desirable that the original source of Paterson's information about the transfer of Glentig to Kennedy by John Wallace should be brought to light. In *The Life and Poems of William Dunbar*, which was published in 1860,[1] Paterson does not specify his source. Fortunately, something is obtainable from an earlier work, his *History of the County of Ayr*, which appeared in 1847. There[2] Paterson writes: 'Walter Kennedy of Glentig (which he acquired from John Wallace of Glentig by charter dated 8th December 1504), parson of Douglas, was the poet. It was always supposed he was nearly connected with the Cassilis family, but the fact was not demonstrable until the recent search through the Ailsa charter-chest brought the matter to light. He replies to Dunbar's taunts about the "laithly luge", that "I haif landis, stoir, and stakkis", showing he was in possession of property and led a rural life.' Here, then, is the same statement about the charter, with the addition that Walter Kennedy's connexion with the Cassilis family had recently been demonstrated by a search through the Ailsa charter-chest. Does this imply that the information as to the acquisition of Glentig as stated is also to be found in the Ailsa charter-chest? Certainty can be reached only when the charters mentioned have been perused, and the present writer, in repeated attempts, has failed to obtain permission to see them or to have them searched.

At present, therefore, the position is that we are entirely dependent on Paterson in the matter of Glentig, and that the source of his knowledge is only very indirectly and obscurely hinted. But there is no reason to conclude that Paterson had any information to the effect that Glentig had been a leper house, and Mackay was going beyond his authorities when he said that it had. For the purpose of dating *The Flyting*, no reliance can be placed upon Paterson's information. If the poet Kennedy did obtain possession of

[1] The date of publication of this work is said to be 1863 by Mackay and by Schipper (S. ed., p. 1). Eyre-Todd, p. 149, gives the date as 1873. [2] p. 280.

Glentig at the date specified, we cannot assume that Dunbar was referring to it, that Kennedy did not own other property as well, nor that he did not own other property previously. It is perhaps noteworthy that Smeaton gives the date of the acquisition of Glentig by Kennedy as 1512, without reference to his source of information. When Schipper came to edit the poems of Kennedy in 1902 with a biographical memoir, he made no mention of Glentig—a curious omission—but he referred[1] to Smeaton's work as a text-book on Dunbar. Why did Schipper keep silent on this occasion? Had he discovered by then how indirect, tenuous, and distorted by accretions, the whole of this line of thought was? Unable to consult original records but nonplussed by the discrepancy of dates between Paterson and Smeaton, did he decide to abandon the whole argument?

Fortunately there are firmer grounds for dating *The Flyting*. In the first place, a portion is included among the separately printed pieces issued from the press of Chapman and Millar in Edinburgh. The licence to engage in printing had been granted by King James under the Privy Seal on 15th September 1507.[2] Some of the pieces, though not the decapitated *Flyting*, bear the date 1508. The piece which includes the *Flyting* fragment bears the device of Millar, who appears to have died before 1510.[3] But it is possible to retract the lower limit further, with certainty. In the closing portion of *The Flyting*, Kennedy tells[4] Dunbar to seek the friendly offices of Stobo as mediator. An entry in the Exchequer Rolls,[5] already referred to in this chapter, shows that Stobo was deceased before 13th July 1505, so that the whole work as at present extant must have been composed before that date. On the other hand, in seeking to fix an upper limit, Laing[6] drew attention to a line[7] in the last poem, in which Kennedy replies to Dunbar's comparison of his opponent's desiccated appearance to that of the bodies of Danes exposed on the wheel. Kennedy warns Dunbar that to speak of Danes is to speak of the King of Scotland's own kin. As James IV was the son of Margaret of Denmark, Laing may be right in concluding that *The Flyting* was written later than James's accession to the throne in 1488.

An important line of *The Flyting*, in this consideration of date,

[1] *The Poems of Walter Kennedy*, p. 1. [2] Livingstone, I, p. 223. [3] See Chapter XIV.
[4] Line 331. [5] E.R., XII, p. 372, '. . . dicto quondam Johanne'.
[6] L., II, p. 429. [7] Line 356, in reply to 51.

is that[1] in which, having told how Dunbar had once fouled so monstrously the ship 'Katryne', Kennedy adds,

> Thy dirt clevis till hir towis this twenty yere.

Paterson rightly rejected the unnatural interpretation that 'this twenty yere' means 'twenty years to come'.[2] Laing makes the doubly unwarranted assumption that this voyage in the 'Katryne' was that of 1491 when she carried the Scots ambassadors to France, and that Dunbar was the priest mentioned in the Treasurer's Accounts as having carried out the secretarial work for this embassy. Yet Laing concludes none the less that *The Flyting of Dunbar and Kennedie* was written during the years 1492-1497.[3] Schipper points out[4] the impossibility of reconciling this conclusion with the line just quoted. No doubt the phrase 'this twenty yere' is not to be taken as a precise numerical computation of the time that had elapsed. The extravagance of *The Flyting* forbids such a view. But to regard the phrase as applicable to a period of, at most, six years, is unjustifiable, as stated in a previous chapter. A long period of years is said by Kennedy to have gone by since Dunbar's seasickness. A date after the opening of the new century is therefore indicated, for Dunbar was still a student at St. Andrews University in 1479.

Further, in denouncing Dunbar, Kennedy says:

> Ane benefice quha wald gyve sic ane beste?[5]

Now, it is possible that Dunbar was seeking a benefice before the old century had ended. But the first dated evidence of his hopes is the grant made to him by the King on 15th August 1500, as described at the close of the previous chapter, of an annual pension of £10 for life or until nominated by the King to a benefice of £40 or more. Many poems of Dunbar show that his campaign to gain the benefice was long and embittered. The later the date of *The Flyting*, therefore, the more painful would be the sting of Kennedy's rhetorical question. The significance of the line was evidently seen by James Chalmers, who wished[6] to date *The Flyting* after 17th March 1503-4, on which date the Lord Treasurer records 'the Kingis offerand at maister William Dunbarris first mes'.[7] Chalmers overlooked the Privy Seal entry of 1500 with its reference to a benefice.

[1] Line 452. [2] *The Life and Poems of William Dunbar*, p. 25.
[3] L., II, p. 420. [4] S. ed., p. 142. [5] Line 505.
[6] L., II, p. 437. [7] See Chapter X.

It thus becomes possible to assign *The Flyting* with some degree of confidence to the period from the opening of the century to the summer of 1505, the poem increasing in effectiveness towards the end of that time. That Dunbar was not too old to travel in these years is clear from his absence in England early in the winter of 1501.[1]

If now we concentrate on the years 1500-1505, and analyse the payments of pension made to Dunbar, referring also to certain passages in *The Flyting* that have not yet been used in this discussion, something further is obtainable. After the short preliminary poems, when Dunbar launches his main attack, he has come home from a long sea-expedition.[2] It is winter. Dunbar relates how Kennedy has had to make his bed in the fields 'this somer',[3]

> Bot now, in winter, for purteth thow art traikit.[4]

Kennedy's reply also suggests winter conditions. In caricaturing the coming expedition of Dunbar to France and Italy, he stresses the wintry state of the Alpine passes and tells Dunbar to give up hope of crossing them.[5] To sum up, in stormy weather preceding winter, Dunbar had gone on the voyage in Scandinavian waters but had returned. Now, in winter, he was about to set out for France and Italy. Unless this proposed journey was for some reason prevented, there must have elapsed a considerable number of months during which he was out of the country and unable to receive the instalments of his pension as they fell due. We must therefore consider these periodic payments year by year during the period from the grant of the pension on 15th August 1500 to 13th July 1505, on which date Stobo was no longer alive.

The pension was to consist of £10 annually, payable in two instalments of £5 each, at Whitsuntide and Martinmas respectively. The first payment is not recorded until 23rd May 1501, 'his pensioun of mertymes bipast be command of ane precept', the payment for Whitsuntide 1501 being recorded in July of the same year, and that for Martinmas in December, 'payit to him efter he com furth of Ingland'. Payments appear for 1502 in July and November, and for 1503 in June and November. In March 1503-4, there is the

[1] T.A., II, p. 95. [2] Lines 89-96.

[3] Line 115. B., 'Thow lay full prydles in the peis this somer.' MF. has faded until it is illegible, but R. reads 'in the heit of summer'.

[4] Line 118, from B. Here also MF. has faded, but R. agrees with B.

[5] Lines 433-438.

record of the King's offering at Dunbar's first mass. During the remainder of the period under review, payments appear in due course in May and November 1504, and in May 1505.[1]

It will at once be apparent that the only prolonged gap, which is unaccounted for, is that which separates the recording of the grant of pension in August 1500 from the first payment, 23rd May 1501, which was in respect not of that Whitsuntide but of the preceding Martinmas, for some reason not previously paid. The first payment was delayed from November to the following May, a period of no less than six months. Hence, since the period from summer, 1500, to the summer of 1505 is the most likely for the writing of *The Flyting*, it can be asserted also that during that time the winter of 1500, before November payments fell due, accords best with the evidence available.

This finding differs from that of Schipper, who favours the winter of 1504-5 instead.[2] He does so because he regards the clause about a benefice in the 1500 grant of a pension as merely formal and usual in such deeds, and not to be taken as meaning that there was any real prospect of a benefice for Dunbar. Therefore Schipper took as the date from which Kennedy's gibe on the subject would acquire much significance, not the grant of 1500, but the first mass of 1503-4, after which, before the date when Stobo is known to have been deceased, only one winter intervened—that of 1504-5. Schipper leans also, far more than the facts as stated by Paterson justify, on the acquisition of Glentig in 1504. Schipper has thus the advantage which has been already mentioned as attaching to the latest possible date before the summer of 1505. But, in the opinion of the present writer, the 1500 clause as to a benefice is not to be swept away so lightly, and the external evidence provided by the gap between August 1500 and May 1501 in the Accounts, is so significant—Schipper overlooked it—that it outweighs completely the merely interpretative advantage which would adhere to a later date.

Though the grant of pension was registered under the Privy Seal on 15th August 1500, the royal precept which it made valid may have been issued some weeks before. It may have been given in recognition of services to be rendered by Dunbar in his voyage. The two preliminary poems of *The Flyting of Dunbar and Kennedie*

[1] See other chapters for the location of these entries in the Accounts.
[2] S. ed., p. 143.

which are extant were probably composed in the summer of 1500, the second of them (by Kennedy) appearing shortly after Dunbar had set sail.[1] Driven far from his course by the gales of late summer and of autumn, Dunbar returned in time to write his long attack on Kennedy in winter.[2] But he was unable to draw his November pension before, having received Kennedy's reply, he presumably set off as planned through England for France and Italy, with the prospect of wintry Alpine passes to be crossed which so delighted Kennedy.[3] The period between the early winter of 1500 and the spring of 1501, by which time he had returned to draw his pension, is certainly not too long to allow, whether he did reach Italy or, as Kennedy prophesied, stayed in Paris.

It is not claimed that these dates are necessarily correct. The evidence is not sufficient to admit of certainty, for there are too many possible, if not entirely probable, loopholes in it. Though 1500-1505 is the most likely period, 'this twenty yere'—not to be too precisely understood—would admit of a year or two earlier, and Dunbar was probably hopeful of a benefice even before 1500. The journey of Dunbar anticipated by Kennedy may never actually have been undertaken, in which case no prolonged winter absence of Dunbar would be necessitated, and so other years would serve equally well. It is even possible that the journey, if undertaken, was completed between the ordinary terms of Martinmas and Whitsuntide. Though Kennedy's last poem must, unless we are to tamper with the text, have been composed while Dunbar was in Scotland, it is possible that the poem to which it was a reply may have been written by Dunbar from abroad. And there are doubtless many other possibilities. But it may be fairly claimed that the date arrived at is the most likely, for it fits the evidence to hand, and fits it more neatly than any other that has been advanced.

Much of the confusion that has arisen over the interpretation of *The Flyting of Dunbar and Kennedie* is due to the manner in which Dunbar's various travels are referred to, not chronologically or systematically, but at random as the spirit of flyting prompts. The earliest such episode is that of his former wanderings as a Franciscan novice, and his journey by sea in the 'Katryne'.[4] These journeys have already been dealt with in earlier chapters. Intermingled with these accounts of long ago are references to the just completed

[1] Lines 89-90. [2] Lines 115-118.
[3] Lines 433-436. [4] Lines 425-428, 449-472.

voyage of autumn, 1500.[1] Thirdly, there are the passages relating to the forthcoming journey by land through England, across the Channel, to Paris, and beyond to Italy, in the winter of 1500.[2] What more can we gather about his more recent itineraries?

It is clear that in the autumn of 1500 Dunbar was not bound for Scandinavia when he was tempest-driven towards it. According to the poet himself, wind and tide drove the ship many hundreds of miles from Scotland, in moonless and murky weather. According to the Bannatyne manuscript, the ship was driven

> By Holland, Seland, getland,[3] and Northway coist.[4]

Zeeland is the district round the mouth of the Scheldt, Sjaelland (Zealand) the island on which Copenhagen stands, Jylland (Jutland) the peninsular province of Denmark, Götaland is the Swedish province around Göteborg on the Skagerrak, and 'Northway' is of course Norway. We must take our choice among these possibilities, and in the end must rest content with conjectures, but Laing is surely wrong in interpreting 'getland' as Zetland, and 'Seland' as Zeeland. 'Seland' is oddly placed in Bannatyne's series, for Holland lies between Zeeland and Denmark, and a southwesterly tempest must have veered very considerably to drive the ship from Holland to Zeeland. The Maitland manuscript is still less intelligible, reading

> By Hilland, forland, getland and Norroway cost.

Fohr is a large island off western Schleswig: Schipper suggested the North or South Foreland of Kent. But the general course followed by the ship is clear enough, whether it was driven into the Skagerrak or not. On the Norway coast, in a wilderness of seas, Dunbar lost the small amount of cash which he had begged from his friends for the voyage. He lost it, along with certain holy relics, when the ship was lightened by jettisoning everything possible in order to escape from the storm. The moneybag thus lay somewhere on the 'Seland' coast,[5] or on the coast of Norway according to the Bannatyne manuscript. Dunbar in vain hired a diver afterwards to dredge for it, and in consequence of the muddle he was in had to sit often hungry, begging for charity, barefoot, and breekless.

If, then, Dunbar was not bound for Scandinavia, what was his

[1] Lines 89-96, 377-384.
[2] Lines 367-376, 429-448, 464, 470, 473-488, 507-512.
[3] M., however, reads 'Yetland'. [4] Line 94.
[5] CM., 'Seland'; 'syland' in MF. and R.; B., 'Northway'.

port of destination? On his return he set about preparations for reaching France through England and, says Kennedy, for reaching Italy. It is therefore possible that his previous expedition by sea was intended to take him part of the way to Italy by landing him in Zeeland. The town of Middelburg in Zeeland was, in 1500, the staple for Scottish trade and shipping, and the Conservator of the privileges of Scottish merchants resided there. From Middelburg Dunbar might have intended to reach Italy by way of the Rhine. On the other hand, he may have been diverted by the storm while on his way from Leith to France.

The second journey, which he was about to undertake after his return from Norway, was to take him through England to France. The sea-passage from England to France would be short, but might yet suffice to deliver him again to the tempests. So many mischances befell Scottish mariners in winter that in 1466 Parliament had prohibited the sailing of ships with staple goods between the feasts of Saints Simon and Jude (28th October) and Candlemas (2nd February).[1] Kennedy affects to believe that Dunbar will find himself at 'Danskyn'[2]—the name invariably given at that time to Danzig.[3] There was a Scottish colony at Danzig, and the city had a considerable trade with Scotland, but it is so far off the route to France and Italy that the only reasonable interpretation would appear to be that Kennedy is being facetious. As Dunbar found himself last time on the coast of Norway, he might on this occasion be blown even to what must have been one of the uttermost of northern ports. And it is in view of what happened on the last occasion to Dunbar's stock of money—no doubt small because of the laws against exporting currency, which were stringent—that Kennedy makes the promise that Dunbar will receive at Danzig from Kennedy's account a pack of flea-skins.[4] Scotland's export trade consisted largely of sheepskins, rabbit-skins, and the pelts of smaller animals such as martens.[5]

If Kennedy's description of the state of the Alpine passes implies that, on the earlier journey by sea, Dunbar was on his way to Italy, it shows that on this second journey, by land, there could be no question of proceeding to Italy from France in mid-winter. The St. Bernard crossing is impracticable, writes Kennedy, on account

[1] *Acts*, II, p. 87. [2] Line 446. [3] Fischer, p. 5.
[4] CM., 'flaskynnis'; B., 'flaskynis'; MF. and R. read 'flay skynnis'.
[5] Innes, p. xl.

of wild beasts, that by 'Mount Scarpre' because of the snow, and the route by 'Mount Nycholas' and 'Mount Godart' because of hurricanes. The advice to Dunbar to stay in Paris, as assistant to the hangman, may be embroidery on a revised itinerary. But this is mere surmise. If Dunbar did go into Italy, his stay can only have been short, for in May he was back in Scotland. If he saw anything of the rich splendour of Renaissance Italy, there are no traces in his poetry.

It may have been during this passage through England, however, that Dunbar visited Oxford and, according to the Maitland manuscript, there wrote a lyric recording his impressions. *Dumbar at Oxinfurde*[1] has already been described. The northerner scrutinised Oxford keenly, and was not enthusiastic about it.

[1] 'To speik of science . . . '. MF. has two copies, on pp. 9 and 317; R., f. 10b. The colophon of MF. 2 reads 'quod Dumbar at oxinfurde'.

CHAPTER VII

LONDON

DUNBAR's visit to England in the winter of 1501 has customarily been associated with the negotiations then proceeding for King James's betrothal to Princess Margaret of England. It has caused the poem that was written, during the visit of the Scots commissioners, in honour of the Lord Mayor and of London, to be attributed to Dunbar.

Reasons have been suggested in the preceding chapter for the delay in paying the first instalment of Dunbar's pension, due at Martinmas, 1500. Payment was actually made on or about the 23rd May 1501, and another payment in July. But the Martinmas payment of 1501 was not paid until 20th December or thereabout, and is recorded in the following terms: 'Item to maister william dunbar quhilk wes payit to him efter he com furth of Ingland—v lib.'[1] We may conclude, therefore, that Dunbar was absent in England over Martinmas, and that his visit was probably connected with the betrothal negotiations concluded in January 1501-2.

The marriage had been under consideration since 1496, but James's support of Warbeck had delayed its fulfilment. Another obstacle had been the consanguinity of the parties due to the marriage of James I to Lady Joan Beaufort. Papal dispensation was at last secured and, after many embassies had been designated and sent, a final commission was issued by James King on 8th October 1501 to Robert, Archbishop of Glasgow, Patrick Earl of Bothwell, Lord Hailes, Great Admiral of Scotland and Warden of the West Marches, and 'Andrew, postulate of the see of Moray', to contract the betrothal with Margaret in the King's name.[2] When the embassy reached London, the court and city were in a ferment owing to the festivities attending the arrival of Princess Katharine of Aragon, the betrothed of Prince Arthur. But two 'faire and large barges', those of the Archbishop of Canterbury and the Abbot of Westminster, had been reserved for the ambassadors from Spain and

[1] For details of these records, see Chapter VIII. [2] Bain, IV, p. 335.

from Scotland respectively, 'besides the kynges two bootes for thayr servauntes'.[1]

The Scots embassy appears, however, to have arrived too late to take part in the welcoming of Princess Katharine after all, for they did not reach London until several days after the wedding of Arthur and Katharine, which took place on the 14th November. But the pre-nuptial ceremonies were such as to throw light on the similar circumstances in which, a little over a month later, the poem attributed to Dunbar was to be produced. An account of the whole proceedings, extending from the arrival of Katharine to the betrothal of Margaret in the following January, is contained in a British Museum quarto manuscript chronicle of the history of England and of the lord mayors of London from 1215 to 1509.[2] It includes a transcript of the poem in question, and was brought to the notice of Laing.

On the 9th November 1501, Prince Arthur with a large company entered London by Fleet Street while Katharine lodged at Lambeth after her journey from Exeter. The Lord Mayor and citizens arranged a series of pageants for her entry into the city, which took place on the 12th. At London Bridge the Princess was welcomed by St. Katharine and St. Ursula, who addressed her from an elaborately carved and gilt wooden structure erected on the drawbridge, the former reciting a poem of welcome and counsel. The poem is given in full in the chronicle. Among other devices was a pageant in Cornhill of the Twelve Signs of the Zodiac, over which sat Raphael the archangel, with Boethius and others, who in turn delivered poetic addresses. A pageant of heaven, with seven golden candlesticks, awaited the Princess in Cheapside, where again poems were recited, the King and Queen listening from a neighbouring haberdasher's shop. In Cheapside also the Lord Mayor, Sir John Shaw, goldsmith, with the aldermen, presented their respects to Katharine. Her ill-fated marriage with Arthur followed in St. Paul's on the 14th, the King and Queen watching from a latticed alcove. After mass, a feast was held in the great hall of the Bishop's palace. On the 16th the Princess went in state from St. Paul's wharf by barge to Westminster, among those present being the Spanish lords,

[1] MS. Cotton Vespasian C. xiv, f. 81. This folio MS. is imperfect; it contains an account of the orders given for the reception of Katharine. It was quoted by Gairdner (*Letters*, I, p. 405).

[2] MS. Cotton Vitellius A xvi, f. 183b onwards. Laing gave some extracts in his *Supplement*, p. 274-275.

but there is still no mention of the Scots ambassadors. A ceremonial jousting was held on the 18th at the palace of Westminster, one of the Spanish lords taking part.

The arrival of the Scots, Dunbar being among them presumably, was on the 20th November.[1] 'Upon Saterday folowyng aboute one of the clok came the Ambassadours of Scotland in at Bisshopesgate and so rode through Cornhill and Chepe and so conveied with lordis and many wele apparayled gentilmen unto Seynt Johannes without Smythfeld, and there loged within the place of the said Lord of Seynt Johannes.'[2] 'And upon the monday folowyng was a goodly Justis ageyne holden, in the forsaid paleis of westminster, where at were present the said Scottissh Ambassadours, the which day the lord marques [of Dorset] before named wan the pre Albe it that the duke [of Buckingham] that day bare hym full valiauntly and breke many Speris but the marques that day brake the moo. And duryng these Justis dyveris nyghtis wer kept in westminster halle noble and costious bankettis with most goodly disguysyngis to the greate consolacion of the beholders. Upon Weddensday folowyng was the said Justis contynued . . . ',[3] and so on Thursday. 'And that nyght folowyng was holden a goodly disguysing and Banket In westminster halle. Upon the morow folowyng beyng friday the kyng Quene my lord prynce my lady pryncesse and all the nobles beyng present att all these forsaid Tryumphes tok their Bargis at westminster Bryge aboute two of the Klok at after none and so were rowed to moretelak where the said astatis tok their horses and Charys and so rode to Rychemount, whom the mair with a treyn of the worshipfull felishippes conveied in Sondry Bargis till the kyng were landed at the said towne of mourtlak and after retourned home to london.'[4]

In Christmas week the Scots ambassadors were no longer onlookers at the festivities attending a foreign marriage, but principals feasted as envoys of the King of Scots, seeking the hand of the Princess Margaret. 'This yere in the Cristmas weke the mair had to dyner the Ambassadours of Scotland whome accompanyed my lord Chaunceler and other lordis of this Realme where sittyng at dyner one of the said Scottis givyng attendaunce upon a Bisshop ambassadour the which was Reported to be a prothonotary of Scotland and servaunt of the said Bisshop made this Balade folowyng . . .'[5]

[1] L. says, wrongly, the 24th (*Supplement*, p. 274). [2] Cot. Vit. A xvi, f. 198b.
[3] ib., f. 199. [4] ib., f. 199b. [5] ib., ff. 199b-200.

The poem which follows, without any further indication of authorship, is in praise of London. It appears in two other manuscripts, where it is anonymous.[1] *The Treatise of London* has been attributed to Dunbar by Laing and others.[2] In the early pages of the Balliol manuscript is a list of contents which includes a description of the poem. This description has apparently not been noticed hitherto: 'A litill balet made by london made at mr shawes table by a skote.'[3] Sir John Shaw, Lord Mayor, 'kept his dyner at the said Guyld Hall which was the first tyme that ever any there was kept or holden.'[4]

Ceremonial banquets, no less than triumphal entries into the city, were normally accompanied by the reciting of 'balets'. Thus, at the coronation feast of Queen Elizabeth of England in 1487, the fruit was followed by 'A Soteltie, with Writing of Balads'.[5] The poem attributed by Laing to Dunbar celebrates the renown and riches of London, its lords, ladies, prelates, and merchants, the beauty of its river

> Where many a swanne doth swymme with wyngis fare,

the ships 'with top-royall', London Bridge, the Tower, and its guns. But it concludes appropriately with praises of the city's incomparable Lord Mayor, at whose table the poem was declaimed.

Is there sufficient ground for regarding this poem as Dunbar's? Certainly the chronicler does not give any encouragement. It is tempting to juggle with the phrasing of the unpunctuated narrative, but its statements are clear enough. The maker of the ballad is stated to be 'a prothonotary of Scotland and servaunt of the said Bisshop'. It is not enough to interpret a protonotary as nothing more than a principal clerk.[6] The protonotary was Andrew Forman, as Mackay states though he regards the attribution of the poem to the protonotary as an error.[7] A protonotary was a papal officer whose duty it was to keep the records of the Church,[8] and Forman had

[1] 'London, thou art of townes A per se.' (Printed by Dr. Mackenzie, p. 177.) MS. Cotton Vitellius A xvi, f. 200; Lansdowne MS. 762, f. 7b; Balliol College MS. No. 394, f. 199b-200 (not No. 395 as stated by S.). In the Lansdowne MS. the poem is headed *An honour to London*. The Balliol MS. title is *A treatice of london*, and its colophon, 'Explicit the treatise of london made at mr shaa table whan he was mayre'.

[2] Quiller-Couch says that Dunbar composed the poem as he stood on London Bridge, 'returning Scotlandwards from his youthful wandering as mendicant-friar in Picardy' (*Studies in Literature*, Second Series, 1922, p. 274).

[3] Balliol MS. No. 394, f. 4. [4] MS. Cot. Vit. A xvi, f. 183b.

[5] Leland, IV, p. 226. [6] M., p. 240. [7] S.T.S., I, p. xxxiv.

[8] Sir J. B. Paul, *Scottish Historical Review*, XVII, p. 178.

held the post of Apostolic Protonotary since 1490 when, acting at Rome as procurator for King James, he received the title from the Pope himself.[1] From that date he is a familiar figure in the public records under that title.[2] In 1498 he received a pension to be enjoyed until his preferment to a bishopric, and in October 1501 he appears among the other commissioners as 'Andrew, postulate of the see of Moray'.[3] In other words, he had been nominated by the chapter of the cathedral, but removal by the Pope of certain impediments under canon law was still awaited. The Pope provided him to the see on 26th November.[4] At the ceremonial betrothal at the end of January 1501-2 he is still described as 'Elect of Murray'.[5] Whether the poem on London is correctly ascribed to him or not, the protonotary among the commissioners was Andrew Forman, not Dunbar.

But the knowledge that Dunbar was in England about this very time, as shown by the entry of 20th December which we have quoted from the accounts of the Scots Lord Treasurer, has made the attribution of the poem to Dunbar persist. Further, two contemporary entries in the English public records have been adduced as referring to Dunbar. They both appear among the privy purse expenses of Henry VII,[6] and were cited by Laing. The first entry is dated 31st December: 'Item to the Rymer of Scotland in rew.[7] £6″13″4d.'. The second entry is on the following page: 'Item to a Rymer of Scotland. £6″13″4d.'. Laing gave to the latter entry the date 7th January, as given by Bentley, and this date has been accepted by later writers; but reference to the manuscript shows that there is no such entry under 7th January, and that the correct date is 27th January, the first digit being so close to the binding of the book that it has been overlooked. Again following the editor Bentley, Laing had little doubt that these entries referred to William Dunbar, and he assumed that they had to do with the writing of the poem on London, which Laing included in his edition of Dunbar as one of the authentic poems. Mackay, for the Scottish Text Society, assumed that the Rymer was Dunbar, and pointed to Dunbar's manner as unmistakable, the poem being written in the aureate style of

1 Herkless and Hannay, II, p. 6. 2 e.g. T.A., II, p. 112. 3 Bain, IV, p. 365.

4 Dowden, *Bishops of Scotland*, p. 166. 5 Leland, IV, p. 258.

6 British Museum, Additional MSS. No. 7099, pp. 71-72. This is an eighteenth century MS., transcribing extracts from the original accounts which are now lost. Laing consulted the printed version in Bentley's *Excerpta Historica* (p. 125).

7 i.e. 'in rewarde', as shown by many other entries.

The Thistle and the Rose and *The Goldyn Targe*.[1] He might have added that Dunbar wrote poems in honour of other towns—Oxford, Edinburgh, and Aberdeen. The possible objection that the poem uses the southern verbal terminations in '-ith' instead of the northern forms[2] is irrelevant, for the English scribe or chronicler would naturally use the southern endings.

None of the arguments for Dunbar's authorship of *The Treatise of London* is convincing. Dunbar had so many manners that his very versatility makes it impossible to ascribe a poem to him on account of a manner unmistakably his and not attributable to someone else; and the aureate style, in particular, cannot be claimed as his own. Mackay knew of only one manuscript version, but in that manuscript the poem is stated to have been composed by the protonotary, who was Andrew Forman. In the other two manuscripts the poem is anonymous except that the Balliol manuscript describes it as made 'by a skote'.

Some difficulty arises, too, in harmonising the English privy purse items with the payment of 20th December made by the Scots Lord Treasurer to Dunbar which was due to him at Martinmas but 'quhilk wes payit to him efter he com furth of Ingland'.[3] The entry occurs at the foot of a folio headed 'anno domini etc. quingentesimo primo', the item at the head of the same folio being dated 20th December. The next item with a date attached is at the head of the next folio, and is dated 21st February. The difficulty of dating precisely the payments recorded in the Treasurers' Accounts has already been mentioned. The accounts were audited at irregular intervals of two years or so, and, in preparation, the extant digest was made from the various day-to-day account books. Thus, payments made on different days might often be brought together under a single date in the digest,[4] and there might even be similar groupings in the original account books. As Dunbar's half-yearly pension was due at Martinmas but was not paid until his return from England, he must have returned later than Martinmas, but how much later? It may safely be concluded that he was back in Scotland before the 20th December, but we cannot be sure that he returned just before that date, nor, on the other hand, that he

[1] S.T.S., I, p. xxxiv.
[2] Baildon, p. xxxiv, points out the southern rhyming of 'white' with 'knyght'.
[3] MS. *Compot. Thesaur.*, 1500-1502, f. 89. Printed edition, II, 95.
[4] T. Dickson, T.A., I, p. xxxiii.

returned some considerable time before it. Edinburgh in those days was some sixteen days' travel from London.[1] The entry in the Treasurer's Accounts does not prove, therefore, that Dunbar could not have gone back to England, after receiving payment of his pension, in time to be awarded a sum from Henry VII's privy purse on 31st December. There must have been many comings and goings between Edinburgh and London during the protracted betrothal negotiations, which involved political issues, financial settlements, and the transfer of very extensive lands as jointure. The Scots Lord Treasurer records on 3rd January a payment to 'Lioun Herald, quhen he cum furth of England',[2] and yet Lyon Herald was present at the final ceremonies in London at the end of January. On the 8th December a payment is recorded to Sir John Sandilands of Hillhouse—obscurely referred to by both Dunbar and Kennedy in *The Flyting*—'quhen he cam furth of Ingland from the Lordis'.[3]

The authority of the English chronicler, who plainly states that the poem in honour of London was made by the protonotary, who was certainly Andrew Forman, can scarcely be overturned without the support of very much better evidence than has been advanced. The evidence so far as it exists is quite definite and is against Dunbar's authorship. As to the identity of 'the Rymer of Scotland' who received King Henry's bounty on 31st December, it is quite likely that he was Dunbar. The later payment of a similar amount by Henry on 27th January 'to a Rymer of Scotland' may also refer to Dunbar, though the indefinite article of the second entry reads strangely after 'the Rymer' of the previous entry. There is, of course, no certainty that the two recipients were the same person. Laing's mistake in dating the second payment 7th January instead of 27th has hitherto obscured its connexion with the public betrothal of King James and Princess Margaret on 25th January. Whether Henry's two payments were made to Dunbar or not, there is little reason to suppose that Dunbar would be absent from the ceremonial consummation, when there would be many gifts.

The betrothal is described by John Young, Somerset Herald, who was later to attend Princess Margaret when, in 1503, she journeyed to Scotland.[4] Margaret was twelve years of age. The marriage contract was signed at Richmond Palace on the 24th of January by Robert Blackadder, Archbishop of Glasgow, Patrick

[1] Conway, p. 20. [2] T.A., II, p. 132.
[3] ib., II, 128. [4] Leland, IV, p. 258.

Earl of Bothwell, and Andrew of Moray.[1] Accompanied by the Queen, the Duke of York, and the lords spiritual and temporal, King Henry heard high mass in the chapel and then proceeded to the Queen's Chamber, where a canon of Glasgow read the papal dispensation for consanguinity. The Archbishop of Glasgow conducted the ceremony of betrothal, Bothwell making the responses as procurator for King James. That done, the trumpeters blew and minstrels played 'in the best and most joyfullest manner'. Dinner was served in the King's Chamber, Blackadder and Bothwell sitting at the upper end of the table, and Forman at the other, while all the other ambassadors dined in the Council Chamber. In the afternoon there were jousts, and a great banquet followed.[2] On the following day, St. Paul's Day, 25th January, the betrothal was proclaimed at St. Paul's Cross, 'Te Deum' was sung, and in the afternoon 'In dyvers placis of the Citie were made greate Fires . . . and at every Fire an hoggeshed of wyne Cowched the which in tyme of the Fires brennyng was drunkyn of such as wold, the which wyne was not longe in drynkyng.'[3] The chief ambassadors received costly presents. Lyon King of Arms was given a horse with a hundred crowns of gold, and a gown of fine satin, and 'to diverse ither Gentlemen of that Company, Gownes of Velvett, in full honourable Manner.'[4] It was on the 27th that the payment, noted above, was recorded, of £6″13″4d. 'to a Rymer of Scotland'.

The ambassadors arrived in Edinburgh before the 24th February, for Blackadder and Bothwell wrote from Edinburgh on that date to express their thanks to King Henry.[5] There is no evidence for Laing's statement that, on his return to Edinburgh, Dunbar received £5 from the Treasurer in addition to his half-yearly pension.[6] But James IV would certainly not fail his servants on this occasion.

[1] Bain, IV, p. 336. [2] Leland, IV, pp. 258-262.
[3] MS. Cot. Vit. A xvi, f. 201. [4] Leland, IV, p. 263.
[5] Rymer's *Foedera*, XIII, p. 54, cited by Sir J. B. Paul, T.A., II, p. lvii.
[6] L., *Supplement*, p. 275. Laing himself makes no mention of such additional payment when he summarises the pension records, I, p. 68. The next pension entry after that of 20th December is not till 9th July.

CHAPTER VIII

'ANE COURTMAN'

HAVING dealt in the two preceding chapters with the circumstances attending Dunbar's travels overseas in the winter of 1500-1, and those probably related to his journey to England in the winter of 1501-2, we return now to his life at the court of King James from the year 1500, when he was awarded his pension.

The only precise dates that are available in his life between the Privy Seal grant of a pension in August 1500 and the writing of *The Thistle and the Rose* are afforded by the entries in the Treasurer's Accounts, recording payments of pension. The pages of the manuscript accounts are now mounted, and there is nothing to suggest that the original sequences have been disturbed in the process. It is usually necessary, however, in order to arrive at the date of a particular entry, to search for a neighbouring item which is dated, as only a few of the items are dated. Some reference has already been made to the pension payments, in considering the probable date of *The Flyting of Dunbar and Kennedie*.

The first half-yearly payment of £5 was made about the 23rd May 1501: 'Item to Maister William William [sic] Dunbar in his pensioun of mertymes bipast be command of ane precept. v lib.'[1] The argument has already been stated that the delay of so many months—from Martinmas to May—in making this payment was probably due to Dunbar's absence from Scotland over the winter, as foreshadowed by Kennedy in the last poem of *The Flyting*. For the next half-yearly payment, due a few days after Whitsuntide, 1501, he had to wait until about the 20th July: 'Item to maister william dunbar his pensioun of the witsonday terme bipast be command of

[1] Printed *Accounts*, II, p. 92. MS. *Compot. Thesaur.*, 1500-1502, f. 85b. The third entry before is dated 23rd May, and the payment to Dunbar, itself undated, is followed by an item dated 22nd June. The sequence of 'precepts' begins in a February, proceeds to the end of a year, and on to September of another year, the Dunbar entry being in the first of the two Mays. Yet the editor assigns all the sequence to 1501 indifferently.

ane precept—v lib.'[1] The next entry concerning Dunbar is that already discussed at some length, recording the payment due at Martinmas, 1501, which had to wait for his return from England. The entry reads, 'Item to maister william dunbar quhilk wes payit to him efter he com furth of Ingland, v lib.'[2] Its approximate date is 20th December 1501. Reasons have been given for concluding that Dunbar's return to Edinburgh was probably only a hasty visit and that he is likely to have been in London again in January 1501-2 and to have been the rhymer of Scotland rewarded at least once by Henry VII. Both the payments of 1502, however, were made at the normal times. About the 9th July the entry occurs, 'Item to maister willam [sic] dunbar sic like—v lib.'[3] A similar item precedes it and refers to 'John Steil', but the explanation of the 'sic like' is given by the entry previous to that again: 'Item to sir donald Rede chapellain quhilk singis in tayn his Witsonday terme—v lib.' This Whitsunday payment was followed by one about 12th November, 'Item to maister william dunbar his pensioun of the said terme of mertymes—v lib.'[4]

This must have been a time of bright hopes for Dunbar. The grant of a pension and promise of a church post had placed him on the first rung of the royal favour. He had around him examples of the swift promotion that might follow. Among them was the case of a fellow-poet, though a man of very different stamp—the grave and learned Gavin Douglas, who had risen rapidly. Born in 1474 or 1475,[5] and therefore very much younger than Dunbar,

[1] Printed *Accounts*, II, p. 95. MS. *Compot. Thesaur.*, 1500-1502, f. 88. The item, undated, occurs in a section of 'pensiones' following the 'precepts' already referred to, and similarly distributed in time. The fourth item in front is dated 20th July, and a later entry (omitted by the editor) is dated 12th September.

[2] Printed *Accounts*, II, p. 95. MS *Compot. Thesaur.*, 1500-1502, f. 89. This item is at the foot of the folio which is headed 'anno domini quingentesimo primo' and which begins with the date 20th December, there being no other date until the head of f. 90, 21st February.

[3] Printed *Accounts*, II, p. 95. MS. *Compot. Thesaur.*, 1500-1502, f. 90b. The Dunbar entry is undated, but at the middle of f. 90 is an item dated 9th July, following the words 'anno domini etc. quingentesimo secundo'. Yet the next date given is at the third item after the Dunbar entry, 'item the thrid day of Junij', which must refer likewise to 1502.

[4] Printed *Accounts*, II, p. 335. MS. *Compot. Thesaur.*, 1502-1504, f. 96b. The entry occurs in a series headed 'Pensiones' which opens with the date 12th November; the next date, attached to the second entry after Dunbar's, is 4th February (i.e. 1502-3), a date omitted by the editor.

[5] Douglas was 48 years of age in 1522 when his will received probate (Small's ed. of Douglas, I, p. cxvii).

Douglas had graduated at St. Andrews in 1494, and taken orders soon after. The powerful influence of the Earl of Angus had helped in his son's rapid preferment. Gavin was rector of Monymusk in 1496, and two years later was designated for the parsonage of Glenquhom. Soon afterwards he was appointed parson of East Linton and rector of Prestonkirk. His progress culminated, for the time, in his preferment to the dignity of provost of the collegiate church of St. Giles, about 1501.[1] In that very year Gavin Douglas stepped into the front rank of Scottish poets with his eloquent and courtly poem, *The Palice of Honour*.[2] Dunbar could scarcely hope for such rapid success, but already, with two of his friends, Kennedy and Quintene, both of *Flyting* fame, he was recognised as a poet of distinction. In *The Palice of Honour*, Gavin Douglas included them in his list of the masters, after the classical poets and the English trio—Chaucer, Gower, and Lydgate:

> Of this natioun I knew also anone
> Greit Kennedie and Dunbar yit undeid,
> And Quintene with ane huttok on his heid.[3]

Loyal service to the King could do much to help Dunbar to preferment, and at court he was in touch with the King.

Dunbar was to face prolonged disappointment and money difficulties, but he could write of them on occasion with good humour, as in the poem *To the Lords of the King's Exchequer*.[4] Perhaps this was prompted by his first efforts to live within the means which the pension provided. There is no evidence that Dunbar ever received payments from the Exchequer. It is unlikely that any money would pass to him from it, as the disbursement of the miscellaneous expenses of the court, including liveries, was the province of the Lord Treasurer. The contents of the poem do not support the view[5] that Dunbar had been summoned by the Exchequer to account for a sum received by him from that department, and was excusing himself. The sum concerned is stated to have been received from the Treasurer. But the annual audit of the Exchequer was con-

[1] Small's ed. of Douglas, I, pp. v-vii. T.A., II, p. 360.

[2] At the close of his translation of the *Aeneid*, finished, he says, on 22nd July 1513, Douglas informs his readers that he wrote *The Palice of Honour* 'weill twelf yeris tofor' (Small's ed., IV, p. 228).

[3] ib., I, p. 36.

[4] 'My lordis of chalker, . . . ' R., f. 6. Presumably to meet exigencies of the rhyme, M. has amended 'clank' in line 8 to 'clink'. L. headed the poem *To the Lordis of the Kingis Chacker*. [5] S., p. 249.

ducted about midsummer,[1] and Dunbar seizes the occasion to address to the Lords of Exchequer—who included other influential officers of state besides the Comptroller and the Treasurer—a jocular presentation of the state of his own finances, with a view to its alleviation.

Of all his receipts during the year there is not a coin left. To ascertain his rents and possessions, they need not tire their thumbs nor make their counters clink nor spend ink and paper. Dunbar had received from the Lord Treasurer a sum of money to spend;[2] he does not know how it has gone, but it is at an end, which afflicts him sorely. When he took the money he had believed it would long support him in comfort in town, but now the remains of it may be bundled up with ease. He has no proof but his purse, he says, but that would not lie if it were looked into. Dunbar does not seem yet to be in serious difficulties, if one may judge from his good humour. There is no suggestion that his life at court is irksome.

The court was dominated by the personality of King James. In 1500 the King was twenty-seven years of age and had ruled for twelve years. He was of athletic build and bore himself well, according to Ayala,[3] the Spanish ambassador, who reported on James's merits to Ferdinand and Isabella in 1498. Of handsome complexion, his portraits show him to have had a face marked strongly with individuality in which there was a touch of sadness. He did not cut his beard, and his brown hair fell over his shoulders. Erasmus records that his personal appearance was such that, from a distance, he was recognisably the King. 'He had a wonderful force of intellect, an incredible knowledge of all things, an invincible magnanimity, the sublimity of a truly royal heart, the largest charity, and the most profuse liberality. There was no virtue which became a great prince in which he did not so excell as to gain the praise even of his enemies.'[4] In the law courts he was a stern judge, especially in cases of murder. Bold in battle and careless of his own safety, he told Ayala that, since the responsibility for peace and war lay with him, he felt bound to be the first in danger. He was affable in conversation, avoided the current fashion of oaths, and was true

[1] Dickson, T. A., I, p. xv. Mackay, E.R., XIII, p. xxxix.

[2] Mackay, E.R., XIII, p. civ, is not justified in regarding the payment as a loan from the Treasurer. [3] Bergenroth, I, p. 210.

[4] *Adagia*, ed. 1558, col. 479. Quoted, Dickson, T.A., I, p. cxxxv.

to his word. In weighty matters he willingly heard the advice of his councillors; yet the final decision was his own, and in Ayala's opinion James's judgment was generally sound. His temperance in eating and drinking impressed Ayala strongly. The ambassador reported that James would be eminently suitable for the hand of a Spanish princess and would prove a faithful ally. Nor was Spain the only Continental power to be interested in the King of Scots. By his ceaseless diplomacy he was establishing the importance of Scotland abroad as a counter to English power.

But the King was far from faultless. Buchanan states that he had too great a desire for popularity, and that, in wishing to avoid his father's reputation for avarice, he maintained an expenditure far more lavish than the country could permanently afford.[1] Ayala, in 1498, did not see these faults, but the Spaniard was alarmed at James's reckless exposure of his person in battle. James esteemed himself, Ayala reported, as if he were master of the world; and, further—an ominous criticism—he was likely to be too much allured by love of war. Ayala learned that James, when a minor, had been led by his advisers into dishonourable courses, and particularly into love-intrigues, but that, to allay the scandal, James was said to have desisted for about a year.[2] The reformation, if there was one, must have been brief. Several of the intrigues persisted for years, and they did not all cease with the marriage of 1503. The poem by Dunbar entitled by Bannatyne, *The Wowing of the King quhen he wes in Dumfermeling*, has already been discussed. Margaret Drummond, daughter of John, Lord Drummond,[3] went to reside in Stirling Castle in 1496 under the charge of the Governor's wife, and in 1497 bore the King a daughter.[4] Many payments were made to her until June 1502,[5] soon after which she and her sister died at Drummond Castle after eating a meal.[6] Her daughter Margaret was brought up at the royal expense, items in the Accounts providing for 'the barne', and she eventually married John, Lord Gordon. For many years masses were sung at Dunblane, by the King's command, for the soul of Lady Margaret Drummond who was buried there. Smeaton's statement that 'strong presumption exists that the *affaire de coeur* was promoted, at least in its initial stages, by Dunbar', is baseless.[7] Smeaton adds, 'I have a strong conviction

[1] Buchanan, II, p. 261. [2] Bergenroth, I, p. 210.
[3] E.R., XII, p. 625. [4] Sir J. B. Paul, T.A., II, p. lii. [5] T.A., II, p. 152.
[6] Sir J. B. Paul, ib., II, p. xxvi. [7] Smeaton, p. 51.

that Dunbar's exquisite poem, *Of Love Earthly and Divine*, was directly inspired by the remembrance of the beautiful Margaret's untimely fate. Only for a reference to the matter have I space in this small volume. Elsewhere I hope to give the arguments leading me to adopt this conclusion.' It would be interesting to know the 'arguments'.

Another mistress, earlier, was Marion Boyd, daughter of Archibald Boyd of Bonshaw,[1] whose son by the King was born about 1493.[2] From 1495 she held an annuity from lands bestowed by the King, who married her in that year to a Mure of Rowallan.[3] Her son by the King, Alexander Stewart, was advanced at the age of nine to be Archdeacon of St. Andrews,[4] became a pupil of Erasmus, and Archbishop at eighteen. Still another affair was with Janet Kennedy, daughter of Lord Kennedy. She bore the King a son in 1500, and a daughter later[5]; the son, James, was made Earl of Moray. Her usual residence was at Bothwell, but in June 1501 James granted her the forest and Castle of Darnaway in the province of Moray, so long as she was without a husband or other man.[6] She did not have them in March 1504-5.[7] The King visited her frequently at Darnaway and at Bothwell; he was at Bothwell with her in April 1503.[8]

James was oppressed continually by a sense of his sins. According to Ayala, he knew the Bible well and other books of devotion, and prayed assiduously. On Wednesdays and Fridays he avoided meat, and on Sundays, even when going to mass, denied himself his horse. Before transacting important business he would hear mass.[9] The part he had played in the faction which had brought about his father's lamentable death at Sauchieburn lay on his conscience. The chronicler's story of the iron belt which, by way of penance, the King wore next to his body, is borne out by an entry in the Accounts.[10] He revered the priesthood, especially the Franciscan Observant friars, to whom he went for confession, we are told by Ayala.[11] His pilgrimages to St. Duthac's shrine at Tain, and to St. Ninian's at Whithorn, were frequent.

Several writers have justly remarked that the King's intense and unceasing physical activity gives, in itself, the lie to charges that

[1] Dickson, T.A., p. clxiv. [2] Dowden's *Bishops*, p. 37.
[3] Burnett, E. R., XII, p. xl. [4] T.A., II, p. 300.
[5] Sir J. B. Paul, ib., III, p. lxxxiv. [6] Burnett, E. R., XII, p. xliii.
[7] ib., xlvi. [8] T.A., II, p. 297 [9] Bergenroth, p. 210 of Vol. I.
[10] Leslie, II, p. 107. T.A., III, p. 240. [11] Bergenroth, I, p. 210.

he lived a life of debauchery. Vigilant in the execution of justice and in the efficiency of his administration throughout the realm, his restless mind drove him continually from place to place. He was therefore very much on horseback, and the courtiers who attended him must have been active men indeed; few roads can have been fit for carriages. But in his journeyings the King turned readily from business to pleasure, and pursued both with a like energy. The year 1501 may be taken as a typical year in the life of the King whom it was Dunbar's duty to serve.

In March the King was at Stirling, but he moved on 8th April to Edinburgh for Easter, riding there in one day. On the 20th he left for Whithorn, going by way of Dumfries and Kirkcudbright and arriving at St. Ninian's shrine on the 22nd. He was at Ayr on the 24th April and at Stirling on the 26th, passing through Glasgow. Two days later he was in Edinburgh, and made an offering in 'St. Anthonis Chapel of the Crag'. He was in Stirling again on the 15th May, showing his interest in some new purchases of Latin classics and religious books—a Life of Christ, the Bucolics, and Quintilian. He amused himself with chess. He was at Falkland on the 19th. From Falkland he went to Perth. He was there on the 26th May, and on the 30th at Stirling. Culross saw him on the 8th June, and on the 12th he was at Linlithgow, returning to Edinburgh by the 27th. Preparations were in progress on the 30th June for his departure for Threave Castle in Kirkcudbright, but instead he was at Cambuskenneth on 11th July and in Edinburgh again on the 14th. On the 12th September he was at Balquhidder on a hunting expedition, and spent at least the next five days in Strathfillan, hunting on Ben More and spending the evenings with music and 'Heland bardis'. Thence he returned to Stirling, and prepared for a pilgrimage to Easter Ross, to the shrine of St. Duthac at Tain. The journey afforded the opportunity of conducting Janet Kennedy to her recently acquired castle of Darnaway in Moray. On the 27th September, feather-beds were sent off for Darnaway from Linlithgow, and cloth was provided on the 2nd October for a riding-gown 'to the lady agane her passage to Ternway'. For his journey the King had a new scarlet hat and a cloak of French brown. They were at Falkland on the 19th, crossed the Tay ferry on the 22nd, and were in Aberdeen on the 26th. Bishop Elphinstone's college was then being built, and Boece, the friend of Erasmus, was already installed as principal. The King was at Strathbogie on the 28th October, and at Elgin on the 31st. The lady's belongings had to wait there until repairs at Darnaway were completed. On the 3rd November the King was at Inverness, where he had several days' hawking and hunting. In the evenings there was music from the portable organ that had been brought north with the King, and the Laird of Balnagowan sent his harper. On the 12th he went by boat to the canonry of Ross, and spent the night with the Bishop. On the 13th he crossed the Cromarty Firth and reached Tain, where he visited the hermit of St. Duthac's. He was back in Inverness on the 18th, and at Darnaway Castle with Janet Kennedy on the 21st. He stayed there several days, and some girls from Forres came to sing; he hunted and played cards. On the 3rd December he was once more in Aberdeen, sending from there to Darnaway a present of Rhenish wine and a silver salt-cellar. He was at Brechin on the 4th, on his way to Edinburgh for Christmas. At Cupar, on the way, he found himself in the midst of the choirboys' festival of St. Nicholas, and made a payment to the boy-bishop of the revels—'to Sanct Nicholais beschop of Coupir in Fiff' and 'to the deblatis' or attendant imps. From Edinburgh he sent a pair of slippers to Darnaway. Christmas was spent in festivities, with minstrels, guisers, and rope-dancers. Leaving Edinburgh after Christmas, he was again in Stirling by the 13th January, and Janet Kennedy paid him a visit from Darnaway, but he returned to Edinburgh for Lent and Easter. Pike and perch were sent to him from Lochleven.[1]

Ayala states that the King spoke Latin very well, and also spoke French, German, Flemish, Italian, Spanish, and Gaelic. He had a good memory, and was well read in Latin and French histories.[2] He was particularly interested in surgery, was a patron of many practitioners, and himself was skilled in the treatment of wounds.[3] We must return later to his dealings with John Damian, the alchemist. The King's most curious research was into the origin of language. In 1493, according to Pitscottie, he had a dumb woman and her two young children taken to the island of Inchkeith to be brought up in seclusion, in order that observations might be kept as to the children's progress in speech as they grew up. 'Sum sayis they spak goode hebrew, bot as to my self,' writes the chronicler wisely, 'I knawe not bot be the authoris reherse.'[4] The King played upon the lute and monochord; on his long journeys he frequently

[1] T.A., II. [2] Bergenroth, I, p. 210.
[3] Buchanan, II, p. 261. [4] Pitscottie, p. 237.

had a portable organ or 'regal' carried with the party. On one occasion he paid twenty-eight shillings to 'ii childer that bure the organis and thair bellysis ouir the month and agane'. To anyone familiar with the paths over the Mounth to Deeside, this is a spectacular entry.

Much of James's boundless energy was directed to sport. In jousting he exercised both himself and his courtiers, and Dunbar was to turn his comic Muse to celebrate certain aspects of these chivalrous encounters. The King's favourite sport was hawking. His falconers usually accompanied him on his journeys. He used peregrine chiefly, and the quarry, whether herons, ducks, or other fowl, were generally not killed but either released or used to train other falcons.[1] Dogs or beaters were used to raise the game, the King following on horseback. Deer were caught in nets and transported in litters to one of the King's palaces, where they were kept in a paddock until the day of the hunt, when they were coursed with dogs. But at the great hunts in Glenfinglas and elsewhere in the Highlands the deer in hundreds were driven from considerable distances on all sides towards a central point where the King, courtiers, and dogs, awaited them with crossbows, javelins, and clubs.[2] James practised sedulously at the butts with his bow. He was also interested in the culverin, which he fired both at Holyrood and elsewhere; with a culverin he shot at fowls on the Bass Rock and the Isle of May, and even tried it on the deer at Falkland.[3] Occasionally he had a round of golf, with a wager on the result.[4] Striking at an anvil was a favourite exercise. The evenings were often spent at cards and dice.

James's munificence to his household and to all who gathered round the court has already been touched upon. The construction and improvement of his palaces and ships involved lavish expenditure on builders and shipwrights, glaziers, painters, goldsmiths, and lapidaries. He generously patronised also the purveyors of amusements, minstrels, musicians, guisers, and buffoons. Ayala notes the great expense of entertaining the nobles, officials, and servants, who accompanied him often on his travels. The Accounts show that, in spite of the concourse of courtiers and the ceaseless activity of the King, he did not overlook his responsibilities to the humblest of his countrymen. He made payment to, and provided a surgeon for,

[1] Dickson, T. A., I, p. cclii. [2] Leslie, I, p. 19.
[3] Sir J. B. Paul, T.A., IV, p. lxx. [4] ib., II, p. cviii.

a boy of the royal kitchen who had broken his leg, and a boy who had fallen and hurt himself in the hall of Holyrood. Similarly, payments are shown to a mariner who fell from the rigging, and to the peasants whose corn was spoilt by the royal hunt.[1] On the St. Andrews road he gave money to a beggar woman on the bridge at Dairsie. The Treasurers' Accounts are full of such incidents. There appear to have been no guards at court, and access to the King was easy for all, whether they came with gifts or complaints.

As a frequenter of the court for many years, Dunbar had ample scope for his shrewdly humorous observation and for his gifts as a 'makar'. He shows, in the poems that are extant, his facility in writing on small and great occasions. Himself accustomed to travel, in the early years at least of his service at court he must have been fully capable of hard riding and interesting conversation. His satirical comment would find much in the intrigues of the household to exercise itself upon. That he had to wait so long without a satisfying provision for his own advancement is surprising in view of his opportunities. But it is perhaps true that James was less interested in men of letters than, on the one hand, in surgeons and alchemists, and, on the other, in the versatile purveyors of entertainment and sport. Dr. Mackenzie quotes the contemporary Hector Boece's complaint that men of letters are not suffered 'to rise in proffit, dignite, or honnouris'.[2]

The King and his courtiers delighted in morris dances and guisings. Examples have already been given, in the account of the London court celebrations in the winter of 1501, of the staging of allegorical pageants with a certain amount of scenic background and 'properties'. This love of pageantry and of allegorical representation is reflected too in the poetry of the time. To describe in verse a procession of allegorical personages, in colourful language and with an eye to scenic effect, would be a suitable means of arresting the attention of patrons. The personages themselves would readily appear to the mind's eye of the reader or listener, without the need for characterisation or description. A mere name would call up the image desired, for the figures of allegorical representations were probably to a considerable extent standardised. Here the modern reader, unaccustomed to these ceremonial processions of embodied

[1] Sir J. B. Paul, T.A., II, p. xlii; III, p. liv, etc.

[2] Bellenden's translation of Boece's *Scotorum Historiae*, Paris, 1526, XVI, p. 355. Quoted by Dr. Mackenzie, p. xvii.

abstractions, is at a disadvantage. Several of Dunbar's poems are of this nature.

The Goldyn Targe[1] takes us back to Chaucer and to the thirteenth century *Roman de la Rose* of William de Lorris and Jean de Meung—the dream-world in May of the medieval allegorist. In the traditional manner it tells of the poet's failing resistance to the attraction of feminine beauty, and his chance escape. It is unknown whether the poem is based upon personal experience, for this was an established poetic mode, and plenty of authority for its use by Dunbar is provided by his citation of Chaucer, Gower, and Lydgate as his models. Even the stanza is Chaucerian, used in the *Compleynt of Faire Anelida upon Fals Arcite*.

The five opening stanzas are an example of the aureate in Scots poetic style. On the usual May morning the poet rests in a rose-garden, delighting in dewy flowers and in the notes of the choirs of birds, and drowsed by the sound of the rushing brook. Genuine observation is shown in the poet's description, as where he points to the play of reflected light from the dazzling surface of the lake on to the boughs of the bank. But to expect simplicity of description would be unfair, for Dunbar states in later verses that his Muse is bent on unfolding the flowers of poetic rhetoric. His word-painting is therefore laid on thickly and unsparingly, with the curious art of the illuminator. Not inappropriately, there is a sleepy redolence and gilded richness,

> With purpur, azure, gold, and goulis gent.

In retrospect we are inclined to look askance at 'the goldyn candill matutyne', but there is music in such verse to lull the receptive reader, as the scene itself soothed the poet. Our literature, and our language, owe much to the aureate craftsmanship which helped to enrich English speech and transform its homespun. It was for later ages to select from and prune this superabundance.

In the poet's fancy as he lay dreaming among the flowers, a white-sailed ship drew near across the lake, and a hundred fair ladies disembarked upon the meadow. From his vantage-ground among the leaves, the peering poet could admire their green kirtles

[1] 'Rycht as the stern of day begouth to schyne . . . ', CM., p. 91; B., f. 345b; MF., p. 84. Apparently the poem was also in the lost portion of the Asloan MS., for the original list of contents refers to Poem xxvi as '. . . goldin ta . . .'. CM. begins, 'Heir begynnys ane litel tretie intitulit the goldyn targe compilit be Maister Wilyam Dunbar', followed by the device of Walterus Chepman.

and golden hair. But not even Homer nor Cicero could, he says, have painted the scene adequately in language. Nature and Venus were foremost, with attendant goddesses, among whom, as stated in a previous chapter, it is interesting to note Apollo, placed there beside Juno; and Dunbar includes in the group not only Pallas, but also Minerva. The birds with amorous notes hail first Nature and then Flora and Venus. Next the pageant is given symmetry by the abrupt introduction of a corresponding band of gods, to form the anti-masque, but, having arrived, they disappear as abruptly from the poem. Among them is Pluto, who appears in green as king of faery.

The poet in hiding does not long escape the watchfulness of the queen of love, and after a momentary confusion among the ladies he finds himself assailed by her archers, though he records that he felt free from fear. Now the allegory begins. The leading assailant, bow in hand, is 'Beautee', with a formidable rout behind her—'Fair Having', 'Fyne Portrature', 'Plesance', and 'lusty Chere'. But Reason, armed from head to heel, throws before the nonplussed poet his targe of gold, and defends him successfully, even against the subtle wiles of 'Dissymilance', 'Fair Callyng' and others. Reason is overcome himself by having a powder thrown in his eyes. Then the poet yields, a prisoner to Beauty. But she and her fickle train quickly tire of him, and he finds himself handed over to 'Hevynesse'. It would have gone hard with his happiness if a sudden blast from Aeolus had not scattered the fair assembly. In the twinkling of an eye they embark and hoist sail, firing a parting salvo of artillery which rudely wakens the poet from his dream, to find the birds singing as before, and the gay sunshine still on the flowers. He concludes with an acknowledgment of his reverence for Chaucer, Gower, and Lydgate, whose golden pens have illumined the desolation of 'oure Inglisch' speech. And he bids his little poem go forth into the world modestly, for it can claim no garland of the roses of rhetoric. It must face publicity fearfully.

There is much in the poem that recalls Chaucer, and also Gavin Douglas's *The Palice of Honour*—not least the opening setting, the entry of the ladies, and the company of allegorical personages. In his own poem Douglas also had written, though less at large, the praises of Chaucer, Gower, and Lydgate; and the closing stanza of *The Kingis Quair* had been phrased very similarly in acknowledgment of the author's debt to Gower and Chaucer.

In spite of the difference in metrical form, there is a close relation in theme between *The Goldyn Targe* and *Bewty and the Presoneir*,[1] a poem which, though anonymous in the only manuscript in which it is extant in its entirety, is attributed in another manuscript in fragmentary form to Dunbar. It also is an allegory of love. But on this occasion there is no targe of Reason to ward off Beauty's influence. On the contrary, the prisoner commends himself through the years to the keeping of 'hir that farest is and best', and Matrimony is invoked to endorse the bond.

The siege of the castle and the release of the prisoner are in the tradition of the *Roman de la Rose*. From another point of view, the poem is a counterpart in verse of a court pageant. The allegorical theme of an assault on a fortress, as Laing pointed out, occurs in several masques recorded by the chroniclers Holinshed and Hall, one of which, *Le Fortresse Dangerus*, was presented at New Year 1512, at the court of Henry VIII.[2] If we may trust the reading of the Reidpeth fragment,[3] Beauty caught her prisoner in the conventional occupation of prying. But he is quickly fettered, and lodged in the 'Castell of Pennance', of which she has the keeping. There the warders treat him with disdain. Scorn, the jester, shakes his bauble at him and makes him a butt for witticisms. Prompted, however, by Good Hope, and helped by Lowliness and Fair Service, the poet succeeds in communicating to the lady herself a 'bill' he has written, which narrates how he has become the prisoner of Beauty. He enlists on his side the forces of Pity and 'Thocht'. With Lust and other followers, these allies lay siege to the castle. The siege-engines bring down the fore-tower in ruins, faggots are piled at the gate, and the defenders in vain parley to be spared. The captain, Comparison, is buried alive, Scorn is shackled by the nose, Languor jumps from the walls and breaks his neck, and Good Fame is drowned in a sack. Beauty's disdainful forces collapse. But the happiness of the prisoner is still in jeopardy, for Slander and Envy raise fresh levies that are subdued only by the host of Matrimony, 'that nobill king', who chases them to their destruction on the west coast—a curious touch. Under his auspices, Beauty and the prisoner are reconciled. There remains the problem

[1] 'Sen that I am a presoneir . . . ', B., f. 214, where the poem is anonymous. R., f. 8, the first 16 lines followed by the words 'et quae sequuntur. Quod dumbar'. L. provided a title from line 112.

[2] L., II, p. 229.

[3] R., line 6: 'So lang to lurk I tuk laiseir.'

presented by the demise of Good Fame: but—a quaint device—Good Fame's heir arrives at court, is awarded all the fiefs of his late parent, and remains, so that the happy ending is untroubled. The whole poem moves with speed, in marked contrast with the usually interminable medieval allegory. The attempts[1] to connect the poem with the history of James IV and Margaret Drummond are mere speculations.

Both these poems belong to the courtly tradition, just as much so as *The Thistle and the Rose*, though their bearing upon the historical circumstances of the court is less definite. But the court, developed though it was under James IV, was small after all, and must have been much in contact with social life outside. This would be especially true in Edinburgh. Besides very often harbouring the King and his household, Edinburgh was frequently the setting for that other national institution, and centre of general interest, the Court of Session. The city itself, for historical and geographical reasons, was hemmed within a very narrow compass, and its area was populous and even crowded. Lying between the Castle and Holyrood, the city was continually traversed by the courtiers, and a satirically minded court poet would have opportunity for studying town life for his special purposes. Antagonisms would arise between the city merchants and the high-spirited nobles. It is only to be expected that the restless mind of Dunbar should have found, in the city and its institutions, matter for his pen. The condition and manners both of Edinburgh and of the Court of Session encouraged invective.

In writing *The Vyce in Sessioun Court*, he is thought to have been describing the Session as it was before March 1503-4, but there is insufficient proof. The hearing of civil lawsuits had been a function of the estates assembled in Parliament, but, as the meetings of Parliament were short, the hearing of civil causes left uncompleted had occasionally in the fourteenth century been deputed to auditors to be dealt with after Parliament dissolved.[2] This procedure had been regularised under James I: the Chancellor and a number of auditors from each of the estates sat three times a year for a month or six weeks to hear civil causes at centres which the King fixed upon, and this institution became known as the Session. But the changes of location must have made their duties difficult for the auditors to undertake, and it became their practice to continue the work which they had been unable to undertake or complete, to be

[1] S.T.S., I, pp. lxxix, clx. [2] Hannay, *The College of Justice*, p. 5.

heard by the King and the lords of the Privy Council. The council likewise was unable to avoid lengthy delays and adjournments, for they were liable at any time to be called away to deal with other affairs of state such as the exchequer and foreign diplomatic negotiations. The grievous expense and delays which had to be endured by litigants 'tarying upon the calling of summondis' remained therefore unremedied.[1] Further, cases still to be heard were usually adjourned to the same day instead of being distributed over a time-table planned ahead. Early in the reign of James IV, reforms were attempted: a number of 'Lords of Council and Session' were appointed, of whom the majority were members of the Privy Council. They were to hear causes at stated terms in Edinburgh, Perth, and Aberdeen, and the distribution was to be planned ahead. But again these duties clashed with other administrative responsibilities of the Lords, cases unheard at the Session in one town were continued elsewhere, and litigants had to suffer many months of delay. An Act of Parliament of March 1503-4 refers to the 'greit confusioun of summondis at ilk sessioun', cases being 'deferrit fra yeir to yeir throw the quhilk thay wantit justice'. The Act set up a new council, evidently intended to sit in Edinburgh or where the King decreed, during intervals between the meetings of the Session.[2] James IV thus appears to have effected much improvement, though an ordinance of Council in 1511 refers to the multitudes that come into the council room and cause noise and misrule.[3] His chief reform was that of March 1503-4 and the deficiencies of the Session would offer fair and safe game to Dunbar before that date especially. But it is impossible to fix the date of the poem with confidence. Duncan Forbes of Culloden, who became President of the Court of Session in 1737, had much the same problems to deal with even in his time.[4] 'Poor Peter Peebles' of *Redgauntlet* illustrates how persisting the evils were of which Dunbar wrote so long before.

Comment on the state of the Session might be less safe if ventured by a litigant, especially if he had not the patronage enjoyed by Dunbar. Hence arises, in the opening stanzas of *The Vyce in Sessioun Court*,[5] the humorously exaggerated secrecy with which the man from a moorland parish, who has just returned from the Session

[1] Hannay, *The College of Justice*, pp. 9-16. [2] ib., pp. 17-19. [3] ib., p. 21.

[4] Menary, p. 124.

[5] 'Ane murlandis man of uplandis mak . . . ', B., f. 59; MF., p. 314; R., f. 37. B. provides a heading: 'Followis certane ballattis aganis the vyce in sessioun court and all estaitis.' Ramsay called the poem, *Tydingis frae the Sessioun*.

in Edinburgh, imparts his criticisms to a neighbour[1]; for at the Session no man trusts another. Flattery, dissimulation, greed, and perjury, are the qualifications for success. His case adjourned from session to session, the pleader must continue to present himself, sick with unfulfilled hope, mortgaging his property in order to find means of subsistence. In the end, bankrupt, he must take to his bed. Owing apparently to the more pressing claims of the courts of criminal law upon the attention of the Lords of Council, even the criminal takes precedence. But when at length the case does receive consideration, justice is overborne by partiality and bribery. Robbed of his due, the unsuccessful litigant must dine on credit while his adversary celebrates the victory. Round these hapless victims the onlookers throng to whom the course of law is a spectacle or an object of profitable study. Among them the pickpurses and cut-throats reap their harvest; and young monks and friars, of whom the white and gray are specially mentioned, find plenty of scope for their amorous desires.

When it met in Edinburgh, the Session was held in the Tolbooth, in the middle of the main street itself, where Edinburgh had its heart. The city began a bowshot from the Castle, and straggled down the long ridge to the east. The long, rectangular strips which stretched down from the ridge to north and south had originally been cultivated enclosures or 'closes', the house of each holder presenting a gable end to the street and having a large gateway at its side; here and there, a path or 'wynd' led down to the back lanes behind the holdings.[2] The houses fronting the street were generally thatched, and of one storey. Built of wood, their upper floor had encroached on the street by an overhead projection of carved timber, supported by beams, and, as the trade of the town increased, the underpart was walled up with stone to serve as booth or shop, an outer stair giving access to the first storey. From the butter-tron or weigh-house at the head of the West Bow, the market stretched as far as the Tolbooth to the east, and would usually be lined with temporary booths. The Tolbooth, a much larger structure than the newer Tolbooth mainly built under Mary, appears to have been originally the collegiate buildings and chapter-

[1] Since the dialogue does not reappear at the conclusion of the poem, it has been inferred (S.T.S., I, p. cxxv) that the poem is incomplete. B., however, concludes with 'Finis q Dumbar'. M. neatly closes his inverted commas after the second stanza, and treats the remainder of the poem as spoken by the poet directly. Ramsay added two stanzas of his own. [2] *Edinburgh*, 1329-1929, p. 384.

house of St. Giles' Kirk. It was the meeting-place of Parliament as well as of the Session. On the south-east it almost touched the buttresses of the church, but the narrow passage was crowded with the stalls of traders; on the north, the Tolbooth must have left only a narrow roadway open between Lawnmarket and High Street. The obstruction thus provided in the street itself was continued eastwards as the building known as the Luckenbooths, through the unsalubrious depths of which an alley-way, the Old Kirk Style, led from the head of Advocates' Close to the north porch of the church.[1] The crooked, dark, booth-lined alley between Luckenbooths and the Kirk, and between the Tolbooth and the Kirk, was the Krames, a notorious resort of thieves. From the east end of Luckenbooths the High Street began, descending eastwards past the Cross and the Salt Tron to the Nether Bow. The centre of the merchant community was thus a compact area. Open fields would divide it from the burgh of Canongate, which had its own gates.[2]

The period of very high building was, however, still to come. Expansion of the town on the north side was prevented by the North Loch, which, artificially dammed, formed an additional protection to the north and north-east of the Castle rock. But Edinburgh had already expanded very considerably on the south. The 'closes' on the south of the Lawnmarket and High Street had originally carried cultivation into the valley of the Cow Gait which terminated them on the south and to which the churchyard of St. Giles also descended. The 'King's Wall', a fortification keeping half way down the southern slope and cutting across these gardens, had not seriously hemmed in the growth of the city, for there were many openings in the wall, which had frequently to be closed up temporarily in time of danger. By Dunbar's time the Cow Gait itself was practically built up. Beyond it, as described in an earlier chapter, on the upward slope to the south stood the great religious houses of the Grayfriars, Blackfriars, and the like. During the poet's own lifetime, important developments had occurred. Gentlemen and merchants were building houses of stone, of considerable height, in the garden 'closes' themselves, which were rapidly becoming built up, so that the close came to be only the passage-way leading to these mansions from the street. The nobility and ecclesiastics, the lesser gentry and the wealthy merchants, were causing a more substantially built city to arise cheek by jowl with the former low

[1] Wilson, pp. 185-198. [2] ib., II, p. 56.

and thatched houses. Edinburgh was rapidly acquiring the dignity of a capital city.[1]

But in his poem *To the Merchants of Edinburgh*,[2] Dunbar draws the city with the pen of a satirist. That he could write otherwise is shown in his *Dirige*, where he tells of its good cheer, and Sir David Lindsay likewise describes the city in complimentary terms.[3] Dunbar's poem is addressed to the guardians of Edinburgh's respectability, the merchants, whose lack of public spirit he blames for the unsatisfactory condition of the town.

Even the principal streets repel by their stench of haddock and skate. The town cross, where silk and gold should be, has only curds and milk; and, at the public weighing-beam or 'tron', cluster the vendors of cockles and whelks, tripe and puddings. Plebeian craftsmen, more particularly tailors and soutars—those unfailing butts of Dunbar—contribute to the filth of the streets. With the experienced eye of one who has travelled abroad, Dunbar notes as peculiar to his own country the cumbersome forestairs projecting into the street and making the houses dark even in daytime. The very school[4] stinks, is dark, and excludes light from the parish church of St. Giles. The less open alley-ways with which the crowded buildings are honeycombed are of evil repute. Among them the 'Stinkand Styll' is singled out, apparently the Old-Kirk

[1] *Edinburgh*, 1329-1929, pp. 396-397.

[2] 'Quhy will ye, merchantis of renoun . . . ', R., f. 1. The blank in the last line of the poem is preceded by the letter 'y'. The title *To the Merchantis of Edinburgh* was supplied by Laing.

[3] *The Testament and Complaynt of the Papyngo*, lines 626-632.

[4] L. regrets, in view of 'stinkand styll' (line 38) that he retained the MS. reading 'stinkand scull' in line 15 instead of emending to 'stinkand styll' (see his *Supplement*, p. 315). M. differs from S.T.S., and rightly prefers the 'scull' of the MS., but is wrong when he says that the word is altered in the MS. from 'styll'. The alteration in the MS. touches only the second letter of the word, and the last three letters ('ull') are unaltered. The word has therefore never been 'styll'; and, had it been so, it is unlikely that Dunbar would have returned to the very same phrase in line 38. Unless we are to prefer a meaningless 'stull' for which there is no evidence, the likeliest explanation is that the scribe, misled by the two first letters of 'stinkand', was beginning the next word with 'st', when he became aware of his slip and corrected the 't' to 'c'. It has been pointed out (S., ed., p. 86) that a 'style' (narrow passage) could scarcely keep light from a church, whereas a school could. Arnot (p. 420) quotes the *Town Council Register*, I, p. 1, to show that the public grammar-school was being officially fostered in 1519. The statement that no school existed in this neighbourhood confuses the Tolbooth with the earlier and larger Tolbooth on roughly the same site, which was big enough to house even the Parliament and Session. If the Old Tolbooth was originally part of the collegiate buildings of St. Giles and had a chapterhouse (Wilson, p. 186), what more likely than that it should have a school?

Style through the Luckenbooths.[1] The streets are filled with the incessant din of beggars, the destitute halt and blind, and with the screams of quarrelsome fishwives at their 'flytings'. Even the town minstrels fail to add to the dignity of the city that employs them: they are such riff-raff that their cunning does not go beyond 'Now the day dawis'[2] and 'Into Joun'. More skilful men must go elsewhere for patronage. If the town does not quickly repair its good name, it may find itself deprived of two sources of its prosperity—the King's court and the Court of Session. In particular, the poet refers to the scandalous overcharging of strangers, by the burgesses, for food and lodging as well as for the general merchandise which visitors are constrained to buy while in the city. This profiteering may involve the decay of the common weal which the merchants disregard. Dunbar's criticism applies of course to the Town Council as well as to the merchants—who formed the bulk of the Council. The Town Council was responsible for fixing and controlling the prices of bread, fish, flesh, ale, and other commodities.[3]

The market-place, presumably of Edinburgh, is the scene for another satire, the poem usually called *The Devillis Inquest*,[4] in which Dunbar writes of the prevalent habit, among all classes, of blaspheming. The practice was the subject of frequent legislation, so frequent that the laws cannot have been effective. In 1551 an Act of Parliament speaks of 'grevous and abominabill aithis, sweiring, execratiounis, and blasphematioun of the name of God; sweirand in vane be his precius blude, body, passioun, and woundis; Deuill stick, cummer, gor, roist, or ryfe thame; and sic uthers ugsume aithis and execratiounis aganis the command of God'.[5]

The only coherent version of Dunbar's poem is that recorded in the Bannatyne manuscript. The poet feigns that he fell asleep and had a dream. He saw the Devil passing through the busy market-place, pausing continually to exult over some impious oath,

[1] Wilson, p. 198.

[2] Small, in his edition of Douglas (IV, p. 246), quotes R. Chambers as to the origin of this tune, and, from a reference to it in *The Life and Death of the Piper of Kilbarchan*, concludes that the air was a common 'réveille' played by the town pipers.

[3] Robertson and Wood, p. 66.

[4] 'This nycht in my sleip I wes agast . . . ', B., f. 132b; MF., p. 55; R., f. 18b. The last two differ very greatly from B. (For the problems of the texts, see Appendix VI, B.) The traditional heading was taken by L. from the original table of contents of the Asloan manuscript, the missing portion of which contained a poem called *A ballat of the devillis Inquest*, which with doubtful validity has been identified with Dunbar's poem.

[5] *Acts*, II, p. 485.

and to whisper into the ear of the swearer a welcome into his service. Dunbar takes the social classes in order of respectability, beginning with the priest who swears by the very God he has received at the altar, and proceeding by way of the flippant courtier and the merchant—most respected of the burgesses—to the various craftsmen in turn. The indictment of the crafts forms the bulk of the poem. In these cases the sin of blaspheming is usually aggravated by the deceit with which each craftsman unduly commends his wares, or by the lies with which he covers up his cheating. The goldsmith delivers himself to the fiend if his goods are not worth much more than he charges for them, and the brewster swears the malt was so poor that he has brewed less than six gallons from a boll instead of sixteen.[1] When the goldsmith, tailor, cobbler, baker, flesher, maltman, brewster and smith have all damned themselves in succession, the poet passes to other equally skilled frequenters of the market—minstrel, dicer, and then thief—ending his survey with the noisy fishwives and hucksters. In the last stanza the reader is left with a picture of the devils clustering, as thickly as bees, at the elbows of the unwary.

Misled by the incoherence of the versions in the other manuscripts, successive editors have assumed a similar defect in the poem as given by Bannatyne. On this assumption a hypothesis has been reared that there have been interpolations and alterations in all the manuscripts. The arguments advanced for this view are unsound, though few of Dunbar's poems could offer easier material for interpolations. The poem deals in series with a number of detailed personages, almost all of them craftsmen, each treated in a uniform manner, the protest and oath of the sinner being followed smartly by the Devil's triumphant reply. It would be easy to insert additional instances in the series, but the prolixity of medieval poetry forbids certainty, and the Bannatyne version shows no sign of having been tampered with as is alleged. The texts of *The Devillis Inquest* are considered in detail in an appendix.[2]

[1] Gregor, S.T.S., III, note on line 64. [2] Appendix VI, B.

CHAPTER IX

THE THISTLE AND THE ROSE

THE royal wedding, the occasion for Dunbar's best known poem, took place on 8th August 1503. Elaborate preparations had begun in Edinburgh and in London in the previous year, for it was to be an event of international political importance. In the autumn of 1502, the Scots nobility and burghs received instructions to prepare themselves fittingly. The Treasurer's Accounts record the preparations. The King's wardrobe was given much attention, and the armourers were busy for the ceremonial jousting. The King was measured for his armour in May by French experts established in Linlithgow. Although the Princess was to bring her trousseau with her from England, rich robes were prepared for her in Scotland too. Even the menials of the court received new clothes. Deer were brought from Falkland to stock the park. Scaffoldings were erected in Holyrood Palace, and the rich tapestries hung in the royal apartments portrayed Hercules, Coriolanus and Solomon.[1] In the Great Chamber, the hangings represented the tale of Troy, and glass windows were inserted which showed the arms of Scotland and England together, and with them a thistle and a rose interlaced through a crown.[2]

The wedding attracted Dunbar as the theme for a triumphal ode. Indeed, though the court was fortunate in possessing such a poet for the purpose, the poet was no less fortunate in having such an opportunity. *The Thistle and the Rose*[3] combines medieval allegory with heraldic pageantry. The new windows of Holyrood may have prompted Dunbar in his choice of devices. But, as Mackay points out,[4] the use of the thistle was already established. Among the contents of the Treasury and Jewel House at the end of the reign of James III was 'a covering of variand purpir tartar browdin with thrissillis and a unicorne'.[5] On the margin of the ratification of his

[1] Sir J. B. Paul, T.A., II, p. lxiii. [2] Leland, IV, p. 295.

[3] 'Quhen Merche wes with variand windis past . . .'. The poem is preserved only in B., f. 342b. The title is Allan Ramsay's. [4] S.T.S., I, p. lxxxi. [5] T.A., I, p. 85.

marriage-contract by James IV on 17th December 1502 is 'a splendid border of roses, thistles, and marguerites, intertwined. In a square compartment azure are the Scottish royal arms and crown, supported by two unicorns argent, collared and chained, horned and unguled, or, standing on a mount vert, with the Scottish thistle flowered ppr. growing on it. Further down the margin are the letters I and M in gold, entwined with a love-knot, beneath a jewelled crown.'[1]

Obviously a May poem, *The Thistle and the Rose* is given a precise date by the poet himself, who records in the last line that he wrote it on the 9th of that month. It has been suggested[2] that the poem may have been composed in May 1502 after Dunbar's return from England. Dunbar would scarcely wait until May 1504, when the occasion would have been long past, but the most likely date would be 1503, in May of which the preparations for the wedding would be proceeding with increased excitement. Admittedly, the most effective time for the appearance of the poem would have been nearer to the wedding, which was due in August. Was there some special reason why the poem appeared so early? Among the Princess's escort through England was Andrew Forman, now Bishop of Moray, with whom, as we have seen, Dunbar may have been associated at the time of the embassy to London for the royal betrothal. It may be that Dunbar was with him again in the Princess's escort and that his poem appeared in May 1503 before he set off with Forman for England again.

In lines richly charged with reminiscences of Chaucer—and especially of *The Parlement of Foules*—the more marked owing to the use of rhyme royal, Dunbar tells of dreaming that he awoke on a May morning to find Aurora, lark on hand, at his window, looking in with pale green face. May appears at his bedside. Smilingly overruling his complaint that the weather that month has been most discouraging to poets, she tells the sluggard poet to rise and pay tribute, as he has promised, to the Rose. He follows[3] May into a pleasant garden flooded with sunshine, where he listens to the cries of the birds. There Dame Nature commands that every bird and beast, flower and herb, shall assemble for the rites of May.

[1] Bain, IV, p. 340. [2] S. ed., p. 93.

[3] Line 46. M. follows L. in reading 'eftir hir' (based on Ramsay's 'after her') to improve a defective line. The line however is not defective in the customary sense of the word, though the 'full haistely' of the MS. is clearly an erroneous repetition by the scribe from the preceding line.

In a moment they have arrived, and the pageant commences.

The noble lion is called forth first, red on a field of gold, and encircled with 'flour delycis'. When she has raised him rampant on her knee, Dame Nature crowns him with a diadem, and gravely advises him to protect his lieges and keep the laws justly and with mercy. All beasts thereupon cry, 'Vive le Roy!' and do him homage. The eagle is similarly entrusted with dominion over the birds, and then the Thistle, hedged with his warlike spears, is crowned with a crown of rubies and bidden to rule discreetly, prizing above all others the Rose, perfect in virtue, beauty, honour, and dignity. Red and white, symbolic of the two noble parent-stocks from which she has sprung, the Rose is exalted above all other flowers, including even the French lily. Her crowning by Dame Nature draws such a shout of acclamation from the assembled birds that the poet awakens where he lies, and turns to see the spectacle. But it has vanished, and he can only write of it.

Nowhere else does Dunbar rise to quite such felicitous expression. Had he written nothing else, *The Thistle and the Rose* would alone have established his fame. The poem harmonises the arts of the courtier and of the poet. The traditional dream-form, decked with gems of Chaucerian phrase and imagery, combines with allegory and pageantry to express the rejoicings of a nation. If a modicum of moral advice is intermingled, it is fitting to the priestly office of the poet and to the impulsive character of the royal bridegroom, and the skill with which it is introduced is equalled by its delicacy and restraint.

> In nervous strains Dunbar's bold music flows,
> And Time yet spares the Thistle and the Rose.[1]

Whether Dunbar was with Forman on the way through England or not, he must have been caught up in the rising tide of expectation as the wedding day approached. The Princess's arrival was eagerly awaited in Edinburgh. In the account of John Young, Somerset Herald, as preserved in Leland's collection,[2] her journey is vividly narrated by a fellow-traveller. Henry VII entrusted her to the Earl of Surrey and Lady Surrey, accompanied by a train of English lords and ladies and also by Andrew Forman, Bishop of Moray, as Scots ambassador. At each halt on the way, the English nobility, clergy, and burgesses were in waiting to do her honour. She rode on a

[1] Langhorne's 'Genius and Valour' (*Poetical Works*, I, p. 56), quoted by Hailes, p. 223.
[2] Leland, IV, pp. 265 onwards.

palfrey, and at other times in a litter. At York, on the 15th July, 'it was grett melodie for to here the Bells rynge thorough the Cite'. On the way to Alnwick, the Earl of Northumberland escorted her through his park, where she killed a buck with her bow. On the 29th she reached Berwick, which she left on the 1st August with a party of 2,000 horse, to be received near Lamberton Kirk on behalf of King James by the Archbishop of Glasgow, Blackadder, who had with him a great company of Scots lords and ladies. The Earl of Northumberland and many others of her escort then returned to England.

The Princess lay that night at Fast Castle, the lady of which was a sister of the Bishop of Moray, while the company lodged in the Abbey of Coldingham. The following night she spent with the nuns of Haddington, and on the 3rd was welcomed at Dalkeith Castle by the Earl of Morton. Here the King came to meet her with sixty horse. He wore a jacket of crimson velvet bordered with cloth of gold. His beard is described as 'somthynge long': it was clipped for him a few days later by the Countess of Surrey and her daughter Lady Gray.[1] The meeting of the King and Princess was in public, at the door of the great chamber; he was bareheaded, and kissed her. She was not yet fourteen years of age, and is described by Bishop Leslie as 'of an honest behaviour, a cumlie countenance, of singular beutie and perfyt portratour'.[2] The King took her aside and they conversed. The board was set, they washed their hands, and all sat down together to supper, after which the minstrels played, and the Princess and the Countess of Surrey took part in the dance. This done, the King took leave of her and returned to Edinburgh, well pleased with the meeting. He visited her again on the following evening. Avoiding the ceremonial train that advanced to meet him, he arrived with a small company and found the Princess playing cards. The minstrels played a round, she and Lord Gray leading the dance. Wine was brought, and the King served her first. Next James began to play for her on the 'clarycordes', and afterwards on the lute, 'and she had grett Plaisir to here hym'. Sir Edward Stanley replied on the clarycorde with a ballade, which the King commended. He kissed his Princess on taking leave, and leapt on his horse without putting foot in stirrup, riding off at high speed, 'follow who myght'. Such visits occurred again on the 5th and 6th.

[1] T.A., II, p. 314. [2] Leslie, II, p. 119.

On the 7th August she left Dalkeith in her litter, with her palfrey behind. The lords, clergy, and gentlemen, wore crimson velvet. Half way to Edinburgh she was met by the King, riding at great speed on a bay horse. He made a humble obeisance, leapt from his horse, approached her litter, and kissed her. He mounted again, but kept near the Princess until they were approaching Edinburgh. Then he mounted her palfrey and, with her behind him on it, rode on. In a meadow half a mile from the town a pavilion stood, where two Scots knights jousted for the company's pleasure, and the King set free a stag, which was coursed by a greyhound but escaped.

At the entrance to the town was a gateway of painted wood, with two turrets, from which angels sang in welcome to the Princess, and from a middle window an angel presented the keys of the gate to her. Within the gate, the priests of St. Giles met her in procession, bearing the arm of the saint, which the King kissed. The town cross was newly painted, its fountain casting up wine. Near by was presented a pageant of Paris and the three goddesses, of whom the fairest, Venus, received the golden apple. There was also presented the Salutation of Gabriel to the Virgin, and, after that, the marriage of the Virgin and Joseph. The town was hung with tapestries. Windows were thronged with the gentry and burgesses, and a multitude rejoiced in the streets, while the church bells pealed. From the town the royal party passed to Holyrood Abbey, where they were met by the dignitaries of the Church, and 'Te Deum' was sung. Bare-headed, the King led the Princess to the Palace, and withdrew to his own lodging. He visited her later in the day, and there was dancing before he bade her goodnight.

On the morning of 8th August, the Princess was brought to the church, wearing her crown. She had the Archbishop of York on her right hand and the Earl of Surrey on her left; the Countess of Surrey bore her train. Her party took up position on the left side of the church. James, with his brother, the Archbishop of St. Andrews, and his nobles, stood on the right. The King wore a gown of white damask, a jacket with sleeves of crimson satin, a doublet of cloth of gold, and scarlet hose. His bonnet was black, and he wore his sword. The Princess's robe was bordered and lined with crimson velvet. Her hair hung loose, with a rich coif between the crown and her hair and hanging down full length. The wedding was performed by the Archbishop of Glasgow, the Archbishop of York reading out the Papal authorisations. The trumpets blew, and the bare-headed King led the bride by the right hand to the altar, where they knelt and prayed. They then drew apart, each to one side, and after the Litany the Queen was anointed and the King gave her the sceptre. 'Te Deum' followed. After bread and wine had been passed round, the King led her to her room and went to his own, where he kept royal state throughout the day, the Queen dining with the Archbishop of Glasgow. After dinner, the minstrels played, and the King and Queen and courtiers danced. Then the company withdrew. That night the bonfires blazed throughout Edinburgh. Festivities and jousting continued for several days.

In the midst of speeches of welcome, we may be sure that Dunbar was not silent. The madrigal, *Welcome to the Princess Margaret*,[1] may be his. Anonymous in the only manuscript in which it occurs, an English collection of music, including songs set to their notes, it is closely paralleled in phrasing by poems admittedly his, and by two other poems on the same theme of Margaret, which may also be by Dunbar.[2] It welcomes her heartily to the throne of Scotland. There are complimentary references to the freshness of her youth and beauty—she is the Rose red and white, of Lancaster and York—to the mighty king her father, and to the joyful expectations of the Scots court for the future.

[1] 'Now fayre, fayrest off every fayre.' The refrain has 'Scotlond', not 'Scotland' as read by M. See Appendix III, 1.

[2] *Gladethe thoue Queyne of Scottis Regioun* and *To the Queen Dowager*. Appendix III, 2, 3.

CHAPTER X

'IN COURT OUR LANG'

THE QUEEN was thirteen years of age, a newcomer in a foreign land, separated from her father and mother, the subject of international negotiation, and married to a restless monarch seventeen years her senior. It is not to be expected that she would fit into her new station with equanimity. Even before the Earl of Surrey returned to England, Margaret wrote to her father, Henry VII: 'My lord of Surrey is in great favour with the King here, that he cannot forbear the company of him no time of the day. He and the bishop of Moray ordereth everything as nigh as they can to the King's pleasure. I pray God it may be for my poor heart's ease in time to come. They call not my chamberlain to them, who, I am sure, will speak better for my part than any of them that be of that council, And, if he speak anything for my cause, my lord of Surrey hath such words unto him that he dare speak no further. God send me comfort to his pleasure, and that I and mine that be left here with me be well entreated, such ways as they have taken.'[1]

The chamberlain was Sir Ralph Verney, son of a London merchant. He was in general charge of the young Queen's household, and his wife was chief lady-in-waiting. In all, there were some two dozen English attendants on the Queen, as stipulated in the marriage contract; James consented to pay them, though he was not bound to do so by the treaty.[2] They were, of course, only supplementary to the main body of the Queen's household, which was distinct from that of the King, very many of the minor officials being duplicated to make this separation possible. In view of the continual movement of King James over the territories he actively administered, it was necessary that the two households should be thus separate. Indeed, the new situation must have provided a much needed element of stability at court, which would be especially welcome to the older courtiers, among whom was Dunbar. The

[1] Ellis, I, p. 42. Quoted Gregory Smith, p. 96.
[2] Sir J. B. Paul, T.A., III, p. xciv.

Queen did on occasion travel with her husband, but it was usually only for short distances. In November 1503 she had twenty-three carts for her luggage in passing from Linlithgow to Edinburgh, as compared with the King's requirement of one baggage-horse.[1] The less active members of the court would tend to cultivate the Queen's interest and favour.

One veteran in the King's establishment who took over an important post in the Queen's household was James Dog, keeper of the wardrobe, who provides the theme for two of Dunbar's poems written in comic vein. Dog had for many years been groom of the King's wardrobe and usher in the hall. A large proportion of the King's disbursements consisted of payments in kind in the form of liveries and lengths of cloth, so that Dog was to that extent equivalent to a royal treasurer and had to be a man of integrity, for the wardrobe which he ruled over was the storeroom of liveries as well as of tapestries and furnishings.

James Dog had the habit of dourly resisting any attempt to obtain articles from his department without clear authorisation. The result of Dunbar's attempt to extract a doublet from his wardrobe is seen in the poem *Of James Dog, Kepair of the Quenis Wardrep*.[2] One would think the demand were for an ample mantle of full proportions, says the poet. Dunbar has had a personal rebuff from the incorruptible wardrober. The latter's name afforded a pun too good to miss. 'Madame,' writes Dunbar, apparently to Queen Margaret, 'ye heff a dangerous Dog.' Even when Dunbar shows him the Queen's seal of authorisation, and speaks ingratiatingly, Dog turns his bark on the expectant poet as if he were chasing cattle through a bog, so that Dunbar fears to be bitten. In another of his poems he has laughed at the mastiff-like proportions of James Dog,[3] and now too, being himself small of stature, he makes use of the same figure. This mastiff is certainly excellent for keeping watch on the Queen's wardrobe overnight, but he is too huge in bulk to be the Queen's lapdog, and she should get a smaller one, for James Dog's heavy tread makes all her chambers shake.

The sequel is in another poem addressed by Dunbar to the Queen,

[1] Sir J. B. Paul, T.A., II, xxxvii.

[2] 'The wardraipper of Venus boure . . . ', MF., p. 339; R., f. 44; each version has the colophon 'Quod dumbar of Iames dog Kepair of the quenis wardrep'. There is no support in the MSS. for the sub-title 'To the Quene'.

[3] *Of a Dance in the Quenis Chalmer.*

Of the said James quhen he had Plesett him.[1] Dunbar begins with an appeal to the gracious princess to show favour to James her wardrober, whose very close and faithful friend the poet now declares himself to be. He is no dog, but a lamb. Has the disputed doublet been delivered? Though Dunbar had jested at Dog's expense in a ballade, he had not written in malice, he says, but all for the amusement[2] of the Queen. She cannot find anywhere a more discreet and efficient wardrober. Then, as on another occasion when Dunbar is making amends, he slyly mixes his compliments with embarrassing ingredients. 'Whether,' asks Pinkerton, 'was it most dangerous to displease, or to please, Dunbar?'[3] It now appears that the lamb-like qualities of James Dog are shown not only in his capacity as wardrober, but in his domestic life also, and Dunbar states that only drowning in a dam is good enough for Dog's wife, who lets fly the tongs at her husband's shins, and that more drastic chastisement still, with a barrow-handle, would alone suffice as punishment for her unfaithfulness.[4] James Dog has so entirely granted Dunbar's requests in all particulars that the poet begs that no misfortune may light on the wardrober to make him sullen. 'He is na Dog; he is a Lam.'

In Dunbar's *Sweit Rois of Vertew and of Gentilnes*,[5] the 'Sweit Rois' may be no other than the Queen herself. She is thus heraldically designated in *The Thistle and the Rose*, and in one of Dunbar's petitionary poems to the King he again applies the same metaphor to her,[6] as it is applied also by the writer of *Welcome to the Princess Margaret*,[7] which has already been considered. The poem would not then be a love-poem but a petition for advancement, directed to one who was Dunbar's powerful advocate, he says. This sweet rose, this lily bountiful in its beauty and in every virtue, is described as lacking nevertheless the quality of mercy. The poet had ventured into her garden that day, and seen fresh flowers both red and white: yet he could find no leaf nor flower of rue. He fears

[1] 'O gracious Princes, guid and fair . . . ', MF., p. 339; R., f. 44b. MF. has the colophon 'Quod dumbar of the said Iames quhen he had plesett him'.

[2] The reading of R. for line 7, ' . . . to do yow game' is preferable.

[3] Pinkerton, p. 409.

[4] Reason is given in Chap. XIII for rejecting Schipper's view (S. ed., p. 201) that Mistress Dog was the Dame Dountebour of the poem *Of a Dance in the Quenis Chalmer*.

[5] MF., p. 320. Two syllables are omitted in line 4, but there is no gap in the MS. Pinkerton called the poem, *To a Ladye*.

[6] *To the King: God gif ye war Johne Thomsounis Man*, line 21.

[7] Line 13: 'Rose bothe rede and whyte'.

that March with his cold blasts has slain that gentle plant, and its death grieves the poet's heart. He would wish to plant the root again, so comforting is its growth to him. There is something of Waller's enamelled perfection in this delicately expressed poem of Dunbar to the Rose.

The connexion of this poem with the Queen is uncertain, but there is no doubt about the petition *To the King: God gif ye war Johne Thomsounis Man*.[1] Laing explains the meaning of the refrain from two works of the seventeenth century, showing that 'Johne (i.e. 'Joan') Thomsounis man' was a current expression to indicate a man who conducted his life in submission to his wife's wishes.[2] Dunbar is appealing to King James to give effect to the wishes of the Queen. The poet says that he is on his knees night and day, praying for this with all the devotion he can summon; for, if it were so, he would not be without benefice and his days of hard misfortune would be over. The King could yield without loss of dignity to one who is the fairest and best in Britain of her day, and, to secure for one year this submission, Dunbar would give all he had—though from his earlier words he seems to have had little. With a skilful return to the metaphor of his bridal allegory, he adds that the mercy of that meek Rose his advocate, who gladdens his heart, would soften the pitiless prickles of the Thistle which have hurt him. More seems to be implied here than mere indifference on the King's part, but rather actual displeasure. The reminder of Dunbar's services in celebrating the royal wedding indicates perhaps that the petition is not long after *The Thistle and the Rose*. Finally, he says that when the King's manner is harsh to him and unsympathetic to his hopes, he prays to God and sweet Saint Ann that James may yet yield to the Queen's influence.

Dunbar's prospect of a benefice was brightened, however, by one new instance of the King's favour. There had been no change in the terms of his pension. About the 14th June 1503, referring to Whitsuntide, the entry occurs: 'Item to maister William dunbar his halfyeris pensioun of the said terme—v lib.'[3] The next payment was on 12th November: 'Item to maister William Dunbar his pen-

[1] 'Schir, for your Grace bayth nicht and day . . . ', MF., p. 194. Pinkerton named the poem, *Prayer that the King war Johne Thomsoun's Man*.

[2] L., II, p. 297.

[3] MS. *Compot. Thesaur.*, 1502-1504, f. 97b. The payment is omitted from the printed edition. The preceding entry is dated 14th June, from the context 1503, and a later entry on the same sheet is of 22nd June.

sioun of mertymes sic like—v lib.'[1] Again, about 28th May 1504, 'Item to maister William Dunbar his pensioun sic like—v lib.'[2] About 13th November 1504, 'Item to maister William Dunbar his pensioun sic like—v lib.',[3] referring to the preceding Martinmas. The next entries are in a new volume of the Accounts. On 4th May 1505, 'Item to maister William Dunbar his pensioun sic like—v lib.'[4] On 11th August appears an extra payment, 'Item to Maister William Dunbar be the Kingis command—xlii s.',[5] but again, about 11th September, 'Item to maister William Dunbar his pensioun of mertymes—v lib.'[6] It will be observed not only that Dunbar received an additional payment in 1505 but that he secured the regular payments before the due dates. Laing obscured this latter fact by inconsistently giving 11th November for the date of the September payment. But the payment to Dunbar which is of outstanding interest in these years is the dated entry of 17th March 1503-4, 'Item the xvii day of merch to the kingis offerand at maister William Dunbarris first mes vii Franch crounis summa iiii lib. xviii s.'[7] This occurs among a series of payments 'pro elemosina et presbiteris'.

It is the first evidence in the records that Dunbar has entered the priesthood. Laing took the view that, having been a Franciscan friar, Dunbar must have been in priestly orders already, and that the grant of a pension in 1500 to be paid to him until such time as he should be given a benefice was also an indication that Dunbar was then a priest.[8] Schipper, on the other hand, rightly rejected

[1] MS. *Compot. Thesaur.*, 1502-1504, f. 98b. Omitted from the printed edition. The eleventh item before, and the fourth item after, are dated 12th November, clearly 1503.

[2] ib., f. 100b. Omitted from the printed edition. This and preceding entries refer to pensions 'of witsonday bipast'. The eighth entry back is dated 28th May, and the sixth later 30th July.

[3] ib., f. 102b. Omitted in the printed edition. The preceding item is of a pension for Martinmas, 1504, and the thirteenth item later is dated 13th November. L. gives the date as 12th November.

[4] MS. *Compot. Thesaur.*, 1504-1506, f. 84. Printed edition, III, p. 117. The seventh entry back is dated 22nd June, and the fifth entry back is of 4th May. The third item succeeding is dated 5th May.

[5] ib., f. 108b. Printed edition, III, p. 154. The entries on either side are dated 11th August.

[6] ib., f. 86. Printed edition, III, p. 121. The fourth entry back is dated 11th September, and the twelfth entry forward 11th November. Yet L. dates the Dunbar payment as 11th November.

[7] MS. *Compot. Thesaur.*, 1502-1504, f. 47b. Printed edition, II, p. 258. Mackay erroneously states the amount as £4 14s. and is followed by Dr. Mackenzie.

[8] L., II, p. 437.

the basis of this view, for he did not admit that Dunbar had been a friar.[1] We have tried to show, above, that the evidence available does not justify the conclusion that Dunbar had been a friar. Further, the prospect of a benefice, held out in 1500, does not prove that Dunbar was already a priest. It happened sometimes that a man was not ordained until immediately before being consecrated a bishop.[2] In *The Flyting of Dunbar and Kennedie*, probably late in 1500, Kennedy refers to Dunbar as 'Dathan devillis sone, . . . Abironis birth'.[3] Dathan and Abiron were punished at Moses' request because they were aspirants to the priesthood.[4] The names would not have stuck to Dunbar if he had already become a priest. But, whatever view is taken of Dunbar's position before March 1504, it is clear that he was then a priest, and officiating at mass whether for the first time as a priest, as seems likely, or for the first time before the King. The sum contributed by the King to the offering was very considerable, though it is doubtful if Laing is right in saying it was unusually large, for on three similar occasions the King contributed fourteen shillings, twenty-eight shillings, and, 'at the persone of Disertis first mes', £14.[5]

There is a disconcerting inconsequence in the character of Dunbar. It might be expected that the poems later than 1504 would reflect the serious outlook of the ordained priest, but there is no reason to suppose that much of his 'sculduddry' was not after 1504. On the other hand, no doubt his priestly status did leave its mark on his religious and on some of his moral poems. It is customary to assign these to his later years, not unreasonably. It would be surprising, however, if the sacred duties he took upon himself in 1504 did not find to some extent a mirror in his poetry, and two of his more serious poems do not give the impression that they were written in old age.

One of these, *An Orison*,[6] only eight lines in length, is a prayer to the Saviour that the poet may recover from the sins of the flesh to which he has been subject. A spiritual light awakens his mind. His conscience, though guilty, pleads for grace and for time in which he may mend his errors, and Dunbar looks forward hopefully to material possessions, which, honourably gained and used, will

[1] S., p. 91. [2] Dowden, *Medieval Church in Scotland*, p. 128.
[3] *The Flyting*, lines 249-250. [4] Numbers, xvi. [5] T.A., III, pp. 59, 56, 290.
[6] 'Salviour, suppois . . . ', MF., p. 326; R., f. 40. L. supplied the title, *An Orisoun*. For the supposed connexion between this poem and the anonymous *The beistlie lust*, see Appendix IV, No. 13.

do harm to none, and to friends, prosperity, peace in this life and bliss in heaven.

Dunbar follows in the medieval tradition of the poetic 'débat' between birds, in *The Disputacioun betuix the Nychtingale and the Merle*.[1] The theme is the rivalry between earthly and heavenly love. On a May morning, as Aurora sprang into the sky, the poet heard the merry notes of a merle or blackbird as she perched on a branch of laurel. She sang of a pleasant life spent in the service of love. Beyond the river, bright from the reflection of an azure sky, a nightingale replied, in sweet notes announcing that all love was lost except when directed to God. But the merle continued to make the woods ring with her joyous welcome to the day, calling upon lovers to awake and see how Flora had caused every spray to blossom and had freshly clothed every field. The nightingale reproved her foolish song. To the argument that youthful saints grew into old fiends, the nightingale replied that young and old alike should regard as most dear the love of God who made us and wrought our salvation. Thus the disputation proceeds to the inevitable triumph of the nightingale. The merle's plea that God would not have made ladies fair unless they were to be loved, is answered by arguing that the Creator of such beauty is the more to be loved. But, protests the merle, we are recommended to love our neighbours, and who than ladies are sweeter neighbours? The nightingale reverts to the danger of forgetting the greater in the less, and she denies that earthly love brings forth the better qualities of the lover: on the contrary, it blinds him with vain-glory. At this the merle gives up the contest, confesses her ignorance, and joins in the nightingale's song. Together, loud and clear, they extol the love of God, as they fly among the green foliage. The pleasant memory brings freshness to the poet's thoughts at all hours, comforting him for lack of love when he can find none.

There was, of course, no possibility that the merle would have the better of the argument. The poem is a lyric, and for its purpose the debate is developed sufficiently. The conventional form and sentiment forbid precise reference to Dunbar's personal circum-

[1] 'In May as that Aurora did upspring . . . ', B., f. 283; MF., p. 165. MF. omits lines 17-32. The poem apparently occurred also twice in the Asloan MS., for, according to the original table of contents, poem xxv was 'the disputacioun betuix the nychtingale and the merle', and poem lxvi was 'the disputacoun (*sic*) betuix the merle and the nychtingale'; both versions are missing from the extant MS. M. follows B., with some corrections which he does not indicate.

stances. Yet the freshness and zest of the poem, and the melody of its lines, indicate a period not late in Dunbar's life.

Among other dream-poems of Dunbar is *How Dumbar wes Desyrd to be ane Freir*,[1] of which the biographical content has already been discussed. It remains to add that there is little in the poem itself to justify the general view that it is a satire on the Franciscan order. It is rather one of the poems which look forward, with varying degrees of hope, to the benefice promised him. He hints slyly that more saints have been bishops than have been friars—an indication that his ambitions are directed to the secular clergy. He states that the apparition which urged him to join the Franciscan order was not St. Francis but a fiend. As the date when Dunbar would, if ever, have become a friar is, he says, 'past full mony a yeir', the poem may best be assigned to the early years of the new century, when the poet had cause to expect that his ambitions as a secular priest were likely to bear fruit. Perhaps the Franciscan authorities had tried to renew their influence over him or had made representations against him in important quarters.

It has been shown that the 1505 payments of pension to Dunbar were ahead of the times when they were due, and that he received an additional payment. These facts give point to his petitionary poems, and also perhaps to three similar poems which discuss in rather more general terms the way of the world in asking, giving, and taking. The three poems together form a series, *Discretioun in Asking*, *Discretioun of Geving*, and *Discretioun in Taking*. Maitland, and Reidpeth who copied from him, arrange the three as one continuous poem without a break, and do not indicate the authorship.[2] The ascription to Dunbar is at the close of the complete version in the Bannatyne manuscript. Bannatyne separates the poems, but at the end of each of the first two pieces he states the sequence so pointedly that the final ascription is clearly intended to cover all three.

[1] 'This nycht, befoir the dawing cleir . . . ', B., f. 115; MF., p. 333; R., f. 42. The last two omit lines 21-25. The title is from B. L. introduced a title of his own, *The Visitation of St. Francis*, which does not accord with the metamorphosis undergone by the nocturnal visitant in the last stanza. M. follows mainly B. except that, without noting the fact, he transfers a stanza to the position of lines 16-20 which in all the MSS. follows his line 30. These five lines, spoken by the fiend, are thus tacked on appropriately to the earlier appeal, and the sudden alternation of speaker is avoided which clashes with the 'Quoth he' and 'Quod I' of stanzas 3 and 5. Dunbar's reply should have been closed at line 45.

[2] J. T. T. Brown erroneously states (*Scottish Historical Review*, I, p. 149) that MF. assigns the poem to Dunbar.

If we judge from the number of his own petitionary poems, Dunbar should have been an authority on the art of asking. There is no profound psychology, however, in *Discretioun in Asking*,[1] but an embittered survey of the mistakes of patrons and the ill success that often attends patient merit. While one man asks more than he deserves and another less, yet a third is, like Dunbar himself (he says), ashamed to ask, and so he starves unrewarded. It is difficult to strike a prudent mean between too much and too little asking, to preserve a correct tone in one's importunities, and to choose the time and place at which the request may be made in sufficient privacy. But the likelihood is that a servant who has long been unsuccessful will succeed. If he does not, to rebel against his lot is foolish. The only hopeful course is to maintain a discreet attitude.

In the second poem of the series, *Discretioun of Geving*,[2] Dunbar is just as clearly drawing upon his own experience in search of favours, and especially of the elusive benefice. Some givers must be dunned so long that the weary asker's thanks are dead before the gift is delivered. It is equally injudicious to be niggardly and to be over-generous. Among the instances of ill-directed giving is one which can perhaps be recognised: old servants remain unrewarded, says Dunbar, but gifts are showered upon strangers with new faces who only yesterday flew from Flanders. This may be a hit at the success at court of John Damian, whom Dunbar has done his utmost to ridicule in another poem in connexion with his experiments in aeronautics. In March 1503-4 Damian was made Abbot of Tungland, and he may already have been studying flight although, needless to say, he had not flown from Flanders. The poet concludes with a complaint about the injustices shown in the distribution of

1 'Off every asking followis nocht . . . ', B., p. 45 (and a second and different version, f. 61); MF., p. 259; R., f. 21. R. applies the refrain of the first poem to the first stanza of the sequel, thus annexing an additional stanza to the first poem. B.1 concludes with the words, 'endis discretioun in asking'. M., who follows B.2, does not indicate that there are two versions in B. He does not show that he has substituted the 'rane' of MF. for 'drene' in line 7, and, while noting that MF. omits lines 16-20, he does not note that MF. makes lines 31-35 succeed line 45.

2 'To speik of gift or almous deidis.' B., p. 46 (incomplete), and also a complete version, f. 61b; MF., p. 260; R., f. 22. B.2 concludes, 'ffinis of discretioun of geving'. In B.1, lines 1-33 reach to the foot of a page, the next leaf of the MS. being missing. M., who follows mainly B.2, does not mention B.1, notes that MF. omits lines 31-35, but does not note that MF. (and R.) reverse the order of stanzas 2 and 3, and of lines 41 and 42. In line 11, B.2 reads 'chereit' (not 'cheritie'), and in line 23 'hie' (not 'he').

church preferments. Great parishes, and kirks of St. Bernard and St. Bride, are so bestowed that men incapable of guiding even themselves aright are entrusted with parish teaching and administration.

In the third poem, *Discretioun in Taking*,[1] Dunbar dwells less upon his own grievances. He deplores the brawls which often attend the occupation of their parishes by newly appointed clerics, and their avarice in having more regard to their rents than to the salvation of souls, He writes of the exactions of barons from their tenants (and, in the Maitland version, of merchants whose ill-won gains do their heirs no good), of the grasping rich, of pirates, and reivers, who will never amend till they mount the scaffold. Though these are insatiable, men who would gladly take little cannot obtain even that. (In such circumstances, adds the poet according to the Maitland manuscript, it is vain to talk of equity, and only his fear of both sanctions, human and divine, restrains him from pursuing the same vicious courses.) If the despoiler is poor, he goes to the gallows; if he is in the ranks of the great, however, he sits at the Court of Session in high esteem.

This radicalism is not frequent in Dunbar. In general, he is more circumspect in his social criticism, or less sweeping. Elsewhere he complains that a certain Mure has made unauthorised alterations in lines of his. Dunbar was jealous of his reputation as a poet. The tone of *To the King: Complaint against Mure*[2] is not that of one who jests, as has been pointed out.[3] Addressing himself to King James, Dunbar complains that Mure has mangled his verses maliciously, and circulated the result in the palace as by Dunbar. Unless James puts the matter to rights, Dunbar will proclaim the offender for what he is, as far as Calais. Mure has disturbed his metre and, much worse, has added defamatory remarks about lords, an offence which does not accord at all with Dunbar's colours, he says. The interpolated lines apparently included an attack on the King, for Dunbar adds the charge of treason. The culprit's ears should be cropped, or he should be supplied with a fool's bauble and motley,

[1] 'Eftir geving I speik of taking.' B., f. 62b; MF., p. 261; R., f. 22b. After the previous poem, B. heads with the words, 'ffollowis discretioun in taking'. M. follows B. He does not mention R. (but it is R., not MF., which has 'thir' in line 6); he includes MF.'s additional lines 16-20 and 36-40, but regards them as intrusions. MF. and R. place lines 41-45 before 31-35, and M. in his notes has confused lines 36 and 42 of MF.

[2] 'Schir, I complane off injuris.' MF., p. 10; R., f. 11. M. follows MF.; but portions of lines 13 and 14 are illegible in MF., including the alleged 'leis', for which R. has 'hie'. [3] Paterson, p. 175.

perhaps in order that the lines complained of may be recognised as the work of a licensed fool. Their author should join the company of Cuddy Rig, the Dumfries fool, before Christmas; the boys may then bait him like a bull, and Dunbar will be mollified. Nothing more is known of Mure. The names 'Cuddy Rig', 'Cudde fule', and 'English Cuddy', occur in the Treasurer's accounts of court expenditure between 1504 and 1512. He performed before the King in Dumfries in September 1504, accompanying him thence to Lochmaben.[1]

The chief figure of the poem named *Of Sir Thomas Norny*[2] is generally taken by the editors to have been likewise a professional jester. But the poem, though it is obscure, seems to say that he was not. Norny appears frequently in the Treasurers' Accounts, receiving sometimes the title of 'Sir' as in Dunbar's poem. One editor has been puzzled why the official records should name a jester thus.[3] The gifts of clothing received by him at various times from the Treasury do not suggest the special garb of a jester.[4] If our interpretation of the poem is correct, Sir Thomas was not a court jester at all, but a braggart, whom Dunbar skilfully ridiculed as *miles gloriosus*, and whom Quenetyne would like to see in motley. The metre, appropriately, is that of Chaucer's *Tale of Sir Thopas*.

Dunbar calls on his audience to listen while he speaks of that noble and chivalrous knight, Sir Thomas Norny, son of a grim giant[5] and a queen of faery. No better knight rode on horse, bore sword or buckler, or entered the court of King James, and Sir Thomas has done many valiant deeds in Ross and Moray. But the poet speaks ironically, for the exploits attributed to Norny are ridiculous by their very extravagance. Hunting down Highland caterans in those gloomy glens, he has driven twenty score of Clan Chattan as oxen before him—though no man has evidence of this deed. At rustic festivals and weddings he bore the gree with his dancing, and in a hundred wrestling bouts he has never been thrown, but for the truth of this the poet's hearers are again referred to Sir Thomas himself, whom the poet compares to heroes of legend such as Robin

[1] T.A., II, p. 457.

[2] 'Now lythis off ane gentill knycht.' MF., p. 3; R., f. 8. MF. is illegible in several places, so much so that Pinkerton, not knowing of R., prints the poem as a fragment and reads 'Moray' for 'Norny'. L. reads 'Norray'. Several lines have to be supplied from R. [3] Mackay, S.T.S., I, p. ccli. [4] T.A., II, pp. 320, 322, 329.

[5] Line 4 in R. reads 'giand keine', and MF., though obscured by fading, more probably had 'gyand keyne' than Sir William A. Craigie's 'grand keyne'.

Hood, Guy of Gisborne, and Bevis of Southampton. Therefore Quenetyne was stupid to speak disrespectfully of

> This wyse and worthie knycht,

and to call him a bellowing bull and worse than a fool. Dunbar prays that a more honourable lot may fall to the knight than Quenetyne proposed—that of assistant to Curry the court fool—though Dunbar admits that Curry is the cleanlier when on horseback. At Christmas and Easter, then, Dunbar always proclaims Sir Thomas Norny the lord of all fools, for Norny lacks nothing in that line but bells.

The records show that Norny went with James to Whithorn in August 1505[1] and, when the King went north to Tain in October, Norny received ten shillings while in Moray, by the King's command. The journey may have led to the tale of his supposed exploits in Moray and Ross. The King was back in Edinburgh by November. Norny figured at court for many years, appearing in the records from 1503, when he accompanied the King over the Mounth, to 1512.[2] Curry died very shortly before 2nd June 1506.[3] The poem may have been composed in the winter of 1505-6.

Much that Dunbar wrote would be inexplicable if account were not taken of the presence at court of these fools and fantastic riff-raff. Irreverent parodies, obscene dances, gross caricatures of tournaments, found a place with poetical masques and chivalric ceremony, and Dunbar could compose wholeheartedly in all these veins. One very curious work is his burlesque on a certain Andrew Kennedy, who appears to have been a physician at court. On the 8th September 1503 someone of that name is recorded as having gone on behalf of the King in May of that year to Wigtown with a relic of St. Ninian.[4] Schipper infers that the relic was intended to cure the King of some illness.[5] Andrew Kennedy figures in the official records between 1501 and 1503.

The Tesment of Andro Kennedy,[6] ascribed to Dunbar in only one of

[1] T.A., III, p. 155. [2] ib., III, p. 166, and IV, p. 358.
[3] ib., III, p. 197. [4] ib., II, p. 393. [5] S., p. 227.
[6] 'I, Maister Andro Kennedy.' CM., p. 193; B., f. 154; MF., p. 135; R., f. 24b. CM. ends with only 'Explicit'. MF. and R., reading in line 1 (instead of 'maister Andro Kennedy') 'I, maister walter kennedie', conclude consistently with 'Finis quod Kennedie'. B. adds the words, 'Heir ends the tesment of maister andro kennedy Maid be dumbar quhen he wes lyk to dy'. M. follows CM. but arranges in stanzas. The insertion of a half-stanza in MF. after line 40 is, as M. notes, superfluous, and its tenor is inconsistent with other lines of the poem. S. (ed., p. 212) was thus led to surmise that the half-stanza is the conclusion of an early draft of the poem, later expanded to the printed form.

the four extant sources, purports to be Andrew's last will and testament. Two of the manuscripts substitute 'Walter' for 'Andro' and attribute the poem to Walter Kennedy. But the version given in the nearly contemporary print, together with the references to Andrew Kennedy in the public records, confirms at least that the poem concerns the physician Andrew and not the poet Walter, though the anonymity of the poem in Chapman's print must cast doubt on Dunbar's authorship, which rests solely on Bannatyne's authority.

The testament put into the mouth of the bibulous Andrew Kennedy is written for the most part in Scots and dog-Latin in alternate lines, forming a medley of traditional character to which, however, Laing[1] refused the name of 'macaronic' because Latin terminations are not engrafted on Scots stems, the two languages being kept apart instead, in comic balance. The indecorous sentiments of the supposed speaker are heightened by the profanity with which the phrases of the death service from the breviary are burlesqued. It is unfortunate that the references to various personages favoured with bequests are obscure.

Andrew gives himself the title of 'Maister', perhaps ironically. The records, usually careful in this respect, deny him it. The line

Curro quando sum vocatus,

together with the later bequest of all his quack remedies,[2] shows that he was a physician. In the pangs of approaching death, having suffered through a sleepless night from chest troubles, he leaves his soul in his lord's wine-cellar, to remain there with the good wine and with sweet Cuthbert—presumably the cellar-master and responsible for the contents—who loved him not. For his body, he leaves it, with the bung of a cask at his bosom, to the town of Ayr, where he hopes it may lie in richness on the refuse heap of a brewery, to be refreshed by new coverings each day. He leaves his heart, always wavering in its impulses except where emptying a pot is concerned, to his friend James, and his property to the head of his family, though he does not know who that may be. He leaves all his quack remedies to his dear cousin, William Gray, Master of the Hospital of St. Anthony in Leith, evidently a physician also, who for his part is never guilty of fraud—except when the holly is green. He bequeaths his pretentions and ill-won gains to the false friars, in

[1] L., p. 318.
[2] Lines 57-58: 'Omnia mea solacia, Thay wer bot lesingis all and ane.'

accordance with the precept to give to the poor, and may the friars suffer for their avarice, lies, and general depravity. To Jock the Fool he grants his folly, of which he claims a more liberal endowment than the said Jock enjoys who, though rich in coin and lands, cuts a poor figure as a jester, the more fool the lord who supports him. Andrew bestows his malison on Master John Clerk, who may, or may not, be the ballad-maker mourned in the *Lament* but whom Andrew asserts to be the cause of his death. Andrew would gladly make him suffer, for an offence which is obscure[1]; it seems to be suggested that Clerk, in spite of his surname, is illiterate.

Finally, Andrew leaves to the head of his family the residue of his goods, together with his children, and gives instructions for his burial in a new fashion. He wants none to be present but his own circle of drinking-companions, with two rustics to bear a barrel on a pole, drinking and weeping together, just as he himself has been wont to mingle maudlin tears with wine. No priests are to chant their *Dies illa, dies irae*, nor must the bell be tolled,[2] but he wants a rousing reel on the pipes, and an ale-house sign borne before him. Instead of banners, let him have four flagons of beer laid in the form of a cross beside him in the grave, to drive off the fiends. Then his friends may recite the last office.

Parallels between this poem and the writings of Villon, published a good many years before, have been pointed out.[3] *Le Lais* is in similar vein, a *testament de voyage* when Villon was preparing to leave Paris, and *Le Testament* is an elaboration on a grander scale, with the poet ostensibly at death's door.[4] But the 'testament' as a poetic form did not originate with Villon, and he had no doubt many French imitators. Dunbar uses the same stanza, but his rhyme-scheme is different. The poem rivals Villon's testaments in its facetiousness only, for it shows nothing of the grave moods and complex outlook of Villon. It is in the tradition rather of the well-known twelfth century Latin drinking-song of Walter Map.[5]

[1] 'Scribendo dentes sine de.' R. has 'sine D'. Hailes (p. 246) says that Clerk, probably an ignorant practitioner, had evidently caught at an imperfectly heard sound, 'ad curandos entes' instead of 'ad curandos dentes'.

[2] It is rash to regard (S., p. 228) these lines as revealing a serious anti-Church bias in Dunbar, or to suggest that he is using Andrew Kennedy as a medium to express without danger his own free-thinking mood (S.T.S., I, p. ccxxxix). Medieval literature abounds in comic detraction of priests, and particularly of friars.

[3] Notes on the poem, S.T.S., III, by Gregor; Mackay, S.T.S., I, p. cxxxi.

[4] *Works of François Villon*, ed. G. Atkinson.

[5] 'Mihi est propositum in taberna mori.'

CHAPTER XI

'TIMOR MORTIS'

COURT life was burdensome at times to Dunbar. He had fits of indisposition which little inclined him to rhyme on request. In a direct and unaffected apology to the King, he excuses himself for being unable, earlier in the day, to set his mind to poetical composition. It is the short poem, of three stanzas, *On his Headache*,[1] preserved in the Reidpeth manuscript. The poet is distressed that he has failed the King. The previous night his head had ached so that he has been unable to compose for the pain, which scarcely allows him to face the light. Just now, after mass, his dull mind has striven in vain, through loss of sleep, to arrange its thoughts. Many a time he rises in the morning unrefreshed, with no mind for the dancing, minstrelsy, and noisy mirth of the court. The poem might be expected to draw the King's sympathy, but is none the less the work of a sick man.

The *Lament: Quhen he wes Sek*[2] has sometimes been regarded as written by Dunbar in his last years,[3] in advanced age,[4] but external evidence renders this impossible. He lived for many years after he wrote this poem. It appears among the pieces printed in 1508 or soon afterwards by Chapman at his Edinburgh press. Towards the end of his procession of 'makars' on whom Death has laid his hand, Dunbar writes:

> And he hes now tane, last of aw,
> Gud gentill Stobo and Quintyne Schaw.

These deaths were evidently recent. Stobo was 'liand seik' on the 6th and 27th May 1505,[5] and is referred to on 13th July as de-

[1] 'My heid did yak yester nicht.' R., f. 6. L. supplied a title, *On his Heid-ake.*

[2] 'I that in heill wes and gladnes.' CM., p. 189; B., f. 109; MF., p. 189. The print concludes, 'quod Dunbar quhen he wes sek etc.'. MF. omits lines 85-88, and in stanzas 13 and 14 reads curiously 'domini' for 'mortis'. M. follows the print, but adopts some of the spellings of MF., as explained in the notes to his edition, and divides the poem into separate stanzas. For further textual matters (relating to the Scots poets named) see Appendix V.

[3] Miss R. A. Taylor, p. 68. [4] Hailes, p. 269. [5] T.A., III, pp. 138, 142.

ceased.[1] The last annual payment of Quintyne Schaw's pension, as shown in the public records, was on 8th July 1504[2]; several people of that name appear in much later records, but none of these can be the poet Quintyne Schaw, and it seems likely that his pension ceased because he died before the next payment fell due. In any case the reference to Stobo shows the poem to be of 1505 or very shortly after. Sickness was rife in 1505 in Edinburgh: the preceptor of the Augustinian house of St. Anthony in Leith, writing in that year to the head of his Order, lamented that the plague had caused the deaths of all the brethren but two, and he asked to be allowed to initiate novices in place of the dead.[3]

Moreover, there is no evidence within the poem itself that Dunbar was at an advanced age when he wrote it, although his illness was clearly a grave one, from the very tone of the poem. When he ends the list of Scots poets whom Death has taken, and recalls that Walter Kennedy is now lying at the point of death, he concludes that his own fate is near also: he must himself be Death's next prey. He is 'feblit with infirmite', but infirmity, conventionally associated with old age, is not peculiar to it, and, a few lines further on, the poet enlarges on the sudden changes of Man's unstable condition,

> Now sound, now seik, now blith, now sary,
> Now dansand mery, now like to dee,

in a manner that suggests rather an unexpected illness which has struck him down when his faculties are by no means yet impaired.

Two of Lydgate's poems offer striking parallels with the *Lament* in particular lines.[4] It is clear that these poems were in Dunbar's mind when he wrote. The refrain, with its suggestion of a death-knell,

> Timor mortis conturbat me,

had been used by Lydgate[5] in a similar poem, illustrated by references to a series of Biblical and classical personages. Dunbar chooses instead the long line of Scots 'makars'. But they provide illustrations rather than the main theme, and the title given to the poem by Lord Hailes, *Lament for the Deth of the Makkaris*, is therefore misleading.

[1] E.R., XII, p. 372. (See also Appendix V, below, No. 21.)
[2] T.A., II, p. 445. [3] Gairdner, II, p. 199.
[4] The parallelism with Lydgate's 'So as I lay . . . ' and with his *Testament* is convincingly demonstrated by P. H. Nichols, pp. 216-218.
[5] Lydgate's 'So as I lay this othir nyght' (MacCracken, II, p. 828).

The religious element in the poem is not so prominent as has been generally supposed. Only in the last stanza, feeling that death is approaching, does Dunbar turn his thoughts to the afterlife. It is true that the refrain has strong religious associations, for it occurs in the Office for the Dead.[1] Laing quotes an interesting passage from a letter written from Lisbon by an eighteenth century traveller: 'I went to the Church of the Martyrs to hear the matins of Perez and the Dead Mass of Jomelli, performed by all the principal musicians of the royal chapel for the repose of the souls of their deceased predecessors. Such august, such affecting music I never heard, and perhaps may never hear again. . . . Every individual present seemed penetrated with the spirit of these awful words which Perez and Jomelli have set with tremendous sublimity. . . . There was an awful silence for several minutes, and then began the solemn service of the dead. The singers turned pale as they sang "Timor mortis conturbat me".'[2] Religious awe must have adhered to these words in Dunbar's mind also, but more omnipresent in the poem is the sense of death as an approaching menace, an ending, an obliteration—a feeling that in its essence is not really Christian at all. It was the sentiment often of Villon, but not only of Villon, for it obsessed the French poets of the fifteenth century.

The shadows are deepening around the sick man, and in retrospect the transitory colours of the world are far away. Death, who takes all ranks and ages, knight and lady, who spares no clerk for his learning, no magician for his art,[3] no theologian for his sly conclusions, takes also the poets 'amang the laif'. They play their pageant and pass to dust—Chaucer, Lydgate, Gower, and the line of Scots poets up to the contemporaries and friends of Dunbar. His metrical restraint is in harmony with his sombre mood. 'All his jewellery of rhythm and colour subdue themselves to a stark, grey, onward movement, like the vaulting of a crypt. It is not the defiant fantasy of a *danse macabre*, but a march of hooded shadows that have been men.'[4]

The identity of these Scots poets, in some cases obscure, is discussed in an appendix.[5]

[1] M., p. 202.

[2] Beckford, *Letters from Spain and Portugal*, 34th letter, 1787, II, p. 253. Quoted by L. in his *Supplement*, I, p. 316.

[3] Professor Bruce Dickins points out that the two words, 'Art, magicianis . . .' (line 37) are to be taken together as a compound, without M.'s comma (*Mod. Lang. Review*, 1933, p. 507).

[4] Dr. A. M. Mackenzie, p. 98.

[5] Appendix V.

It is customary to relate to this period of illness and despondency a number of Dunbar's other seriously reflective poems, among them *Erdly Joy Returnis in Pane.*[1] The metrical form is the same as that used in the *Lament.* This sermon in verse is quaintly represented as being sung to the poet by a bird, in the early morning of Ash Wednesday. Man is reminded that he is but ashes, and to ashes must return. Age follows youth, death follows life, and, though May is fresh, the succeeding January will be wild and snell. Health gives place to sickness, mirth to heaviness. Forests disappear, and towns decay. Freedom, truth, honour, degenerate with the other virtues. Since earthly joys do not last and are vanity, all that is left to man is to work for the heavenly joy that lasts for ever.

There is a similar note of disillusionment in *Inconstancy of Love*,[2] which occurs in the Bannatyne manuscript as the first of a new series of poems, the transition from the preceding group being shown by the scribe in the words, 'Heir endis the prayiss of wemen And followis the contempt of Blyndit Luve etc.' This opening poem, by Dunbar, analyses the blindness and futility of love. The candid observer will not fail to agree, says the poet, that no assurance can be placed in a sentiment so insecure. Its pleasures are brief, and it readily forgets the old in the new. The poet forswears Love's observance, which accords only with an ignorant and unbalanced mind. To demand faith in love were as exacting as to require a dead man to dance in his grave. Point and emphasis are added to the poem by the recurrence of only two rhymes throughout.

A sense of ultimate values is mingled, in *Meditation in Winter*,[3] with

[1] 'Off Lentren in the first mornyng.' B., f. 48b; MF., p. 319. M. follows B., but is mistaken in stating that MF. omits lines 17-20. Apparently by a printer's error, the inverted commas are closed after each stanza, in M.

[2] 'Quha will behald of luve the chance . . . '. B., f. 281. B. concludes with 'ffinis q dumbar'. The first of these words is in the same ink as the poem, and 'q dumbar' is in darker ink but the same as the next poem but one, as if, when writing out the latter poem, the scribe had gone back to this and entered the ascription. L. headed the poem *Inconstancy of Luve*. Presumably M.'s reading 'care' for 'cure' in line 16 is a printer's error, for it spoils the rhyme.

[3] 'In to thir dirk and drublie dayis.' MF., p. 3 (lines 23-50 only), and p. 318 (the whole poem); R., f. 1 (lines 1-22 only). The MF. fragment begins at the top of a page. The preceding page, on which were the earlier lines, 1-22, is now lost. Pages 1-2 of MF. as at present paginated belong strictly to a later part of the volume. In transcribing from MF. 1, R. reached the foot of MF.'s page (the last stanza of which is now partly illegible) and then proceeded not to the top of p. 3 of MF. where this poem is continued with line 23, but to the top of the first page of a lost quire (wrongly inserted in this place in MF.) beginning with line 55 of *The Petition of the Gray Horse, Old Dunbar*. R. omits line 9. Pinkerton called the poem *Meditatioun Writtin in Wyntir*.

consolation offered by the earth in its changing seasons. In the wet days of winter, the poet writes, when the skies are sombre and laden with mist, he has no heart to compose 'sangis, ballattis, and playis'. His mournful spirit languishes for lack of summer and its flowers. He wakes and turns but cannot sleep, vexed with heavy thought, and, the more he seeks a remedy for his position in the world, the more his unrest deepens. Presences are around him on all sides. Despair counsels him to provide himself quickly with some means of livelihood lest his wretched lot should be to stay permanently at court. Then Patience on the other hand enjoins him to hold fast to Hope and Truth, letting Fortune exhaust her rage, since no reasoning may assuage her. Prudence asks why he should try to hold to illusions, or crave what he may possess for no considerable time in view of his steady journeying to another place. And Age in friendly tones summons the poet to take his hand, bearing in mind that he must make account of all his days spent on earth. Death in turn casts up his gates wide to receive him; however robust he may be, under that lintel he must stoop. Thus, in fear, the poet's spirits droop all day. No store of gold, no wine in cup, no lady's beauty nor love's bliss, may obscure his knowledge of what is to be, however gladly he dines or sups. Yet, when the nights begin to shorten, his spirit, which was oppressed by the rains of winter, is comforted, and he hails the approach of lusty summer with its flowers.

Dunbar distrusted the seeming stability of human life. In the lines written in spring, known as *On the Changes of Life*,[1] he says he can find no other quality so characteristic of the world as its deceptiveness. Only the day before, spring, soft and fair, came in as fresh as a peacock's feather: to-day the cold stings as an adder. Yesterday the flowers were springing, and birds sang clearly in the forest: now the flowers are dead with the rain and the birds are listless, stricken in nest and bower by the cold. In the same way comfort is suddenly followed by anxiety, and joy by sorrow.

Another poem, written for Ash Wednesday, is *Of Man's Mortality*,[2]

[1] 'I seik about this warld unstabille.' MF., p. 5, and another transcript not quite the same on p. 315; R., f. 8b. R. has transcribed MF. 1. Pinkerton gave the poem a title, *On the Changes of Lyfe*. M. follows MF. 1, adopting R.'s line 16, that line having been cut away in MF. 1; but M. does not note that his reading in line 14, 'walkis', is from MF. 2.

[2] 'Memento, homo, quod cinis es,' B., f. 47; MF., p. 193. M. follows B. He does not note that the poem is anonymous in MF. Hailes called the poem *The Contemplatioun of Manis Mortalitie*.

attributed to Dunbar in the Bannatyne but anonymous in the Maitland manuscript. On that day, the first in Lent, the priest removed from the altar after their consecration the ashes of palms blessed on Palm Sunday, and, inviting the penitents to advance and kneel, made on their foreheads the sign of the cross with the ashes. In doing so, he used the solemn words with which Dunbar—if he is the writer—opens his poem, *Memento, homo, quod cinis es*, and the refrain, *Quod tu in cinerem reverteris*. Gravely the poet proceeds with the grim lesson. To dust have come alike, he says, Hector and Hercules, Achilles and Samson, Alexander, David, and Absalom. Of all the possessions of man, only his good deeds accompany him after death, and there is only one firm anchor in life.

A similar sentiment is found in the poem of seven lines, *Of Life*.[1] What is this life, the poet asks, but a straight way to death, an unceasing flow, in which we are offered a choice between Paradise and Hell? It is a short torment which gives place to eternal gladness, or it is as short a time of joy with enduring misery beyond.

Of the Vanity of the World[2] is a warning not to delay too long in turning from worldly interests. The pilgrim should set forth from the wilderness while daylight remains to him, and make haste, for the pursuing night comes. He is to bend his sail and make the port of grace, lest he should have cause to lament that Death overtakes him in trespass. Nothing is stable in the flux of this world.

Vanitas Vanitatum, et Omnia Vanitas.

[1] 'Quhat is this lyfe . . . ', B., f. 75b; MF., p. 310. Anonymous in B. Laing called the poem, *Of Lyfe*. M. states erroneously that the poem is in MF. only.

[2] 'O wreche, be war . . . ', MF., p. 195. L. supplied a title, *Of the Warldis Vanity*.

CHAPTER XII

'ANE AULD HORS'

In the later months of 1506 it became known that the Queen expected to give birth to a child. The birth took place on 21st February 1506-7. Invitations to the christening were sent out previously, and on the 20th the Town Council of Edinburgh made final preparations for celebration. 'The Provest, baillies, and counsall hes ordanit the serjandis to pas throw the toun, and charge every honest man, merchand, and craftsman, that they have, ilk ane, ane new tortys (torch) reddy and pas in thair best array to the Abbay with the provost and bailies quhane God sall provyde the Quene to be deliveret, and that ilk man be reddy to sett furth thair fyre quhane thai sall be chargit be the bell.'[1]

The Queen, who was only seventeen years of age, gave birth on the next day to a 'bony barne',[2] and the news was despatched immediately to her father in England.[3] On the 23rd the Prince was christened James, by Blackadder, Archbishop of Glasgow. The King was 'very blithe' to have an heir, says Bishop Leslie. The 'Lady Maistres', who announced the happy event to the King, was very richly rewarded, and the nurse and midwife also were not forgotten; William the taborer arranged a dance for the occasion.[4] But when it became clear that the Queen was herself in grave danger, the King was in grief 'sa sair that he wald not be conforted'.[5] When the danger was over, he set off for Whithorn on pilgrimage, to pray at the shrine of St. Ninian. But the heir in whom such high hopes were placed lived scarcely a year, dying at Stirling on 17th February 1507-8. The ill-fated Queen was to have many other such blows. A daughter born in 1508 died soon after she was christened, and Prince Arthur, born in the next year, died in 1510. The only one of her children to survive infancy was the future James V, born on 10th April 1512. The daughter born in 1513 died after a few days,

1 *Extracts from Records of Burgh of Edinburgh*, p. 111. 2 Leslie, II, p. 123.
3 T.A., III, p. 369. 4 Sir J. B. Paul, T.A., III, p. xxxi.
5 Leslie, II, p. 123.

and the boy born after the death of the King did not reach two years.[1]

The poem which begins, 'Gladethe thoue Queyne of Scottis regioun',[2] celebrates the approaching birth of this first child of the Queen. The poem occurs only in a volume of the Aberdeen *Minute Books of Seisins*, alongside and on the same page as Dunbar's *The Twa Cummers*. The latter poem has, below it, the customary form of attribution to Dunbar, but in such a position that it could refer also to the poem which concludes alongside it. A further indication of Dunbar's authorship is thus provided, though there can be no certainty. The poem has been assigned to Dunbar by the editors on general grounds of theme and style, and because it occurs in the same volume as *The Twa Cummers*, but they apparently did not know that the two poems are not only in the same volume but on the same page. A comparison of the phrasing of the poem with that of pieces that are accepted as by Dunbar, especially with poems on the subject of Margaret, and with the anonymous madrigal, *Welcome to the Princess Margaret*, and *To the Queen Dowager*, shows striking parallels. The stanza was a favourite one with Dunbar. The poet plays as elsewhere on the name of Margaret, 'our perle of price', 'precius mergreit', and bids her be glad. He prays that her subjects may be granted at last what they have long desired, a prince. She is 'Our Roiss Riale', 'Roiss red and quhit'. The dates of neighbouring deeds in the manuscript confirm, as shown in the appendix, that the child yet unborn was the prince born in 1506-7.

Dunbar chose, about this time, another theme from matters of national concern, but a less happy one. He had little opportunity for political polemics, for King James had mastered his early opponents in the lowland parts of the country at least. But a source of continual unrest remained. The Highlands and Islands were far from pacified, and the long struggle with Donald Dubh, or Donald Owre, had probably sharpened Dunbar's dislike of the Highlanders. John, Lord of the Isles, had forfeited the earldom of Ross by his intrigues with the English Yorkists in the reign of James III, and the later attempts of John's son, Angus Og, to re-establish himself had led to the forfeiture of the lordship of the Isles itself by James IV in 1494. Angus's son, Donald, had been held by the King at court in the succeeding years,[3] and he must have been a familiar figure to

[1] Sir A. H. Dunbar, p. 219. [2] See Appendix III, 2.
[3] T.A., I, pp. 273, 380, 381.

Dunbar. He was at large, however, in 1501, headed the dispossessed Highland vassals, and laid waste to Badenoch in 1503.[1] Elaborate expeditions had to be prepared against him, and perhaps Sir Thomas Norny's fantastic exploits in Moray and Ross had some basis in connexion with these campaigns. But Donald fell into the King's hands again and was placed under lock and key, in 1505. He was at the mercy of the law.

Dunbar's poem, *For Donald Oure: Epetaphe*,[2] is a denunciation of Donald as a vicious traitor. The poet feigns that he is already writing Donald's epitaph. It behoved a courtier to denounce treason, which, he says, is horrible and unnatural as a fiend under the cowl of a friar. And Donald's past perhaps justified Dunbar's warning that to give him a second respite would be to invite further civil turmoil.

> Ay rynnis the fox
> Quhill he fute hais.

The whirling metre accords well with the poet's fanaticism. In spite of the doubts of one editor,[3] Dunbar is unlikely to have been so outspoken after James's decision to spare his enemy, and more probably he put forward his plea for ruthlessness while Donald's fate was still in the balance. The captive was still alive, in Stirling Castle, in the summer of 1507,[4] and lived to make more trouble in the next reign.

Meantime Dunbar's own personal position was giving him acute concern. His pension of 1500, to the amount of £10 a year, was to be for life or until he was awarded a church benefice of £40 or more. The continued payment of his pension in 1505 shows that he had not yet obtained such a benefice, and it has been shown above that he was drawing the pension before the due dates, and received an additional payment in August. He did not fare very much better in the following year. An interesting entry occurs in the records on 27th January 1505-6: 'Item to maister william dunbar be the Kingis command for caus he wantit his goun at Yule—v lib.'[5] On 2nd June 1506 he received his usual Whitsuntide award: 'Item to

[1] Terry, p. 141.

[2] 'In vice most vicius he excellis.' B., p. 53; MF., p. 11; R., f. 11. B. concludes with 'q dumbar for donald oure epetaphe'. M. follows B., the superior version (cf. MF.'s 'sa terribill' in line 8), but does not mention the versions of MF. and R.

[3] S. ed., p. 207. [4] T.A., III, p. 415.

[5] Printed T.A., III, p. 81. MS. *Compot. Thesaur.*, 1504-1506, f. 125. The fifth entry back is dated 27th January, and the entry following is on the 28th.

maister William Dunbar his pensioun of the terme forsaid—v lib.'[1] About the 11th August he obtained a further additional payment: 'Item to maister William Dunbar be the kingis command—v lib.'[2] The Martinmas payment occurred about the 12th November: 'Item to Maister William Dunbar his pensioun of the said terme—v lib.'[3] But an extra sum of the same figure was paid to him that Christmas, on 4th January 1506-7: 'Item to maister William Dunbar in Recompensacioun for his goun—v lib.'[4] The regular pension remained, however, as before. On the 23rd May 1507, for Whitsuntide: 'Item, to Maister William Dunbar his half yeris pensioun of the said terme—v lib.'[5] And now at last comes a change, the sums paid in pension being 'new ekit' to double the former amount, to reach £20 a year, though no authorisation for the increase is extant in the Privy Seal register. The first payment under the new dispensation is recorded on 12th November 1507 for Martinmas: 'Item, to maister William Dunbar his pensioun of the said terme—x lib. and new ekit.'[6] The most likely period, therefore, for the importunate complaints and petitions of Dunbar to the King, is that which leads up to the autumn of 1507 when relief was at last granted. Several of them, however, which suggest an earlier date, have already been discussed.

Of Folkis Evill to Pleis[7] is an example. It was written at Christmas.

[1] Printed T.A., III, p. 125. MS. *Compot. Thesaur.*, 1504-1506, f. 88b. The fourth item back is a Whitsuntide payment dated 2nd June, and the fifteenth succeeding item bears the same date.

[2] Printed T.A., III, p. 331. MS. *Compot. Thesaur.*, 1506-7, f. 72b. The thirteenth entry back is dated 11th August, and the thirteenth succeeding is of 13th August.

[3] Printed T.A., III, p. 327. MS. *Compot. Thesaur.*, 1506-7, f. 68. The second item preceding has the date 12th November, and the thirteenth succeeding is dated 1st February, i.e. 1506-7.

[4] Printed T.A., III, p. 361. MS. *Compot. Thesaur.*, 1506-7, f. 86. The previous entry is dated 4th January, and the second succeeding one 5th January.

[5] Printed T.A., III, p. 327. MS. *Compot. Thesaur.*, 1506-7, f. 69b. The preceding entry and the fifth succeeding are both of 23rd May.

[6] Printed T.A., IV, p. 69. MS. *Compot. Thesaur.*, 1507-8, f. 59b. The third entry preceding is dated 12th November, as is the third succeeding item.

[7] 'Four maner of folkis ar evill to pleis.' R., f. 3; B., p. 47 and also f. 66b, both of them incomplete, and anonymous (owing perhaps to the lack of the last stanza). B.1 begins with line 13 at the head of a page, the preceding page being lost and with it the beginning of the poem; B.1 consists of lines 13-16, 9-12, 17-24. B.2 has lines 1-8, and thereafter is as B.1, though the wording is not exactly the same. Both B.1 and B.2 end at line 24 with only 'Finis'. R. seems to have transcribed from a lost portion of MF. which attributed the poem to Dunbar. M. follows R. but writes 'goes' for 'gois' in line 24, and does not repeat the final couplet as does R. Perhaps because of the anonymity of the incomplete versions in B., the poem is omitted from S.T.S., and from the chronological list of poems in that edition.

James, generous towards his dependants, had on this occasion neglected Dunbar. Four types of people, says the poet, are ill to please. The rich man with store of coin, grain, and cattle, is still disposed to take from others. A powerful lord whose estates are already so vast that he cannot administer them adequately, will still try to add to them. The husband of a fair, noble, and virtuous lady will yet covet another. And, lastly, the man who has already drunk deep, continues to call for ale and wine. Presumably Dunbar would be more easily pleased in such circumstances. But this Christmas, wherever Sir Gold may have disposed his favours, the poet will not applaud his largesse, for he passed over Dunbar.

He was not always inclined to self-commiseration. In *One who is his Own Enemy*,[1] he prescribes wine and jollity as compensation for neglect. He comments on the prevalent folly of making oneself miserable in spite even of good fortune. A rich man lives in wretchedness of mind. A comfortable bachelor plunges rashly into marriage with a 'wicket' wife. And another man has remained loyally in the service of a master who will never take pity on his needs. This appears to be Dunbar's own mistake. Now he will live merrily and care not a cherry for the world.[2] So long as good wine is obtainable, to the devil with all who gnaw the dry bread of unhappiness!

In *The Dream*,[3] written early in a New Year, Dunbar uses the traditional dream-procession of allegorical figures in order to press his claim to a benefice. The previous night as he lay half-asleep, it seemed to him that the walls of his room were freshly adorned in many colours with noble legends old and new. Into the brightly lit room came a procession of old and young, singing, dancing, and playing on instruments. Though astonished, the poet took little comfort, for the damsel Distress and her sister Heaviness oppressed him. The wan-visaged Languor sat at his bed's head, playing doleful music. When the dance drew nearer, Nobleness, who headed the

[1] 'He that hes gold and grit riches.' B., f. 115b; MF., p. 212. M., who follows B., does not mention MF. The other editors do not indicate that in MF. the poem is anonymous. Ramsay supplied a title: *On anes being his Own Enemy.*

[2] Line 22 reads 'And sett nocht by this warld a chirry.' An identical line, with the same rhyme, occurs in *Of Cuvetice* (line 42). See Chapter XVI.

[3] 'This hinder nycht, halff sleiping as I lay.' R., f. 3b. L. called the poem *Dunbar's Dream*. M., without indicating the fact, makes several corrections, notably of 'with' to 'quoth' in line 73; one of these at least ('aird' to 'air' in line 113) is less justified. Apparently by an oversight, the poem is omitted from the chronological list of Dunbar's works, in S.T.S., I.

ladies, sent Comfort and Pleasance to cheer him with their harps and song, but in vain. Discretion, a lady of benign countenance, then pronounced that he would not recover heart unless she and Nobleness repaired to the court where he had long given fruitless service, and obtained for him some reward in honour of the New Year. Here 'Blind Effectioun' interposed, claiming that at court his influence was supreme. But Reason replied that the misrule of Blind Affection in the distribution of rewards was ended, that he himself could superintend their allotment, and that a reward was due to the poet for his service to the King. Never descending to flattery, he had patiently endured his lot, presenting his humble complaints in the form of ballades. Now he was to take heart, for Nobleness would aid him. The lady Discretion applauded the speech of her brother Reason, whose help, she believed, would be of great profit to the whole realm if he sat on dais with the Lords of Session. But further opposition to the poet's hopes arose, for Importunity declared he was prepared to deafen the King in order to be served before the poet. Next Sir John Kirkpakar, a mighty collector of benefices, vowed that, though he had already seven churches, he would have eleven before a single cure should fall to Dunbar, 'yone ballet maker'. Sir Bet-the-Kirk had four or five assiduous servants who were only waiting for the deaths of incumbents, and he expected soon to have tidings. At this, Reason protested that the distribution of benefices was out of balance, and the world a prey to greed. But the most interesting comment is that made by Temperance. She will not accept blame for the poet's position. Though she holds the balance even for him by the offer of the only benefice available, Dunbar himself upsets the scales by wanting another instead. Here Patience advises him to be of good cheer and to rely humbly on the King, for she knows the nobility of the King's intentions and that James will not for a bishop's rent leave Dunbar unrewarded for another six months. The poem concludes suddenly. The allegorical personages rush out of doors tumultuously and fire a gun on Leith Sands, and the earth-shaking report awakens the poet from his dream.

We come now to one of the direct appeals, *To the King: Quhone Mony Benefices Vakit.*[1] There has been, metaphorically, a feast of

[1] 'Schir, at this feist of benefice . . . '. MF., p. 7, and a second transcript, spelt differently, on p. 316; R., f. 9b. MF.2 concludes with 'Quod Dumbar quhone mony Benefices vakit'.

benefices. The vacant benefices must have been likely to go to men already well endowed, for Dunbar asks whether it is better to offer wine to him that is dying of thirst or to fill to bursting point a man that has already drunk. It is no glad banquet where one makes merry and drains his cup while another sits thirsty, with downcast looks. The cup must once circulate if the feast is to be acclaimed.

The protest of Temperance in *The Dream* shows, however, that when offered a benefice on this or another occasion Dunbar intemperately refused it, hoping for a better.

He adopts again the metaphor of the banquet, in the poem *To the King: Off Benefice, Schir.*[1] One man devours swan, and another duck, but Dunbar fasts piteously in a corner. This is the way of the world, where the rich always cast their nets before the poor and regard all waters as their own. He who has nothing can obtain nothing. The well endowed supplicants care little for the benefices committed to them. Provided they have the revenue, they take little account of book and bell, and are indifferent to the lot of the poor. But when they are in the pangs of death they will repent, and repent in proportion to their wealth. From this thought Dunbar draws some consolation.

Another poem, *To the King: Schir, yit Remembir*,[2] begs the King to call to mind that Dunbar's youth has been quite spent in his service. The King's conscience must itself feel the need for rewarding so faithful a servant. To remind James of services rendered, Dunbar reverts to the conception he employed in *The Thistle and the Rose* of James as king of birds. Provision has been made on all sides for the King's clerks, but Dunbar is like a discarded hawk, no longer allowed to rest on its master's wrist, and that too at a time when its plumage is beginning to deteriorate. It is always thus, he says, with the nobler fowls: while the lesser hawks and kites feed fat, the gentle goshawk must go undined. The song of the nightingale is imitated feebly by the parti-coloured magpie—there may be a reference here to some particular rival poet—and the fairest plumage of all is in the possession of birds from the most distant places of origin. Though these cannot sing, they enjoy silver cages in the place of honour. If this is not a tilt at the Abbot of Tungland, it

[1] MF., p. 8, and another copy on p. 321; R., f. 10. M. follows mainly MF.2 but does not indicate all his departures.

[2] B., f. 94b; MF., p. 295; R., f. 34. M. follows MF., pointing out his departures from it except in line 19, where MF. has 'hasknes'. He prints B.'s third stanza in his notes (but B. reads 'unkynd', not 'undynd', in line 14).

refers to some other foreign recipient of the King's favours. And so Dunbar invokes the King as the 'gentill egill'. In *The Thistle and the Rose* the eagle had been urged to show justice no less to whaups and owls than to peacocks, popinjays, and the like, and—another metaphor—the lion had been directed to administer the laws faithfully. Now Dunbar asks why the eagle does not come to the support of the lieges and cherish them according to their degree. He admits his limitations: he can boast of few virtues, and yet he has the same essential needs as other men, and would fain live like them. His talents are only in poetry, an art that is reputed as childish against his competitors. His services are admittedly light, but let the King apply the remedy from a merciful disposition rather than as due of right. A benefice can cure his malady. In very early years, when dandled on his nurse's knee, Dunbar says, by fond anticipation he was addressed as bishop: yet now that age oppresses him he cannot attain to be a mere vicar. By contrast, Jok, who once herded the stirks, can draw in a whole batch of churches by a false card up his sleeve worth all Dunbar's 'ballattis under the byrkis'. Michell, who recently drove his oxen in landward parts, has several benefices and a bundle of the necessary dispensations. Thus it is to be fortunate with the dice. How is Dunbar to live when he has no lands and no benefice? He speaks in this manner, he says, not to reprove the King,

Bot doutles I go rycht neir hand it!

Like a soul in purgatory living in painful hope, he anticipates the King's compassion.

Perhaps the most poignant petition is that *To the King: On the World's Instability*.[1] Here he sets his own misery in a framework of general wretchedness. He laments the vain activities, the fleeting joys, and the insincerities around him, where humble service gains little reward. In the poet's judgment this is true not only of Scotland but also of France, England, Ireland, Germany, Italy, and Spain. It applies in all walks of life; the honourable usages of old have gone.

As for the clergy, their piety may be measured by the latitude of their conscience, on which eight oxen and a waggon could turn. And then, by a swift transition, Dunbar comes to his own wrongs.

[1] 'This waverand warldis wretchidnes.' MF., p. 178; R., f. 27. M. follows MF.: in lines 61 and 66 he has altered 'cuming' to 'cumen' without indication. Pinkerton headed the poem *On the Warld's Instabilitie*.

The distribution of benefices is unjust when some men have seven while he has none; and one man, unworthy to enjoy a cure, is unsatisfied by even a bishopric and would climb to cardinal's rank. Though Dunbar's benefice is on its way, now by the King's influence and now by the Queen's, it is at long range still. It might have come to him in shorter time, he adds sadly, from Calicut[1] or Newfoundland[2] or the far south lands. By this it might have reached him from the deserts of Ind over all the great ocean, from Persia[3] and the East, or from the isles of Africa. It is so long in coming that he dreads that it is not coming at all but is receding. In connexion with it, Dunbar has certainly the promise of much good gold, but all men are asking when the benefice is coming. He has no wish to gather in the fruits of great abbeys. A kirk scantily covered with heather will suffice, for he would be glad with little. As for his holding benefices in plurality, he says ironically that the help of the King's grace will obviate any danger to his soul from that sin. Yet he has hopes of the royal favour, and thus finds some alleviation of his pain.

The poem *To the King: Complane I Wald*[4] expresses Dunbar's bitterness. His complaint again is that worthless churls receive every honour. He attacks all these in true 'flyting' manner. One undeserving courtier dons the cowl and undertakes to maintain a great monastic house in piety, though it is the wealth of the benefice which weighs with him if the truth is told. Is this again John Damian? Another, on whom a parsonage is bestowed, will remain discontented until he is a lord bishop. What must be the thoughts of the highly educated son of earl or lord, who is fitted from birth to wield authority[5] as were his forefathers, and has three times the talent of the upstart and informer? He sees an ignorant wretch, whose task was once 'to muk the stabell', set far above him at the board. Let James have an eye to the welfare of old and faithful servants.

The throng at court is described in more detail in the *Remon-*

[1] M., in his notes to the poem, erroneously identifies 'Calyecot' with Calcutta.

[2] 'The new fund Yle.'

[3] L. conjectures that 'Paris' is probably an error in the MS.

[4] MF., p. 16; R., f. 13. MF. is illegible in many lines, which have been supplied from R. M. mentions R. with reference to line 21 only (where R. reads 'mastif', not 'mastyf'); in line 69, however, he has adopted a composite reading. In line 19, both MSS. have 'dyouris'.

[5] 'And he is maister native borne.' The line may, however, refer to a graduate of a Scottish university as compared with a foreign clerk such as Abbot Damian.

strance to the King: Schir, ye have Mony Servitouris.[1] Among them are

Kirkmen, courtmen, and craftismen fyne.

Doctors of law and medicine, philosophers, astrologers and diviners, orators and masters of arts, have all a place, with valiant knights and many others, forming a goodly company. Musicians, minstrels, singers, and dancers, find patronage, as well as craftsmen, among them carvers in wood and metal, carpenters, masons, shipwrights, glaziers, goldsmiths and lapidaries, printers,[2] painters, and apothecaries. All are skilled and busily engaged in their crafts, bringing much honour to the King their master. They deserve all the recompense that the King bestows on them, says Dunbar. But, though he may be unworthy himself to have a place among them—does he speak with modesty or irony?—yet he is confident that his poetry will be remembered as long and as fully as any of their works, even though his reward is small.

The King is so gracious and kind that another sort follows him, dissimulators and flatterers, 'Monsouris of France' (connoisseurs in claret), importunate self-seekers out of Ireland, purloiners of food from the hall, and others of whom little good is known. These men have no skill in the crafts, and will listen to none who tries to instruct them in good breeding. Those who experiment in *quinta essentia* are fantastic fools, mendacious and insatiable, able to multiply very far indeed—in folly. Few, the poet adds, of all this sort would dare, without a special writ of pardon, to venture near the Tolbooth when the courts of justice are in session. It rankles that they also are rewarded while Dunbar is not.

He turns to the hereafter for consolation when he writes *In This Warld May Non Assure.*[3] How does God will him to dispose of the days remaining to him, since no reward comes to him for long

[1] MF., p. 196. There is a blank in line 10, before 'flingaris'. L. heads the poem *His Remonstrance*. In the MS. the poem is not divided into paragraphs as by M. At the end is written 'Quod dunbar', and below this again, at the foot of p. 198, is the catchword 'To the o mercyfull', referring to the next poem, *The Tabill of Confessioun*, which begins on the next page with these words. S. connected the catchword with the preceding colophon, to read 'Quod dumbar to the unmercyfull (k)ing'.

[2] In the context it would be rash to assume that these printers were printers in the modern sense, and not merely artists in the stamping of designs on fabrics, wood, or metal.

[3] 'Quhom to sall I compleine my wo?' B., f. 84; MF., p. 331; R., f. 40b. R. omits lines 31-35. M. has followed MF. generally; his reading of 'in' (line 81) is, however, from B., and he states wrongly that in the sixth stanza B.'s refrain begins with 'So'; the refrain there is 'For in etc.'.

service? His life may not endure long, and his time hitherto has been wasted. At court, worthless men rise to favour, and drones enjoy benefices. There is no pity in princes. Yet again he remembers that all must appear before judgment. Ill-gotten wealth will be little help when the angel blows his trumpet. To describe more powerfully the torments that await such damned souls, Dunbar passes for several lines into Church Latin. Why then should he seek to acquire world's trash when one day flood and fire will sweep it all to destruction? The day of resurrection will come. He prays for a seat in heaven rather than an earthly cure.

We come now to the best known of Dunbar's appeals to the King, *The Petition of the Gray Horse, Old Dunbar*,[1] which has the distinction of being followed by a short poem that is probably the composition of King James himself. From a consideration of the manuscript texts it is evident that this petition has been mishandled by the poet's editors, and that the true beginning of the poem, as Sir William Craigie points out, is at the twenty-third line of the text shown in the various printed editions. Of the two manuscript sources, Maitland begins unmistakably with this line, and Reidpeth follows suit. Owing to the loss of a quire in the former manuscript, the poem is incomplete there, but Reidpeth, in transcribing from Maitland, made use of the quire now lost but then only misplaced, and clearly shows the ending of the petition, attributes it to Dunbar, and follows on with the *Responsio Regis*.

[1] 'Schir, lett it nevir in toun be tald.' MF., p. 18 (lines 23-53 of M.'s version); R., p. 1 (lines 55-65; 1-24; 67-74) and p. 14 (lines 23-24; 25-54). L. erroneously says (II, p. 326) that the R. fragments are in three different parts of the volume. That the MF. fragment consists of the first part of the poem is shown by its beginning not at the top of a page but after the colophon of *To the King: Complane I Wald*. The fragment breaks off at the foot of the page, the succeeding quire being lost which began with line 55. In Reidpeth's day it had not yet been lost but only inserted at the wrong place. In transcribing, on p. 1 of his manuscript, Dunbar's *Meditation in Winter* (taking it from the first of the two copies in MF.), Reidpeth reached the foot of the page in MF. and then proceeded not to the continuation at the top of p. 3 in MF., but to the top of the first page in the lost quire, beginning with line 55 of the poem now under consideration. Having transcribed lines 55-65, R., evidently following MF., gives 1-24 and the colophon 'Q:dumbar', after which the *Responsio Regis* follows. When in due course R. came to p. 18 of MF., he began with the true first line of the poem (line 23) and, on reaching the foot of Maitland's page at line 54, he stopped, adding no colophon because he had already given it on his p. 2. The true order of the lines is therefore 23-66, 1-24, 67-74. Sir William Craigie, in editing MF. has pointed out the error (II, p. 40). Pinkerton began correctly with line 23 but did not go beyond the MF. fragment. After the initial couplet, line 25 is a convincing first line as compared with the weak beginning of the printed texts. M. follows MF. so far as available, but reads 'Yuillis' for the 'yowllis' of MF. in line 24. The title of the poem is Laing's.

The poem opens with a detached couplet which recurs as refrain:

Schir, lett it nevir in toun be tald
That I suld be ane yowllis yald

The meaning is obscure, but the context shows that Dunbar is appealing to the King for new attire for the approaching Yule.[1] As already stated, a payment to Dunbar is recorded on 27th January 1505-6 'for caus he wantit his goun at Yule', and there is another payment to him on 4th January 1506-7, 'in Recompensatioun for his goun'.

If he was an old and worn-out horse turned out into the wilds to crop the clover, he would, he says, be brought indoors under cover at Christmas, even if he could browse on the grass of all Strathnaver.[2] He is indeed an old horse, as the King knows, and lives in drudgery, the great court horses shouldering him from the stall to live on the moss of field and heath. On this bare pasture he has existed for a long time. Now, on account of age, he should be taken indoors, for his teeth are failing. His mane has turned white, and the fault is the King's: when other horses had bran to eat, he had only grass. He was never made much of in stable, ill strewn straw sufficing for his hide; but he begs the King, if he should die in James's service, at least not to let the soutars have his skin to gnaw with their gums. Life at court has dimmed his ardour and overdriven him, but he would willingly be spurred unmercifully if he might have trappings to wear at Yule. At this season, when the young mares ridden by lords and commons are decked and apparelled, why should not palfreys also make a brave show? In the days of his youth, when he stepped high, he might have been bought in neighbouring realms if he had consented to be sold: now, when he would fain graze alongside steeds of quality, he is driven off to consort with plebeian coal-hacks that are scabbed,

[1] L. explains the term as 'a Yule jade', 'yald' or 'yaud' being strictly a mare but meaning also 'old and worn-out horse'. Gregor (note in S.T.S., III) derives it from Old Norse 'jalda', a mare. Cf. *The Flyting*, line 246, 'yad' meaning 'mare', and also the next line of the present poem, 'yaid aver', with which cp. *The Flyting*, line 229. The word 'yald' rhymes with 'gnawit' at line 60 (the MS. reading 'gnawin' being probably a scribal error). Professor Dickins has drawn the writer's notice to a recent discussion by Mr. A. S. C. Ross of this phrase and of similar phrases of Scandinavian origin, in Vol. XII of the *Saga-Book of the Viking Society*.

[2] The MSS. have 'Streneverne', which, as Dr. Mackenzie points out, would spoil the rhyme. Strathnaver is mentioned apparently as an extreme instance. It drains into the north coast. Leslie describes it as famed for the breeding of livestock (I, p. 43). Cp. *Of a Dance in the Quenis Chalmer*, line 13: MF. 'Stranaver', R. 'Straverne'.

lame, and rheumatic. Though he is not clapped in stall like coursers in their silk housings, he would like to be wrapped in new attire against the Christmas cold.

The short poem of eight lines, in couplets and headed *Responsio Regis*, gives a favourable reply to Dunbar's appeal. The King gives his Treasurer instructions, according to a royal prescript, to take in this gray horse, old Dunbar, whose hair has turned gray during his loyal service. Let the Treasurer deck him this Christmas like a bishop's mule, for the King has given authority with his own hand to pay whatever sum his clothes may cost.

In commenting on this poem, Laing leaves the reader to decide whether it is really by the King or only by Dunbar, but he notes that Chalmers regarded it as genuinely the composition of James IV. Mackay, on the other hand, regards the *Responsio Regis* as in Dunbar's manner. Schipper thinks that Dunbar would not have dared to feign royal authorship and that the poem is therefore to be ascribed to James IV. It is true that Dunbar might have devised it as a piece of ingenious suggestion, but the evidence of the manuscript, which has apparently not been considered, points to the other view. As has been stated, Reidpeth closes the petition itself with a definite attribution to Dunbar, but the *Responsio Regis* has no colophon, the scribe evidently thinking the title sufficient in itself to show who was the author. If Reidpeth had considered the reply to be also Dunbar's, he would have reserved his 'Q: dumbar' for the end. As Reidpeth copied from the lost portion of the Maitland manuscript, it is strongly to be presumed that Maitland held the same opinion and had indicated it in the same manner. This, in turn, would suggest that Maitland's source was equally explicit, and the inference is justified that the *Responsio Regis* is probably the work of King James IV. There is no reason to think that James's royal position would make him unwilling to try his hand at versifying. He had before him the illustrious example of his ancestor James I. His own son, James V, certainly wrote verses, as is shown by Lindsay's poem, *The Answer quhilk Schir David Lindesay Maid to the Kingis Flyting*.[1]

[1] S.T.S. edition of Lindsay's works, I, p. 102.

CHAPTER XIII

GROTESQUERIES

THERE was a dramatic element in the frequent pageants and other similar entertainments of Dunbar's time, but there was probably little that could be called formal drama. Plays of a sort were performed at Perth in connexion with the feast of Corpus Christi, and also in Edinburgh, but Herod and his followers may have been little more than participants in the processions.[1] In 1504, money was 'payit to James Dog, that he laid doun for girs on Corpus Christi Day, at the play, to the Kingis and Quenis chamires'.[2] At the marriage celebrations of 1503, 'a moralitie was played' by 'John Inglish and his companyons' in the presence of the King and Queen.[3] In the early nineties of the preceding century, Patrick Johnstoun and 'the playaris of Lythgow' had been active. How far these entertainments were in dramatic form is doubtful. Dunbar has left no play. The fantastic monologue known as '*The Droichis pairt of the play*' or '*The manere of the crying of ane playe*' has been attributed to him, but on quite insufficient evidence.[4]

Processions, pageants, guisings, and dances, were very much in the spirit of the age. The morris dance was a favourite entertainment at court. There is a record of 'Colin Campbell and his marowis that brocht in the Moris dauns'.[5] Guising was traditionally associated with the dance. Payment was made 'To the gysaris of Edinburgh that daunsit in the Abbay', and 'To gysaris dansit in the Kingis chamir'.[6] The King and Queen themselves took part in mummings. Of the innumerable minstrels of the time, many entertained with mime and dance.[7] We have mentioned in preceding pages what a prominent part was played by allegorical shows in public celebrations, and how the poets mirrored these shows in such allegorical poems as *The Goldyn Targe* and *Bewty and the Presoneir*. The annual return of the various festivals of the calendar provided regular

[1] Mill, pp. 68-73. [2] T.A., II, p. 438. [3] Leland, IV, p. 299.
[4] Appendix IV, No. 9. [5] T.A., II, p. 414.
[6] ib., II, p. 418; III, p. 141. Quoted Mill, p. 15. [7] Mill, p. 44.

occasions for processions. An example was the ceremony of bringing in the May, at Edinburgh.[1]

Some of these recurring celebrations were burlesque. On Twelfth Night, the revelry was presided over by an elected King or Queen of the Bean, with dance and guising. Each December, St. Nicholas' Eve brought the indecorous revels of the boy-bishop, elected by the choirboys of St. Giles. In full vestments, the mock-bishop headed the procession of farcical figures, with attendant imps, on his visit to the King. At Yule there was the similar revel of the Abbot of Unreason, who frolicked with his attendants, not without violence if we may judge from the public accounts: 'To the barbour helit Paulis hed quhen he wes hurt with the Abbot of Unreason.'[2] Herod and his train, in the processions of Corpus Christi, would be grotesques. As the Virtues would present a noble front in the allegorical pageants, the Vices would be appropriately hideous and often obscene. When 'Wantonness and hir Marowis' sang before the King, they would offer a ribald spectacle, and so would 'Janet Bair-ars'.[3] Laing quotes the account of a procession at Heidelberg in 1613, when 'came in the Seaven Deadly Sinnes, all of them chained, and driven forward by a dragon, who continually spet fire'.[4] Dunbar's grotesque poems must be read in the context of the entertainments of his day.

The three poems, *The Dance of the Seven Deadly Sins*, *The Turnament of the Tailliour and the Sowttar*, and *Amendis Maid to the Telyouris and Sowtaris*, are closely connected and were all written within a short space of time. The Bannatyne manuscript has no break, other than the ordinary spacing between stanzas, between the first and second of the poems. In the list of contents of the manuscript, where a separate title occurs for the second poem, the title is expressly linked with the first line of the preceding poem.[5] The words *The Dance*, written in a large hand, are in the right margin opposite the opening lines, and *The turnament* in the same hand appears similarly in the margin before the opening of the second poem. The Maitland manuscript ends *The Dance* with the customary form of ascription to Dunbar, and then begins the next poem, without title, with the first and last stanzas of *The Dance*. The

[1] T.A., III, p. 197. [2] ib., II, p. 432.
[3] ib., IV, pp. 314, 108. [4] L., II, p. 257.
[5] B., f. 372, 'Off februar the xv tene nicht callit the turnament of the tailliour and the the [*sic*] sowttar.'

complicated metre is the same in both poems, the scene of both is in Hell, in the presence of Mahound, and the trance into which the poet falls at the beginning of *The Dance* is not ended until the close of *The Turnament*. Finally, the opening line of the second poem,

> Nixt that a turnament wes tryid,

is proof that it is an adjunct to another poem. The connexion of the last poem, *Amendis*, with *The Turnament* is plain. The three poems may therefore be taken as forming a series of approximately the same date.

Based upon the first nine lines of *The Dance of the Seven Deadly Sins*, inferences have been drawn as to the date of composition. These findings do not agree. In the manuscript of Bannatyne the poem begins:

> Off Februar[1] the fyiftene nycht,
> Full lang befoir the dayis lycht,
> I lay in till a trance;
> And then I saw baith hevin and hell:
> Me thocht, amangis the feyndis fell,
> Mahoun gart cry ane dance
> Off schrewis that wer nevir schrevin,
> Aganis the feist of Fasternis evin
> To mak thair observance.

Fastern's Even was the last day of carnival before Lent was ushered in with Ash Wednesday. The dance was on the night of the 15th February, and on the occasion of Fastern's Even. But was it on the night preceding Tuesday, or on the Tuesday night? In the first case the 15th would be Monday, in the second case Shrove Tuesday. Different decisions on this point lead to different conclusions as to the particular year concerned. The editors of Dunbar differ, but do not discuss the issue. In dating Fastern's Even (Shrove Tuesday), Laing cites without comment the views of Hailes and Chalmers as being for the 15th and 16th respectively.[2] Mackay[3] agrees with Chalmers, but Schipper[4] with Hailes. Dr. Mackenzie[5] assumes that Fastern's Even was the 16th.

What was Dunbar's purpose in writing *The Dance of the Seven Deadly Sins*? He may have intended it as a literary counterpart of the carnival scenes of Shrove Tuesday. It may have been composed for recitation on the Tuesday as part of the revelry. *The Dance* may,

[1] The 'feber-yeir' of MF. is transcribed by R. as 'fever yeir'.
[2] L., II, p. 255. [3] S.T.S., I, p. clxiii. [4] S. ed., p. 107. [5] M., p. 219.

on the other hand, have been composed some time later by way of reminiscence and description, and been followed up with the account of the mock tournament which came 'nixt' on Fastern's Even as the first line of *The Turnament* states. Certainly the precise dating of the night of the trance seems odd if it refers only to the preceding evening. But we do not know enough to be sure about these matters. Lent began, however, on the evening of Shrove Tuesday, not on the morning of Ash Wednesday. It appears, therefore, that the poet's supposed trance on the night of the 15th must, if we are to avoid putting it into Lent, and with it the carnival it involves, have been on the night of the Monday. Early on Wednesday would be too late. We conclude, then, that Fastern's Even fell on the 16th February.

As Fastern's Even was the seventh Tuesday before Easter Sunday, its date varied in successive years with that of Easter. Two considerations have to be borne in mind in consulting the calendar. In the first place, since the civil year in Scotland before 1600 began on the 25th March instead of 1st January, the Fastern's Even relevant to any particular Easter is that of the previous year. Secondly, in dealing with leap years, care is necessary to see that the 'leap' due to the extra day at the close of February is computed not according to the civil year but according to the 'historical' year beginning on 1st January.[1] An instance of the necessity for this latter method is afforded by two entries in the Treasurer's Accounts. In 1496 'the vij day of Februare was Fasteringis evin', and, a few weeks later, in 1497 'the xxvj day of Marche was Pasche day.'[2] These dates will not agree unless we assume there was no leap at the end of February 1496—or, as it is more clearly named in historical works, 1496-7—though 1496 is divisible by 4 in accordance with the well known rule of thumb. The months of January, February, and part of March, which together are for historical purposes denoted as 1496-7, must, for purposes of the 'leap', be considered as belonging to the year 1497, which was not a leap year. The leap came instead at the close of February 1495-6, which ranked in this connexion as 1496.

Between the years 1480 and 1530, Fastern's Even fell on 16th February in the common years 1506-7 and 1517-18, Easter Day being then on the 4th April, and in the leap year 1495-6, with

[1] Members of the staff of H.M. General Register House find that only in this way will such calculations square. [2] T.A., I, pp. 319, 326.

Easter Day on 3rd April.[1] Of these three calendrical possibilities, only 1506-7 is at all likely for the three poems we are now concerned with. The years 1495-6 and 1517-18 are much too early and much too late respectively. The date 1506-7 is nearest to the period of Dunbar's greatest poetic activity. Mackay[2] declares for 1506-7, but largely on the unsatisfactory ground that, when Dunbar says the Devil bids his followers

> kast gamountis in the skyis
> That last came out of France,

he is referring to the attempted flight from Stirling Castle of the Frenchman, John Damian, in that year. The flight was, however, in September or October,[3] a date after that chosen by Mackay for the poems. Besides, the lines quoted refer only to the latest dances from France.[4]

The spring of 1506-7 may, with some degree of confidence, be taken as the date of *The Dance of the Seven Deadly Sins*, *The Turnament of the Taillìour and the Sowttar*, and *Amendis Maid to the Telyouris and the Sowtaris*.

As Dunbar lies in a trance on the night of Monday, the 15th February 1506-7, long before daylight on the 16th, he sees Mahound summon fiends to a dance in Hell to celebrate Fastern's Even. *The Dance of the Seven Deadly Sins*[5] is thus an example, but a strange one,

[1] *L'Art de Verifier les Dates*, p. 30-31. Sir A. H. Dunbar, p. 355. L. (II, p. 255) quotes a MS. note supplied to him by Chalmers, indicating these dates. S. wrongly attributes to Chalmers the statement that these years had Fastern's Even on the 15th, not the 16th, whereas Chalmers rightly says on the 16th. S. concludes that Fastern's Even was on the 15th, but, by means of this misapprehension of what Chalmers said, arrives inconsistently at 1506-7 (S. ed., p. 127).

If Fastern's Even was on 15th February in a common year, Easter Sunday was on 3rd April. Between 1480 and 1530, the Februaries of 1484-5 and 1490-1 meet the requirements. In a leap year, Easter Sunday would have to fall on 2nd April: here the only year available is 1479-80. None of these years can be considered as late enough.

[2] S.T.S., I, p. clxiii and p. ccxlvi. [3] Leslie, II, pp. 124-5.

[4] Somerset Herald records (Leland, IV, p. 281) that, having escorted Princess Margaret towards Scotland in 1503, 'The Lord of Northumberland made his devoir, at departynge, of gambades and lepps'. The lines quoted of the poem are 11-12 in B. MF., however, has 'gambaldis . . . as verlottis dois in france' (p. 12), and (p. 161) 'gawmundis . . . Of the new use of france'. R. has 'galmandis'.

[5] 'Off Februar the fyiftene nycht.' B., f. 110; MF., p. 12; R., f. 11b. L. called the poem *The Dance of the Sevin Deidly Synnis*. Each long stanza is divided in MF. into two, so that some of the rhyming subtleties are lost, though lines 25-30 and 103-108 no longer have the appearance of fragments; R. follows suit. R. has a number of marginal emendations in old, pencilled characters. M. follows B. mainly, but omits the marginal rubric titles of the successive sins; in lines 50 and 89, M. departs from B. without indicating the fact. L. has confused the readings of line 50.

of the medieval dream-poem. Pride is first in the dance, in all his wastefulness of attire, the rout behind skipping through the searing flames. Shaven priests are among them, and the watching devils respond to the humour of the situation.[1] Ire follows, with his train of desperados in accoutrements of war. Next comes Envy, trembling with secret hate. At sight of the dissimulators, flatterers, backbiters, and whisperers that press behind their leader, the poet usurps the choric function to lament that the courts of kings can never be quit of these rogues. 'Cuvatyce' comes next, with followers whose throats vomit molten gold but are replenished continually with gold coin by the attendant fiends. Sloth requires a second summons before he comes sleepily like a sow from the dunghill, with his unwilling supporters. As they deploy for the dance, Belial lashes their loins with a bridle-rein, and the surrounding flames also quicken the dancers. Lechery and his diseased companions follow. Gluttony is last of all, at his heels a drunken rout

> With can and collep, cop and quart,

like Falstaff larding the ground under them, and plied by the devils with hot lead for drink.

Hell was devoid of minstrels, but Mahound had not far to seek for the hellish equivalent. He cried out for a Highland pageant. As elsewhere, Dunbar does not spare the Celt. A devil runs to fetch Macfadyen from his nook in the far north, and, when the latter has raised the coronach, the Erschemen gather in a multitude. With their Gaelic cries they so deafen the Devil that he smothers them hastily in the deepest recess of Hell.

The poem which thus concludes in the Maitland and Reidpeth manuscripts is grotesque and startling, but it bears clearly from start to finish the mark of the comic style. And apart from the unmistakable tenor of the poem itself, the occasion on which it was written—the time of carnival—is evidence of its comic intention. Lowell is wide of the mark when (as quoted by Mackay) he seems to assume some serious moral purpose behind *The Dance*: 'It would be well for us if the sins themselves were indeed such wretched bugaboos as he has painted for us. . . . The uninitiated foreigner

[1] Lines 25-30, describing the proud bearing of these followers, and the fiends' derisive reaction to it, form a detached half-verse which L. transfers needlessly to follow line 13, regarding the half-verse as a fragment of which the remainder has been lost. The significant connexion with Pryd is thus lost. None of the MSS. offers support for the emendation, and L. retains in position a later half-verse, lines 103-108.

puts his handkerchief to his nose, wonders, and gets out of the way as soon as he civilly can.'[1] Lowell is not entitled to regard Dunbar as a simpleton because he has used as poetic material one of the established pageantries of medieval times. Nor does a payment on 16th February 1506-7, 'To Wantonness, that the King fechit and gert hir sing in the Quenes chamir', justify the suggestion that Dunbar was directing a moral satire against the King and his courtiers, who would probably, it is added, be the last to see any reflection on themselves.[2] Schipper saw more clearly the spirit of the poem and its appropriateness to the season.[3]

The relation of *The Dance* to *The Turnament of the Taillíour and the Sowttar*[4] in the manuscripts has already been discussed. The two poems had an organic connexion in the minds of the scribes of the only two manuscripts which contain both poems. Apart, however, from the adventitious links of the poet's trance, the scene, and the metre, there is in truth no organic unity unless we follow the version of Maitland, who succeeds in short-circuiting the dance entirely; for his first stanza lays down the occasion of the poet's trance and of the carnival in Hell, and his second passes to the Highland pageant: then follows naturally enough the first line of *The Turnament* proper. The best arrangement would therefore be to preserve the separation from *The Dance* but to lead up to it as in Maitland's version.

Whatever personal grudge Dunbar may have harboured against the two crafts is not now to be discovered, but others also of his poems show his love of pouring ridicule on tailors and soutars. In the eyes of derisive courtiers they may have stood for the undistinguished crowd of humble artisans, the 'stinking multitude', just as, with other crafts, they came under the scorn of the socially superior merchants of the burgh. Ordeal by battle might be applied to tailors and soutars just as to the knightly class, but such displays of arms would be ludicrous to the practised chivalry that frequented Edinburgh. Sir David Lindsay has a poem in a similar vein, *The*

[1] Lowell, *Literary Essays*, IV, p. 269.
[2] S.T.S., I, p. ccxlv.; T.A., III, p. 369.
[3] S., p. 199.
[4] 'Nixt that a turnament wes tryid.' B., f. 111; MF., p. 161; Asloan MS., f. 210. B. concludes with, 'Heir endis the sowtar and tailyouris war maid be the nobill poyet maister william dumbar'. Asloan's heading is 'The Justis betuix the talyeour and the sowtar'. Asloan is closer to MF. than to B., but he has no recapitulatory stanzas from *The Dance*. M. in general follows B., but separates the poem from *The Dance*, and in several lines follows MF. without indication; he misreads MF. in line 95 ('steyll').

Iusting betuix Iames Watsoun and Ihone Barbour, narrating the encounter in the lists of two servants of the court, at St. Andrews, in the presence of King James V and his Queen. The tone of Dunbar's poem is one more indication that his interests lay with the higher ranks of society for which he wrote and from which he had sprung.

The jousts of the tailor and soutar had been proclaimed long before in Hell, in the presence of Mahound, and the lists were prepared. Each combatant was convoyed to the barrier by a mob of plebeian associates, a banner farcically characteristic of his craft being borne before him. The tailor as challenger appeared first, and received knighthood at the hands of the Devil, but, at sight of the lists and of his opponent, his fear made him disgrace himself lamentably. The soutar, similarly initiated, faced the prospect in a manner not quite so unseemly, though the Devil, who was close by, had cause to rue his proximity. The burlesque combat began. At the first shock of onset, the tailor's slippery saddle was his undoing, and the crash of his fall so scared the soutar's horse that it took flight in the direction of the presiding Devil. Eager to requite the soutar, the Devil took the opportunity in a way which must be sought in the poem itself. The poet had intended to write more on the subject, but the sight of the consummation of Belial's retaliation on the soutar seemed to him so irresistibly comic that he was overcome with laughter, and thus awoke from his trance. Attempts to prevent him from recording the episode failed, for the occasion was too savoury to omit.

Now trow this gif ye list.

Pinkerton[1] says, 'The flames alone can cleanse the filth of this poem. But such were the standing jokes of the time. Sir Thomas More has his epigrams *De ventris crepitu*, etc.'

The *Amendis Maid to the Telyouris and Sowtaris*[2] is ironical, being far from amends. The information is provided by Maitland that the poem was recited by Dunbar 'quhone he drank to the Dekynnis for amendis to the bodeis of thair craftis', and the poem itself mentions that the setting is in the busy mart on fair-day, where the booths of tailors and soutars would have their place and where the deacons

[1] Pinkerton, p. 452.

[2] 'Betuix twell houris and ellevin.' Having ascribed the preceding poem to Dunbar, B. adds 'Followis the amendis maid be him to the telyouris and sowtaris for the turnament maid on thame.' MF. omits lines 5-8.

of their crafts would be prominent. Gregor[1] surmises that, at the close of his mock-apology, Dunbar may have pledged them in a jorum. The poet says that he dreamed that an angel from heaven proclaimed a blessing on the two crafts, promising them a place above beside God Himself, since they succeed in mending what God has mismade. The soutar can make amends for ill-made feet with a well-made pair of shoes, and the cut of the tailor's workmanship can reshape an ill-fashioned man. The poet lingers on this idea for some time, and not out of mere prolixity, for the suspense heightens the mocking effect of the sting with which the poem concludes. Since on earth these crafts can perform such miracles, they will merit precedence over the saints in heaven—though they be knaves in this country.

Telyouris and sowtaris, blist be ye!

Reference has been made more than once to the guisings that were at various times held in the Queen's chamber. The tone of the three poems just discussed is matched by that of Dunbar's poem *Of a Dance in the Quenis Chalmer*.[2] That the dance should have been described in such terms as Dunbar uses is certainly surprising. There is nothing in the poem, however, to suggest that the Queen herself was present, though it would be rash to assert that she was not. In either event, it is to be hoped that the poem arises from burlesque poetic convention rather than from the actual manners of the court. Perhaps an entirely respectable dance might in pothouse mood be caricatured in this fashion, even if the Queen were present. What would have shocked Victoria may not have troubled Margaret, over four hundred years earlier.

Shorn of its garnish, the poem can be described as giving a picture of the Queen's circle in which Dunbar moved. The tipsy roisterers make their entry in succession, and can scarcely keep their feet. Sir John Sinclair leads off, as befits one who has recently returned from France. But his feet betray him, and Master Robert Schaw the physician fares no better, nor the Master Almoner—to the glee of John Bute the jester. At this point 'Dunbar the Mackar' enters in his turn, inspired, he tells us that the onlookers believed, by his love for one of the ladies taking part—and astonishing all present,

[1] S.T.S., III, p. 207.

[2] 'Sir Jhon Sinclair begowthe to dance.' MF., p. 340; R., f. 45. MF. closes with 'Quod dumbar of a dance in the quenis chalmer'.

if we may believe him, by his agility. He is brought to a halt by the loss of a slipper.

> A mirrear dance mycht na man se.

The lady herself, Mistress Musgrave, follows him in the dance, and what Matthew Arnold calls the 'lyrical cry' emerges incongruously from the indecorous setting. The tender yearnings of the author of *Mary Morison* are attempted nowhere else by Dunbar; but here, forgetful of the curiously impersonal way in which he has just described his own antics, Dunbar speaks in the first person, from the heart-strings:

> Quhen I schau hir sa trimlye dance,
> Hir guid convoy and contenance,
> Than, for hir saek, I wissitt to be
> The grytast erle or duk in France.

It is only for a moment, and then the glow is gone.

Next in the dance, the sour-faced Dame Dounteboir is treated in the same spirit as were the earlier figures. James Dog, Keeper of the Queen's Wardrobe, who appears last in the dance, is figuratively introduced as the 'Quenis Dog', and his mastiff-like movements, together with less reputable canine qualities, provide the poem with a full close.

If we may judge from Dunbar's bearing in this company, these were his close associates. Sir John Sinclair of Dryden had attended at court for many years, occasionally playing bowls with the King and Andrew Forman the protonotary, and cards with the King.[1] Like Dunbar, he had been on a mission to England in the autumn of 1501 when the royal betrothal was being negotiated.[2] Dunbar's description of him as 'the Quenis knycht' shows that Sinclair was now attached to the Queen's household. He was still attending on the Queen in 1513.[3] 'Maistir Robert Scha' was a physician in the royal service, his name appearing in the Accounts from 1502 to 1508. In 1504 he attended Lady Janet Kennedy at Bothwell, and in February 1504-5 prescribed for the Queen herself 'for bleding of the ness'.[4] In 1508 the King gave a large sum as offering at Master Robert Shaw's first mass.[5] The 'Maister Almaser' was the Queen's Almoner. Dr. Babington,[6] an Englishman who, like Sir

[1] T.A., II, pp. 112, 459. [2] ib., II, p. 121. [3] Ellis, I, p. 73.

[4] T.A., II, pp. 436, 477. [5] ib., IV, p. 41.

[6] ib., II, p. 336. Mackay (S.T.S., I, p. xcix) believes that the poem cannot have been written until some years after Margaret's marriage, and that the reference in the poem to Dr. Babington indicates a date before 1507 when he became Dean of Aberdeen; but the reference is only to a 'Maister Almaser'.

John, had been employed in the business of the King's betrothal and marriage contract,[1] had remained in Scotland with Margaret and held the post of Queen's Almoner for some time. He was a doctor of theology, and in December 1505 was nominated to be Dean of Aberdeen, but is referred to in May 1507 as deceased.[2] It may have been he who offended the nose of John Bute, the fool, according to the poem. Bute figures in the records for many years from 3rd November 1506. His assistant was called Spark.[3] As for 'Maesteres Musgraeffe', she has been identified with the wife of the Englishman, Sir John Musgrave, who came to Scotland with the Queen, and also with the 'Lady Maistres' who, unnamed in the records, was the Queen's chief lady-in-waiting. It is doubtful, however, who this court beauty was who called forth Dunbar's emphatic admiration. As early as September 1501 there is mention of a Lady Musgrave at court.[4]

As for 'Dame Dounteboir', Schipper[5] thought she was probably Mistress Dog, wife of James Dog the Queen's wardrober, because the editor of the Exchequer Rolls referred to the Privy Seal Register as stating that on 12th May 1500 Dog had purchased the lands of Duntober in Perthshire.[6] Certainly her sour looks as described in *The Dance in the Quenis Chalmer* recall the shrewish conduct related in *Of the Said James, quhen he had Plesitt him*. The unfaithfulness alleged in that poem might have made appropriate the apparent pun here on the word 'Dounteboir', which as used by John Knox seems to have a disreputable significance.[7] But, of course, the crux is the similarity of 'Duntober' and 'Dounteboir'. In fact, the entry in the Privy Seal Register[8]—dated 20th May, not 12th—refers to Dunrobyn, not Duntober, and is confirmed by the original manuscript of the Register, which moreover has no entry as to 'Duntober'. Thus Schipper's whole case for identifying Dame Dounteboir with Mistress Dog falls to the ground. There is no entry relating to Dog under the date 12th May.[9]

As with *The Dance of the Seven Deadly Sins* and *The Turnament*, the

[1] Bain, IV, p. 338. [2] Livingstone, I, 1172; II, 1478.
[3] T.A., III, pp. 301, 308. [4] ib., II, p. 120. [5] S. ed., p. 201.
[6] Mackay and Burnett, E.R., XIII, p. lxxxi.
[7] 'Madame Baylie, Maistres to the Quenis Dountibouris (for Maides that Court could not then weill beir).' Knox, *History of the Reformation*, 1732, p. 335. Quoted by Dr. Mackenzie, p. 210. [8] Livingstone, I, p. 76.
[9] The writer is indebted in this matter to Mr. C. T. McInnes, Curator of Historical Records, H.M. General Register House, who kindly consulted for him the MS., *Reg. Secreti Sig. Regum Scot.*, II, 1498-1504, p. 1.

riotous night of Fastern's Even is the occasion for another of Dunbar's poems, *To the Queen: Madam, Your Men Said thai Wald Ryd.*[1] The title *To the Quene* was added by Pinkerton and the other editors following him. The person to whom the poem is directed is addressed as 'Madam', and the Queen is so addressed in the refrain of the poem *Of James Dog, Kepair of the Quenis Wardrep*. It is reasonable, therefore, to regard the poem as meant for the Queen, though neither manuscript gives any such indication. In parts the poem is obscure,[2] and especially the refrain in its relation to the context of successive stanzas. The Queen—if it is the Queen—instead of staying in town on that licentious night, had apparently intended to ride off with her court to some quieter place. But the wives of her gentlemen had flocked to protest against being deprived of their husbands during the festivities of Fastern's Even, and the Queen had relented. The poet shows how much better it would have been for these profligate gallants, and for the health of some of their wives too, if the Queen had adhered to her first resolution, for the wenches they frequent would be better lodged[3] in the stocks. Dunbar concludes by underlining the moral. But is he serious?

The spread of the disease known then as 'the Grandgor' was so alarming at the time that the Lords of Council in 1497 had ordered measures to be taken against the contagion: all persons in Edinburgh afflicted by the disease were to assemble at a stated time on Leith Sands, to be conveyed to the island of Inchkeith, with supplies of food, 'thair to remane quhill God prouyde for thair health'.[4]

We have seen that tournaments found a place in the revels of Fastern's Even, though they can rarely have been of the nature described by Dunbar. Tournaments were, however, at all times a feature of King James's court. Sir David Lindsay includes among the glories of his reign, which made the King famous throughout Europe,

> Triumphant tourneys, jousting, and knightly game.[5]

The tournaments were in the main brilliant spectacles, accompanied by fanciful pageants, and even the armour of the knights who took

[1] MF., p. 342; R., f. 46.

[2] MF. in line 4 reads, 'And baid tham betteis som abyd', but 'som' might be 'soin'. R., 'betties [or 'bettres'] soñ'. It is tempting to surmise that 'betteis soin' or Beattison was the name of a surgeon whose services might be sought.

[3] M. unnecessarily alters the 'lugget' of MF. to 'ligget'.

[4] *Extracts from Burgh Records of Edinburgh*, I, p. 71.

[5] *The Testament and Complaynt of the Papyngo*', line 502.

part was highly ornamented. The King himself wore armour specially prepared for him by experts in France.[1] In Edinburgh the lists were usually placed on the ground immediately south of the cliffs of the Castle, and near the King's Stables. Pitscottie relates how, on one occasion, the King cast his hat from the window of an apartment of the Castle, as a signal to stop the tilting.[2] The tournaments were proclaimed throughout Scotland and sometimes at foreign courts as well. The site was railed in by a wooden barrier. As each knight approached, he was welcomed by the heralds and trumpeters, and the shield bearing his armorial bearings was hung on the barrier or on a tree. A challenger sought out the shield of the knight he wished to encounter, and struck it with his lance. A fantastic element was traditional. The knights were announced under fictitious names, and their attendants were grotesquely disguised[3]. A long wooden barrier crossed the lists. The tilters, as they galloped towards each other, were on opposite sides of it in such fashion that each lance was pointed across the horse's neck. The lances had blunted heads and shivered easily on contact.[4]

In *The Turnament of the Tailliour and the Sowttar*, Dunbar had produced a caricature of such a scene. In another of his compositions, *Of ane Blak Moir*, he made use of one of the most brilliant tournaments of the reign. The occasion lent itself well, for the 'blak lady' who presided was one of the court negresses.

This tournament is placed in 1505 by Pitscottie,[5] who says that it was presided over by Lord Bernard Stewart of Aubigny, then on a visit from France to Scotland. But Aubigny's visit was in 1508,[6] not 1505. Moreover, the Treasurers' Accounts show that on the 31st May 1508, when Aubigny was indeed in this country, there was a tournament held in honour of the 'blak lady'.[7] Pitscottie has evidently mistaken the year. But the jousting of 1508 was only a repetition of a tournament held for the 'blak lady' in Edinburgh in the preceding year, in June 1507, and duplicated many of its details. The prime mover in the whole matter appears to have been the French knight Sir Anthony d'Arcy, Sieur de la Bastie, a native of Dauphiné who had distinguished himself in the Italian wars and for whom King James came to have a warm affection.[8] He is said[9]

[1] Sir J. B. Paul, T.A., III, p. xxxviii. [2] Pitscottie, p. 234.
[3] Arnot, p. 72. [4] *Scot. Hist. Review*, IV (Oct. 1906), p. 111.
[5] Pitscottie, p. 242. [6] Leslie, II, p. 126. [7] T.A., IV, p. 119.
[8] Michel, p. 304. [9] ib., p. 334.

to have been in Scotland at James's wedding, and to have issued at Edinburgh, in 1505, a general challenge, but the official records do not mention him at these times. In 1506 he engaged with Lord Hamilton in the lists, wearing a white scarf in honour of the Queen of France, and received rich gifts from the King in money and kind.[1] He left Scotland for France in January 1506-7, bearing with him an illuminated proclamation of a tournament, 'the justing of the wild knycht for the blak lady', to be held in Edinburgh in the following August.[2] But the Accounts of the Treasurer do not mention him when the tournament was held in June, not August, and he seems therefore not to have been present, though a messenger from him was in Edinburgh on the 21st August.[3]

According to the articles of the tournament, which was the 'Emprise du Chevalier Sauvage à la Dame Noire', the 'Wild Knycht', with his two companions, challenged all comers for the space of five weeks to combat, on foot or on horseback, 'pour l'amour des dames'. The jousts were to be held in Edinburgh in the Field of Remembrance, situated between the Castle and the Secret Pavilion. Within this field was to be the Tree of Hope, growing in the Garden of Patience, and bearing the leaves of Pleasance, the flower of Noblesse, and the fruit of Honour. All comers were to proceed straight to the tree when the joust opened, and to touch the white shield which was in the keeping of the Black Lady, 'accompagnée de Sauvages, trompettes, et tous instruments'.[4] The programme is confirmed in several particulars by the Treasurer's Accounts for 1507. Payment is made for pears 'to the tree of esperance' on the 26th June, and on the preceding 17th May for doublets, hose, and bonnets, of the attendants on the 'wild knycht'. Winged monsters were made from canvas.[5]

When repeated on 31st May 1508, the arrangements were on an even more elaborate scale. La Bastie was present on this occasion,[6] having returned from France in April, according to Leslie,[7] though the same chronicler is wrong in stating that La Bastie left again for France on 27th May, for it was on 27th June.[8] The jousts were graced by the presence of the illustrious Stewart of Aubigny, newly arrived from France; we shall have to return to him later.

[1] Sir J. B. Paul, T.A., III, p. xli; pp. 358, 312.
[2] T.A., III, pp. 366, 365, 372. [3] ib., III, p. 412. [4] Mill, p. 326.
[5] T.A., III, pp. 394, 258, 259, 394. [6] ib., IV, pp. 117, 124.
[7] Leslie, II, p. 126. [8] ib., II, p. 128. Cf. T.A., IV, p. 128.

On 10th May, payment was made for hose and belts of the attendants on the 'wild knyght', which were to be of yellow and black, and for their bonnets of scarlet. The black lady was to have a green kirtle, with black leather sleeves and gloves, and her maidens were to have gowns of satin, bordered with yellow taffeta. There is an entry 'for tagging, grathing, and bukkilling of the wild bestis', and also for leaves and flowers and pears for the Tree of Esperance.[1] On 31st May itself, the day of the tournament, payments are recorded to the fourteen men 'that bure the blak lady fra the Castel to the barres and syne to the Abbay'.[2] If we are to believe Pitscottie, King James jousted in disguise as the Blak Knyght, fighting with spear, sword, and mace, and was adjudged the victor, and winner of the lady, by the heralds and by Aubigny as judge.[3]

Dunbar's poem in honour of the black lady was evidently written on the eve of one of the two tournaments at which she held so high a ceremonial position, but whether that of June 1507 or that of 31st May 1508, it is impossible to say. There are continual references to blackamoors at King James's court. In November 1504 two black girls, 'the More lasses', arrived, and one was baptised in the following month.[4] Without justification, Laing identified the black lady of 1507 with one of these and also with Black Elen, one of the two blackamoors at court in 1511-1513. Dunbar says that the black lady has 'landet furth of the last schippis', which can scarcely apply to arrivals of 1504. The black lady of the tournaments is not named. There is, of course, no reason why the same negress should have acted at both tournaments.

Dunbar begins his poem, *Of ane Blak Moir*,[5] by saying that he has for long composed poems about white ladies. This time his inspiration is a black lady whom he would fain describe in all her perfection—

My ladye with the mekle lippis.

The description leaves no doubt that she was of genuine negro blood, and that the word 'Moor' is not to be taken in the strict modern sense. Her mouth protrudes and gapes like that of an ape, and her short 'cat-nose' turns up merrily; her skin shines as with

[1] T.A., IV, pp. 64, 129, 120-121. [2] ib., IV, p. 119.
[3] Pitscottie, pp. 242-243. [4] T.A., II, pp. 465, 469.
[5] 'Lang heff I maed of ladyes quhytt.' MF., p. 341; R., f. 45b. MF. concludes, 'Quod dunbar of an blak moir', and R., 'Quod dumbar of ane blak moir'. M. does not notice R., from which, however, he has taken his title.

soap. When she is dressed in rich apparel, she shines still more brightly—as a tar-barrel. Doubtless she was born in the darkness of an eclipse. Whoever, in her name, proves mightiest in the field with spear and shield, must kiss and embrace her, and the vanquished are to be requited by her in less seemly fashion.

Pitscottie probably exaggerates when he says that the tournament attended by Aubigny, and therefore the one held in 1508, lasted for forty days, and that it was followed by banquetings in Holyrood which lasted for three days. But there was certainly a banquet there, and it would be to adorn the banquet that the fourteen men carried the 'blak lady' from the lists to the Abbey, as recorded above. After praising the lavishness of the feast, Pitscottie tells of a quaint final episode concerning the negress. 'Betuix everie service thair was ane phairs or ane play', some of them merely spoken but some contrived by 'Igromancie', 'quhilk causit men to sie thingis aper quhilk was nocht'.[1] The characteristic of the 'phairs' was not the same as that of a modern farce. It was rather the introduction of an ingenious device operated spectacularly by mechanical means.[2] In this instance, at the final banquet on the third day, a cloud was made to descend from the roof of the hall; it opened, and 'cleikkit up the blak lady in presence of thame all, that scho was no moir seine'. This 'farce' was devised for the King's pleasure, says Pitscottie, by Bishop Andrew Forman, 'quha was ane Igromancier'. Doubts have been cast upon this part of the chronicler's story, but there seems to be a peep afforded into the mechanical arrangements behind the scenes by an entry in the Accounts on 27th June 1508 'for bukkilling and grathing of Martin and the blak lady agane the bancat'.[3]

There was, however, in court circles, a much more ingenious contriver than the Bishop of Moray. John Damian, Abbot of Tungland, has been referred to more than once in the preceding pages, and, since this chapter deals largely with 'sculduddry', it will be convenient to close with a consideration of this remarkable foreigner and of the two poems which Dunbar wrote about him and his experiment in flight.

Damian appears in the Treasurers' Accounts from 1501-2 as a physician, described as 'Maister Johne the Franch leich' or 'medicinar', expenses being incurred on his behalf for a pestle and mortar,

[1] Pitscottie, p. 243. [2] Mill, p. 77.
[3] T.A., IV, p. 129.

drugs, urinals, and the like. It was no doubt the King's interest in medicine and surgery which in the first instance made him Damian's patron. But the Frenchman's studies in natural science went further, to include chemistry and alchemy. In 1502, payments are recorded for saltpetre and coals, and later for glass flagons 'and stuf', at the King's command. In 1503, at Stirling, he received a sum of money, probably 'to multiply'.[1] The King was interested in the pursuit of the 'quinta essentia', the transmutation of other substances to gold, and the chemical multiplying of gold into more gold. Bishop Leslie says ungraciously that Damian, an Italian, 'was sa disceitful, and had sa craftie and curious ingin to begyl, that he persuadet the king of his gret cunning in al thing natural, cheiflie in that politik arte, quhilk quha knawis tha cal him an alcumist; bot his intentioun only was to milk purses'.[2] The Accounts, on 27th July 1507, state that a large sum has been 'lent be the Kingis command to the Abbot of Tungland, and can nocht be gotten fra him.'[3] Damian's servants were often sent abroad on his business, and he himself went for some months in 1502,[4] probably to keep in touch with kindred spirits on the Continent. But Damian knew also the ways of the court. He could take a hand at cards with the King.[5] James bestowed his favours generously, and Damian was appointed Abbot of Tungland, in Galloway, early in 1504.[6] Dunbar was not the only rival whom Damian thus outdistanced. His enemies must have been many. Being hated by all, says Leslie, the Abbot tried in the autumn of 1507[7] to gain favour with the King and the nobility. Perhaps the disappearance of the sum of money which, presumably spent on the attempt to multiply it, the Treasurer had failed in June to regain from Damian, had cooled the King's regard for him. Damian now let it be known that on a stated day he would fly through the air from Stirling Castle and reach France before the ambassadors who had left for that country, or were due to leave for it, on the 27th September.

Dunbar's first extant reference to the projected flight of the Abbot is the poem called, by Laing, *The Birth of Antichrist*.[8] It is an ironical forecast of the monstrous consequences to be expected

[1] T.A., II, pp. 395, 144, 139. [2] Leslie, II, p. 125.
[3] T.A., III, p. 406. [4] ib., II, p. 149.
[5] ib., II, p. 138. [6] ib., II, pp. 422, 423.
[7] Leslie, p. 125; Michel, p. 315; Gairdner, *Memorials*, p. 105.
[8] 'Lucina schynnyng in silence of the nicht.' B., f. 133; MF., p. 334; R., f. 42. B. omits line 40. Hailes called the poem, *Dream*.

from the flight, combined with an attempt to exploit the approaching fiasco for purposes of personal advancement.

The poem opens beautifully in a smooth and quiet rhythm. The poet is so oppressed with heavy thought that no sleep has come to his bed; and as he watches Lucina, the star associated with childbirth, shining tranquilly through the silent night, he complains of his adverse fortune. At length he falls into a light sleep, and dreams that Dame Fortune stands before him, coldly reminding him that the movement of her wheel is inexorable. Soon, she says, his troubles will end and his fortunes rise; but he will not prosper, and the eagerly sought benefice will not be gained, until an abbot clad in feathers flies up into the air among the cranes. There the abbot will meet a she-dragon, with Lucina's aid beget Antichrist in the clouds, and in company with Simon Magus, Mahound, Merlin and a band of witches on broomsticks—a horde truly medieval in its heterogeneity—will descend to earth to preach the tenets of Antichrist. Needless to say, this world will then end.

Having delivered this enigmatic message, Dame Fortune withdraws, her irony a little lost upon the poet, who can scarcely feel comforted that his fortunes must depend on such fantasies as a human flight up into the air. When he awakes, he keeps his dream secret until he hears that unquestionably an abbot is about to make a flight, and that his coat of feathers is already made. Then the poet's heart is comforted and he knows his luck will mend, since an abbot is to fly above the moon, or, which in point of probability is equivalent, two moons will be seen in the sky.

On the appointed day, 'From all partes mony gatheris to se that sycht. Ye the king amang the rest to recreat his mynd wald se gif he war sinceir. To be schort, the day cumis; to baith his schouders he couples his wings, that of dyvers foulis he had prouydet, fra the hicht of the castel of Sterling as he wald tak Jornay, he makis him to flie up in the air; bot or he was weil begun, his veyage was at an end, for this deceiuer fel doun with sik a dade, that the bystanders wist not, quhither tha sulde mair meine his dolour, or meruel of his dafrie. Al rinis to visit him, tha ask the Abbot with his wings how he did. He ansuers that his thich bane is brokne, and he hopet neuer to gang agane; al war lyk to cleiue of lauchter, that quha lyk another Jcarus wald now flie to hevin, rycht now lyk another Simon Magus mycht nott sett his fute to the Erde. This notable Abbot, seing himselfe in sik derisioun, to purge his crime, and mak al cleine, the wyte he lays on the wings, that tha war not uttirlie egle fethiris bot sum cok and capoune fethiris, sais he, war amang thame, nocht conuenient to that use. In rest and quyetnes, this was, and hitherto hes bene a sport to lauch at in mirrines throuch al Scotland.'[1]

Dunbar's account of John Damian's enterprise is in *Ane ballat of the fenyeit freir of tungland how he fell in the myre fleand to turkiland*,[2] a scurrilous piece. In traditional fashion Dunbar falls into a dream at dawn. As a preliminary to the main narrative, he relates what he sees of Damian's former hisory. The abbot is declared to be a Turk in origin. To medieval Christendom, Mahound was synonymous with the Devil. Having reached Lombardy as a vagabond, Damian is represented as having slain a friar and clothed himself in the religious habit of the dead man, thus avoiding the ordeal of baptism. Dunbar, as has been seen, knew much of life in the garb of a friar. Being able to read and write, Damian supported the disguise successfully for a time, and affected to apply himself to medical science, for which Bologna was famous. The deception being discovered, he fled to France, where he posed as a physician until he became too notorious for the energy with which he severed the veins of his patient victims. Again a fugitive, he came to Scotland, with equally dire effect on those who trusted in his skill, though Dunbar now rather inconsistently refers to his talents, marking him down as a Jew and the progeny of giants. His laxatives would kill a stallion, and a thief thus treated would certainly be spared the gallows. It was no laughing matter when he opened the chest in his surgery, full of instruments of slaughter. For one night's attendance he would exact a horse as payment, together with the sick man's very hide—a statement which prompts the thought that Damian's scientific research may have included anatomy as well as aeronautics, and that he found means of obtaining in this way the material for dissection. But besides his extortionate charges, Damian is blamed by the poet for other social misdemeanours not entirely unexpected in the natural scientist. The sound of the church bell failed to bring him forth to mass, prelate though he was, and he easily dispensed with matins. His attire was not of

[1] Leslie, II, p.125.

[2] 'As yung Aurora with cristall haile.' B., f. 117, thus entitled. Asloan MS., f. 211b, cut short at the foot of a page, at line 69, after which a later hand has added the words, 'Cetera desunt'; the succeeding pages are lost.

clerical dignity: instead of wearing stole or maniple, he preferred to strip for sport at the anvil, 'battering at the study', or perhaps he was at his mysterious work in lurid flames and smoke, which Dunbar considers a suitable environment for him.

According to Dunbar, the failure of the Abbot in his chemical experiments with 'quinta essentia' caused the adventurer to try to make good by undertaking the desperate enterprise of flying—with poetic exaggeration—to Turkey. And so, clad in coat of feathers, he mounts on high to the wonderment of the birds, that speculate with mythological precision as to this intruder in their element. As the birds pass to active resentment and collect from all quarters of the sky for the attack on the Abbot, Dunbar's mood and his verse quicken to a fierce glee. The sky becomes dark with the multitude of birds. The hooded crows tear forth the impostor's hair, a kestrel has him by either ear, and the buzzard snatches at him more indelicately. In the extremity of physical torture, the bird-man puts in jeopardy, in accordance with Dunbar's usual style of invective, a hundred cattle that graze below. When the poet's extensive ornithological knowledge has been sufficiently exhibited, the Abbot contrives to slip from his coat of feathers. Leaving it to be torn to pieces by the birds, he plunges up to the eyes in a swamp where he hides from their vigilance three days 'amang the dukis'. Such is the clamour of the disappointed birds that the poet awakes from his dream. He has never since ceased to curse them, so overpowering is his sense of the ridiculous when he calls to mind their attack.

When Damian leapt from Stirling Castle in the attempt to fly, he deserved more than the derision of an outraged ecclesiastic and of a jealous rival. His venture is worthy to be included in the history of aeronautics. It can scarcely have been unrehearsed or carelessly planned. Michel suggests that Damian may even have known something of Leonardo da Vinci's work on the possibility of human flight.[1] The records show that King James continued his favour and close friendship towards this pioneer of aero-technology. On 13th October 1507, the Abbot of Tungland received a puncheon of wine with which to make the elusive 'quinta essentia', and several cakes of glass at Christmas. He is recorded as playing cards with the King in November and December, and dicing with the King to the Abbot's gain. In February 1507-8, he obtained more material for

[1] Michel, p. 332.

alchemy. In March he spent an evening with the King in the hall of Holyroodhouse, shooting with the culverin, and again winning money from James; and he engaged the King again in this sport, with like result, in the hall at Stirling in April. Two months later he received, without doubt for experimental purposes, a gallon of 'aqua vitae'.[1] In September he obtained the King's permission to leave the realm for five years to study, without prejudice to his abbacy at Tungland.[2] But he was back in 1513, receiving money in March for expenses in connexion with a project at Crawford for mining gold.[3]

[1] T.A., IV, pp. 79, 83, 89, 91, 101, 103, 111, 112, 122.
[2] Livingstone, I, p. 259.
[3] T.A., IV, p. 408.

CHAPTER XIV

'BUKIS EFTER OUR AWIN SCOTTIS USE'

THE succession of payments made to Dunbar, as recorded in the Treasurers' Accounts, has been followed to the 12th November 1507, when the pension due to him in terms of the Privy Seal authorisation of 1500 was increased from £10 a year to £20 a year. The increase may be regarded as measuring the enhancement of the esteem in which Dunbar was held. His remuneration was still much below the equivalent of the benefice of £40 a year or more which it was intended ultimately to award him, as stated in the grant under the Privy Seal. But even if the additional sums which he received now and again, and the various perquisites in kind which would fall to him at court, are neglected, his income was no mean sum. When Dunbar's pension amounted to only £10 a year, it was equivalent, according to the editor of the Exchequer Rolls,[1] to the salary paid at court in 1499 to such officials as the clerk of accounts, the King's steward, the steward of the household, Ormond and Kintyre pursuivants, and the King's butcher, tailor, furrier, head cook, barber, and cutler. When his pension was raised in 1507 to £20 a year, Dunbar had more than was received in 1499 by any official of the royal household except the principal keeper of the King's silver vessels, who also was paid £20 a year. Hector Boece, when he became Principal of King's College, Aberdeen, in 1498, received from Bishop Elphinstone a salary of 40 merks,[2] which was equivalent, if we take relative values to be as stated by the editor of the Rolls, to £27″6″8d. (Scots) a year.

Dunbar was therefore of some consequence at court. He would be expected to provide poetry to celebrate outstanding ceremonial events in the royal circle. Such an event occurred in the summer of 1508, when King James was visited by Lord Bernard Stewart of Aubigny, ambassador from the King of France. Aubigny was a leading soldier, with a European reputation won in Italy in the wars of the French against the Spaniards. Besides Aubigny in Berri, he held

[1] Burnett, E.R., XI, p. xxxvii. [2] Dr. W. D. Simpson, p. 9.

fiefs in Italy and Normandy. He came of a family of soldiers of fortune. Grandson of a Renfrewshire knight, Sir John Stewart of Darnley, who had risen in the French service, Bernard followed his father as Captain of the Scots Guard. Once before, in the previous reign, he had come as an ambassador from France to Scotland, and had later fought at Bosworth in command of the French allies of Henry Tudor. In spite of recurring ill-health he had campaigned with distinction in Italy against the Great Captain, Gonsalvo de Cordova, had experienced the vicissitudes of fortune undergone by the French arms, and had been Viceroy of Naples and Governor of Calabria.[1] He came to Scotland in 1508 at a critical time in European affairs, to confirm the French alliance and obtain Scottish support for the League of Cambrai. Having travelled through England with a large following, Aubigny arrived in Edinburgh on 9th May, according to Pitscottie, who, however, as we have seen, mistakes the year as 1505.[2] On the 12th, rich presents were exchanged with King James.[3] Aubigny was accompanied by the President of the Parlement of Paris.[4] James set him at his own table, says Pitscottie.[5] The repetition on 31st May, in his presence, of the 1507 tournament of the 'blak lady' has already been described.

Dunbar's poem was composed in honour of the illustrious soldier on his arrival in Scotland. *The Ballade of Lord Barnard Stewart, Lord of Aubigny*[6] is extant only in the volume of prints of 1508 or shortly after, from the press of Chapman and Millar, and is incomplete. Its ceremonial character is heralded by the high-sounding title: 'The ballade of ane right noble victorious and myghty lord Barnard stewart lord of Aubigny erle of Beaumont roger and bonaffre consaloure and chamerlane ordinare to the maist hee maist excellent and maist crystyn prince Loys king of france knyght of his ordoure Capitane of the kepyng of his body Conquereur of Naplis and umquhile constable general of the same Compilit be Maistir Willyam dumbar at the said lordis cumyng to Edinburghe in Scotland send in ane ryght excellent embassat fra the said maist crystin King to our maist Souverane lord and victorious prince James the ferde Kynge of Scottis.'

The poem owes to the circumstances of its composition, and to

[1] Michel, pp. 274-287. [2] Pitscottie, p. 242. [3] T.A., IV, pp. 117, 118.
[4] Mackay and Burnett, E.R., XIII, p. lv. [5] Pitscottie, p. 241.
[6] 'Renownit, ryall, right reverend, and serene.' CM., p. 171. The fragment ends at the foot of p. 174.

the official character of the sentiments expressed, its absence of the shrewd thought and homely directness of expression which are the salt of Dunbar's best works. It is an entirely laudatory poem and, deprived of its accompaniments of trumpets and blazonries, loses much, there being little in it of intrinsic interest, so formal is the language of ceremonial welcome. But there is a noteworthy pride in the fame of a great Scotsman. As the poem progresses, Aubigny is likened in succession to Achilles, Hector, Arthur, Agamemnon, Hannibal, and Julius Caesar, and an outline of his horoscope enumerates the favours showered on him by various classical deities. Lest he should be prolix, the poet refrains from describing Aubigny's victories in France and Italy, but announces that he intends to narrate them at length and with diligence before Aubigny departs from Scotland. If this undertaking was fulfilled, no trace of it remains. The fragment concludes with an array of complimentary epithets, beginning with the successive letters of the name 'Bernard', and Laing surmises that the lost continuation dealt with Aubigny's surname similarly. It cannot be claimed that the poem rises to grandeur nor that it is too short. The classical allusions are not without ingenuity, and the diction and metrical effects have dignity, but Dunbar's Muse, on this occasion, has not had the scope for a characteristic utterance.

The festive mood of the court and city was quickly changed to mourning. Shortly after his arrival, Aubigny fell suddenly ill, and died on the 11th June.[1] On the 15th, King James made an offering 'at my Lord Awbignes saule mess'.[2] The veteran's heart was buried at the shrine of St. Ninian at Whithorn, to which he had vowed long before that he would make pilgrimage.

Aubigny was struck down at the height of his fame, and in the midst of the proud rejoicings at his homecoming. Dunbar marked the occasion with his *Elegy on the Death of Bernard Stewart, Lord of Aubigny*.[3] It has been well said[4] that this sudden recoil of fate was of a nature to appeal to a poet whose work shows a sense of the uncertainty of human life. There is in the *Elegy* much ornate eulogy, as in the preceding poem of welcome, but the poem of mourning is fittingly short, and does convey the impression of personal feeling. The loss to King Louis, the monarch whom Aubigny has served so

[1] E.R., XIII, p. 123. [2] T.A., IV, p. 42.
[3] 'Illuster Lodovick, of France most Cristin king.' R., f. 6. The title is Laing's.
[4] Mackay, S.T.S., I, p. cviii.

conspicuously, is shared by all who esteem valour and nobility of soul. Why has gloomy Death set his hand on such a peerless leader? All who loved him must intercede with God for him; but especially all of Scots birth, whom he always trusted most, will make their orisons on his behalf, for he was the flower of chivalry.

Dunbar's position at court in 1508 shows that he was a man of note, and his poetic address of welcome to the Lord of Aubigny that he was active in maintaining his position. It is not surprising, then, that about the same time, almost certainly in the same year, he had the further honour of figuring prominently in the poetical prints published—some of them, at least—in 1508 and forming the first extant productions of the printing-press in Scotland. Walter Chapman and Andrew Millar, the Edinburgh burgesses who undertook the important venture of introducing printing into this country, did so at the request of the King, who granted them a patent on 15th September 1507. They had agreed 'to furnis and bring hame ane prent, with all stuff belangand tharto, and expert men to use the samyne.' They were to print the laws, Acts of Parliament, chronicles, mass-books 'efter our awin scottis use', and other publications, and sell them at suitable prices.[1]

Walter Chapman was a merchant of substance, trading with foreign parts in wood and textiles especially. He had also been a notary for many years, engaged in secretarial work for the King, with whose signet he was entrusted. In this work he was closely associated with the King's secretary, Patrick Panther, and with Sir John Rede or Stobo, who was also one of the King's writers. Stobo we have met already in *The Flyting of Dunbar and Kennedie*, and Dunbar had included 'gud gentill Stobo' among the deceased poets in his *Lament: Quhen he wes Sek*.[2] It has been surmised[3] that Stobo was the link in bringing together Dunbar and Chapman, and in securing the inclusion of several of Dunbar's poems among the pieces printed by Chapman. But Stobo died in 1505, and in any case the supposition is needless, for Chapman and Dunbar could scarcely fail to be well known to each other. Chapman's part in the printing enterprise was that of general business management, and especially the arrangements for initial expenses and for importing the plant and experts, the technical details being in the hands of Andrew Millar, an experienced printer. One of Chapman's pro-

[1] Dickson, pp. 9, 94. [2] See Appendix V. [3] Mackay, S.T.S., I. p. xliii.

perties in the Southgait—now the Cowgate—at the foot of Blackfriars Wynd, was brought into use as the printing premises.[1]

Andrew Millar appears in the Treasurer's Accounts in March 1503[2] as supplying several Latin works to the King, but between that date and 1507 he was evidently in Rouen, engaged in the printing trade. The city was at that time an acknowledged printing centre, and its typographical foundries supplied many other cities with a type recognisably Norman. English liturgical works were printed at Rouen for the London booksellers. Such a book, with a colophon dated 10th June 1506, and entitled *Expositio Sequentiarum*, contains the same device bearing the name 'Androv myllar' as was later used by Millar in the prints he produced in Scotland. It represents a miller ascending the ladder of a windmill, with a sack of corn on his back, and, among other details, includes Millar's monogram and several fleurs-de-lis.[3] The town where the book was printed is not stated, but the type used appears to be that of a Rouen printer; it is disputed which printer.[4] In 1505, John Garland's *Multorum Vocabulorum Equivocorum Interpretatio* has a colophon stating that its printer and reviser was 'Andreas Myllar Scotus'[5]; again the town is not indicated, but the type is apparently that of a printer of Rouen.[6] Millar would, therefore, when backed by Walter Chapman's capital, be a very suitable person to make arrangements abroad 'to furnis and bring hame ane prent, with all stuff belangand tharto, and expert men to use the samyne'. The device of Walter Chapman, on the Scottish prints, is itself imitative of that of a Parisian printer and may have been brought to this country by Millar.[7]

One of the main aims of the Scottish printing concern was to print the Aberdeen Breviary for Bishop Elphinstone. The first volume of it was printed in Edinburgh at the expense of Walter Chapman in February 1509-10, and the second volume likewise in June 1510, but Millar does not figure at all in these works. Still more surprising, perhaps, is the omission of any reference to Millar when, early in 1510, Chapman appealed to the Privy Council against an infringement of the privileges granted to him and Millar by the letters of patent of 1507. It is reasonable to conclude that Millar

[1] Dickson, p. 17. [2] T.A., II, p. 364. [3] Dickson, pp. 83, 78, 32, 44.
[4] ib., p. 32. Gordon Duff, *Edinburgh Bibliographical Society Publications*, Vol. I (1896), No. 13. Stevenson, p. xviii.
[5] Dickson, p. 39. [6] Duff, op. cit. [7] Dickson, pp. 44, 69.

had died before 1510. Chapman lived for many years more, but nothing is extant from his printing-press with a date later than that of the Breviary,[1] from which date there is a long gap in Scottish printing.

Before printing the Breviary, however, Chapman and Millar had issued the separate poetic prints in quarto—some of them containing several poems—which, discovered in the form of a bound volume in Ayrshire in 1785 and presented to the Advocates' Library, have been mounted and rebound and form the volume now in the National Library.[2] Six of Dunbar's poems are included, and also the poem *Kynd Kittok* which, without any valid reason, has been attributed to Dunbar.[3] Three of the prints, the first, second, and sixth, which do not include poems of Dunbar, bear colophons dated 20th April, 8th April, and 4th April respectively, all of the year 1508, but the other prints are undated. The fourth print consists of Dunbar's *Goldyn Targe*, with the device of Andrew Millar below the concluding lines of its last page. The seventh print opens with a fragment of *The Flyting of Dunbar and Kennedie*, followed immediately by two other poems, after which the device of Andrew Millar occurs overleaf at the close of the whole print. The ninth print consists of the unfinished *The Ballade of Lord Barnard Stewart*, with the device of 'Walterus Chepman' on the same page as the lengthy title, and after that poem are three blank leaves, on the last page of which appears the device of 'Androv myllar'. The tenth print begins, after three blank leaves, with the later portion of Dunbar's *The Tretis of the Tua Mariit Wemen and the Wedo*, and, after its conclusion, proceeds without heading to Dunbar's *Lament: Quhen he wes Sek*, each poem being attributed to Dunbar in its own colophon. The anonymous *Kynd Kittok* follows on immediately without title, and the print concludes with Dunbar's *The Tesment of Maister Andro Kennedy*, without heading and without attribution to Dunbar.

It is clear from the colophons of the first, second, and sixth prints that the order of the prints in the volume is not the chronological order of printing. Some writers have assumed too readily that the undated prints are contemporary with those that are dated. The ninth print, consisting of *The Ballade of Barnard Stewart*, cannot

[1] Dickson, pp. 71, 74.

[2] Reprinted and edited for the S.T.S. by G. Stevenson, in 1918. The earlier reproduction by Laing appeared in 1827. A photographed facsimile, edited by Mr. William Beattie, was published in 1950.

[3] Stevenson (p. 303) speaks of *Kynd Kittok* as Dunbar's, but see Appendix IV, No. 8.

have been printed in April 1508, for Stewart did not arrive in Edinburgh until 9th May. On the other hand, the interest of the poem depending largely on the occasion which it celebrates, it is unlikely that this print was much later than May. For this, as well as for the fourth and seventh print, the presence of the device of Andrew Millar makes it possible to conclude that the prints were issued before January 1509-10, when Millar was presumably dead; and on the other hand they are most unlikely to have been issued earlier than April 1508, as letters patent were granted to Chapman and Millar in September 1507, and they had their material and experts to fetch from abroad, and their plant to set up, before issues could begin. The position is not so clear, however, as to the dating of *The Tretis of the Tua Mariit Wemen and the Wedo*, the *Lament: Quhen he wes Sek*, and *The Tesment of Maister Andro Kennedy*, for this print does not bear the device of Andrew Millar and might therefore be later than 1509. Further, it has been doubted whether this tenth print and the eleventh are from the Scottish press at all. It is unnecessary here to consider the question of the eleventh, which does not include works by Dunbar. As to the tenth print, Dickson states that it is printed with the same type as is found in many parts of the *Expositio Sequentiarum* of 1506, and that this tenth print is therefore to be attributed to the press of Andrew Millar when he was still abroad,[1] at a date earlier than September 1507. There appears, however, to be no good ground for casting doubt on the authenticity of the tenth print as a Scottish issue. Dickson himself states that the first nine prints of the volume are printed with types genuinely Norman in character, though probably cut specially for the Scottish press; and, indeed, this Norman characteristic of the type used in Edinburgh is only to be expected in view of the typographical importance of Rouen. If the device and name of Andrew Millar did not appear in the foreign *Expositio* of 1506, we might reasonably assume that the tenth print, printed in the same type as the *Expositio*, was itself foreign. But Andrew Millar himself provides a sufficient explanation of the whole matter. In his hands lay the task, in September 1507, of setting about 'to furnis and bring hame ane prent, with all stuff belangand tharto'. If he brought from abroad, as part of the 'prent', type he had apparently used for the *Expositio Sequentiarum* or a type modelled on it—and he is quite likely to have done so—then there is no reason

[1] Dickson, p. 52. Stevenson (p. xviii) is non-committal.

to assume that our tenth print is foreign, and therefore no reason to assume that the three poems contained in it by Dunbar were printed before 1508, though they may, as already suggested, have been printed after 1509.

CHAPTER XV

'PENSIOUN MOST PRECLAIR'

THE increase of Dunbar's pension on 12th November 1507 from £10 to £20 a year was followed by further good fortune, but not until years had elapsed. On the 15th March 1507-8 he received an extra payment apart from the terms of his pension: 'Item to maister William Dunbar be the kingis command—v lib.'[1] The entry occurs among the 'Bursa Regis' payments. On the 15th June 1508, or soon after, he was awarded the usual payment of pension: 'Item to maister William Dunbar his pensioun of the said term—x lib.'[2] This was the month following the poem of welcome which he composed for the arrival of Lord Bernard Stewart, and also the month following the second tournament of the 'blak lady' whom he celebrated. On the 11th June, Aubigny had died, and Dunbar had written a fitting elegy. Almost certainly, some of his poetry, particularly *The Ballade of Lord Barnard Stewart*, had just been awarded the distinction of being printed. On the 26th he received an additional sum of £3″10/-: 'Item the xxvi of Junij to maister william Dunbar be the kingis command—iii lib. x s.'[3] When he was in this comparatively happy position, Dunbar disappears from the records for some time, for all payments came to him through the Lord Treasurer, whose accounts are not extant from 8th August 1508 to 25th August 1511. But in the interval much greater prosperity had come to him, his pension being raised from £20 a year to the very large sum of £80 a year, on 26th August 1510.

The record is in the Privy Seal Register: 'A lettre maid to maister William Dunbar of the gift of ane yerely pensioun of iiiixx lib. to be pait to him at mertymes and Witsonday of the kingis

[1] Printed *Accounts*, IV, p. 106. MS. *Compot. Thesaur.*, 1507-8, f. 81b. The fourth item back is dated 15th March, and the fifth succeeding entry has the date 16th March.

[2] Referred to, only, in the printed *Accounts*, IV, p. 69. MS. *Compot. Thesaur.*, 1507-8, f. 61 b. The third item back is dated 15th June, and refers to 'the terme of Witsonday'; the next dated entry, the eleventh succeeding, is of 4th July.

[3] Printed *Accounts*, IV, p. 127. MS. *Compot. Thesaur.*, 1507-8, f. 94.

cofferis be the thesaurare that now is and beis for the tyme or quhill he be promovit to benefice of 100 lib. or abone etc. with command to the said thesaurare to pay[1] the sammyn and to the auditouris of chakker to allow etc. at edinburgh the xxvi day of august the yere forsaid. Per signaturam.'[2] The 'yere forsaid' is specified four entries back[3] as the twenty-third year of the reign. This year began on 11th June 1510,[4] so that the award to Dunbar was on 26th August 1510. As in the case of the original grant of 1500, the word 'gratis', written beside the entry, shows that Dunbar was not charged the usual registration fee when given the sealed writ. The reason on this occasion would certainly not be poverty, but the fee was often waived as a personal favour, or in deference to an influential patron. Bishop Elphinstone, Keeper of the Privy Seal, had instructions in the form of a letter bearing the royal signature, as is shown by the words 'per signaturam'.[5] The poet could now look forward to years of affluence, whether as recipient of the £80 pension or, failing that, as incumbent in a benefice of £100 or more. The degree of Dunbar's good fortune may once again be measured by a comparison. The pension which was given under the Privy Seal to the celebrated Hector Boece, Principal of King's College, Aberdeen, in 1527, amounted to £50 a year.[6]

As the Treasurer's Accounts are not extant for this period, it is impossible to be sure of the first date of payment under the new arrangement, but normally payment of £40 would be made at Martinmas, and the poet would be comfortably provided before Christmas. The Lord Treasurer at Martinmas 1510 was Andrew Stewart, Bishop of Caithness and Commendator of Kelso Abbey.

This first payment seems to have been the occasion for the poem, *Welcom, My Awin Lord Thesaurair*,[7] expressing gratitude or confident expectation. The poet has been despondent while waiting for the homecoming of a certain lord from whom he hopes to claim a favour, and whose propitious name he is happy to disclose:

Welcom, my awin Lord Thesaurair!

Dunbar's salute to him is more heartfelt than to any other man of

[1] The word 'allow' has been written originally but struck through, and, in the same ink as the original, 'pay' has been written above.
[2] Livingstone, I, p. 323. MS. *Reg. Secr. Sig. Regum Scot.*, IV 1508-1513, f. 80b.
[3] MS. *Reg. Secr. Sig. Regum Scot.*, IV, 1508-1513, f. 80.
[4] Sir A. H. Dunbar, p. 222. [5] Livingstone, I, p. viii. [6] ib., p. 565.
[7] 'I thocht lang quhill sum lord come hame.' R., f. 5b.

rank[1] except his royal master. He sought payment of a noble sum from the Treasurer, who promised to return at an early date to Edinburgh. The Treasurer fulfilled his tryst so punctually that Dunbar considers him true as steel, and is sure that none needs to despair of payment from him. The poet has been perturbed lest the Treasurer should take the shortest route from Stirling to the circuit courts of justice, instead of coming to Edinburgh on the way. In that case Dunbar would have lacked his wage until Christmas and his poem would have been doleful, whereas now he sings with carefree heart. He gives a joyful welcome to his benefice, his 'rent', and all the substance bestowed upon him—in particular, to his illustrious pension.

The crux is in the penultimate stanza:

> Welcum, my benefice, and my rent,
> And all the lyflett to me lent;
> Welcum, my pensioun most preclair;
>   Welcum, my awin Lord Thesaurair!

This seems at first sight to mean that Dunbar has received both benefice and pension. But there is ambiguity, and Schipper takes the lines to mean only that Dunbar is reminding the Treasurer of his promise and calling him his benefice and rent and pension.[2]

The joy expressed in the poem is too emphatic to be thus explained. No mean gift was welcomed in such language. By 'rent' he presumably means the stipend of a benefice. The stipend would not come to him through the Treasury, nor would the benefice itself. But the pension of £80 a year would come to him through the Treasurer and could very well be called the 'pensioun most preclair', in comparison with the smaller sums the poet had received previously. On the other hand, both pension and benefice would not be granted. The royal coffers were not so overflowing that, contrary to the express injunction in the King's warrant under the Privy Seal, both benefice and pension would at the same time be given him. On receipt of the benefice, the pension would stop. Dunbar probably means that he is overjoyed at the payment of pension just received or about to be received, and that the pension is all the benefice and 'rent' and substance that he possesses. It is not the Treasurer, but the pension, that he is addressing

[1] The word 'raik' in line 5 is obscure in the MS. It seems to be an alteration from 'rink'. M. suggests it may be derived from 'rike' (rich, powerful).

[2] S. ed., p. 229.

in the first two lines of the stanza as in the third line; the fourth line is the refrain to which the poet has adhered throughout the poem.

In view of Dunbar's appeal *To the King: God gif ye war Johne Thomsounis Man*, it would be interesting to know how far, if at all, the King's munificence to Dunbar was due to the influence of Queen Margaret, with whose household his poems show him to have been closely concerned. At any rate, not long after he received his new rate of pension, Dunbar is found celebrating, as an eye-witness, the Queen's ceremonial entry into the burgh of Aberdeen in May 1511. The King does not appear to have been with her. It was the Queen's first visit to the town, which was probably the second in the kingdom.

The port of Aberdeen had a busy trade in wool with the Low Countries and the Hansa towns, and imported wine and other luxuries from France. Its merchants and craftsmen were organised and led an active corporate life. Bishop Elphinstone had given the town some distinction in the world of letters with the foundation of King's College and the printing of the Aberdeen Breviary. The magistrates determined to welcome the Queen in such a manner as to do honour to the town. Elaborate preparations were made, and Dunbar's poem supplements in its details the records of the town council. The provost, bailies, and council, took measures for the cleansing of the town 'agane the quenys cumming'. On the 30th April it was decreed that the bellman should go through the town and charge all persons who had middens on the road in front of their gates and doors to remove them, on pain of a fine, before the following Sunday. Each of the town officers was to take two witnesses with him, and, in his own quarter of the town, see that the main street was cleared of all pigsties, on pain of forfeiting the pigs as well as of paying a fine. A few days later, the provost, bailies, council, and burgesses, warned by the handbell, met and unanimously decided 'to ressave oure soverane lady the queyne als honorablie as ony burgh of Scotland except Edinburgh allanerlie'. At the same time a committee was set up to raise some £200, for a gift to the Queen, on certain leases and fishing-rights belonging to the town. Further measures were taken to 'clenye the toune of all myddingis'.[1] On the 10th May it was decreed that outside stairs should be hung with arras, and that 'personis that bringis ony byrkis,

[1] *Extracts from the Burgh Records of Aberdeen*, 1398-1570, p. 81.

holingis, gyrss, herbis, or ony uthir grene flouris, haf common passage, and sal haue fre mony and redy silver for the samyn'.[1] That these were not the only preparations is shown by Dunbar's poem, which is concerned mainly with the dramatic spectacles produced for the occasion. There is no mention of these pageants in the burgh records; they would be the work of the craft gilds, not of the town council. The town records show that religious plays were performed by the crafts at Aberdeen in the preceding century. But it has been pointed out that the organising of pageants for royal visitors was customary at the time, and that, so long as no important innovations were involved, the burgh records would not require to take cognizance of such preparations.[2]

In *The Queen's Reception in Aberdeen*,[3] Dunbar hails Aberdeen as the beryl of all towns, renowned for its virtue and wisdom. It is suited to receive the illustrious young queen. He relates the incidents witnessed at the ceremony. The Queen was met by the burgesses, richly attired, having chosen from among them four young men of note, dressed in gowns of velvet, to bear the customary canopy of crimson velvet above her head. The artillery gave her a royal salute. Wearing a cap of silk and gold, she was received at the gates by a brilliant procession, and, as she proceeded through the streets, a succession of pageants provided entertainment. The Salutation of the Virgin was performed first. The music of minstrels rose to the sky. A representation followed of how the Three Kings of the East humbly presented to the infant Christ their gifts of gold and frankincense and myrrh, acknowledging him as their King. The next pageant showed the expulsion of Adam and Eve by the sworded angel. After that came the valiant Bruce, riding on horseback with crown on head, a magnificent figure of martial strength. A blank in the manuscript leaves unknown the nature of the next performance, but Laing may be right in supplying the words 'nobill Stewarts'; bearing green branches, they made a glorious show, to the delight of the citizens. A band of four and twenty maidens, beautiful in their mantles of green, came next, their golden hair in plaits, and their white hats bravely embroidered. They played on

[1] *Extracts from the Burgh Records of Aberdeen*, 1398-1570, p. 70. These entries are wrongly dated 1501 instead of 1511; but the error is pointed out by the editor himself in the 'errata', in the list of contents, and in his preface.

[2] Mill, pp. 62, 99-100.

[3] 'Blyth Aberdeane, thow beriall of all tounis.' R., f. 7. Laing headed the poem *The Queinis Reception at Aberdein*.

timbrels and sang most sweetly in welcome to the Queen, saluting her with reverence.[1]

The streets, Dunbar says, were all hung with tapestry. The pigs and middens had evidently disappeared. A great gathering of the lieges greeted the Queen respectfully, while the pageants proceeded. Great barons and fair ladies formed her escort, and the commons hailed her with a great shout. At the Cross, wine ran in abundance. Convoyed to her lodging by the citizens, who left nothing undone to honour her, the Queen was presented with a rich gift, a costly cup filled with gold coin. In conclusion, Dunbar bids the Queen never to forget the honours paid her by the noble burgh.

At the time of this visit to Aberdeen, in May 1511, the poet would be expecting the Whitsuntide instalment of his first year's pension at the new rate. It has already been said that the accounts of the Lord Treasurer are not extant for the period from 8th August 1508 to 25th August 1511. As the grant of the new pension had been registered under the Privy Seal on 26th August 1510, Dunbar would draw £40 at Martinmas of that year, and another £40 in May or June 1511, on his return to Edinburgh from Aberdeen. In fact, his name appears again in the accounts rendered in August 1512 for the preceding twelve months. It is in the list of 'Annue pensiones', recording the payments of pensions for the period as a whole: 'Item to Maister William Dunbar takand termlie fourtj lib. of Martimes and Witsonday last summa—lxxx lib.'[2] From the details of successive payments made to other pensioners and recorded at the same time—'Maister James Sympsone' and 'Maister Johne Chesholme' preceding Dunbar, and 'Schir Alexander Makesone' following him—it is clear that the account was made up after Whitsuntide 1512, and that the payments to Dunbar which are thus recorded are for Martinmas 1511 and Whitsunday 1512. There is no reason to suppose that the earlier payments due had not been made with equal regularity. It is interesting to note in the same list of 'Annue Pensiones' the first payment of pension to Sir David Lindsay, at the rate of £40 a year.[3] Lindsay was involved that autumn in a dramatic entertainment at court, for we read of 'ane play coit to David Lindesay for the play playt in the King and Quenis presence

[1] The MS. says that they 'Did meit the Quein hir husband reverentlie'. As L. points out, had James indeed been present he would not have been referred to so casually. L. substituted 'saluand' for 'husband'.

[2] Printed T.A., IV, p. 268. MS. *Compot. Thesaur.*, 1511-12, f. 74b.

[3] T.A., IV, p. 269.

in the Abbay'.[1] He was in due course to become usher to the young Prince, later James V.[2]

In the same account of 1511-12 is a section dealing with liveries given to the King's henchmen and other servants, disbursements for each person being grouped together though they were separated considerably in time in some cases. Two payments are recorded to Dunbar, and would, of course, be in addition to the pension. For Christmas 1511 there is the entry: 'Item to Maister William Dunbar for his Yule leveray vj elnis ane quartar Parise blak to be hyme ane gowne price elne xl s. Summa—xii lib. x s.' Presumably this is the basis for Smeaton's fanciful statement that Dunbar 'received each year his robe of red velvet fringed with costly fur'.[3] Immediately after this Christmas entry is the record of a further allowance, for livery over and above ('attour') the Yule gown, and apparently given him before or after Christmas, but still in 1511: 'Item allowit to the said maister William attour his leveray was tane at yule in anno v^{c}xj v quartaris scarlete price—iii lib. ii s. vi d.'[4]

The Bishop presented a second account as Treasurer for the period from August to 29th October 1512. According to the editor of the Accounts it is a slovenly production, and the Bishop either resigned or was dismissed from the Treasurer's office, having proved unsatisfactory.[5] Dunbar's name does not appear in this account. The new Lord Treasurer was Cuthbert Baillie, Rector of Sanquhar and Commendator of the Abbey of Glenluce. His account was audited on 8th August 1513, not long before Flodden. Dunbar's name occurs in it several times, but does not appear in any later account. The first occasion is the payment, rather late, of his Martinmas pension: 'Item the xxiiii day of december to maister William Dunbar his mertymes fee be the Kingis command—xl lib.'[6] It was the last Christmas Eve he was to spend with his royal master. In the following year, three payments to him are recorded, but all are small. Two are in April 1513: 'Item the first day of aprile to maister William Dunbar—xlii s.' and 'Item the xiiii day of aprile gevin to maister William Dunbar—xlii s.'[7] Last of all is the entry: 'Item the xiiii day of maij to maister William Dunbar in his pen-

[1] T.A., p. 313. [2] ib., IV, p. 441. [3] Smeaton, p. 58.
[4] Printed T.A., IV, pp. 249-250. MS. *Compot. Thesaur.*, 1511-12, f. 60.
[5] Sir J. B. Paul, T.A., IV, p. xi. Mackay and Burnett, E.R., XIII, p. clii.
[6] Printed T.A., IV, p. 442. MS. *Compot. Thesaur.*, 1512-13, f. 90.
[7] MS. *Compot. Thesaur.*, 1512-13, ff. 93, 93b. Referred to in the printed T.A., IV, p. 442.

sioun—lvi s.'[1] This payment of 14th May 1513 is Dunbar's last appearance in contemporary records. The next mention of him is in 1530, when Lindsay writes of him as deceased, though it must be added that there are several extensive gaps in the records during these years.

It is tantalising that just at this point, in May 1513, we should be thus brought to a stop, a few months before Flodden. As has been said, this particular account of the Treasurer goes on to 8th August. What has happened, then, to the £40 due to Dunbar at Whitsuntide? Why was he paid only £2″16/- instead? The editor of the contemporary Exchequer Rolls attributes the smallness of the sum to the poverty of the exchequer. He also suggests that the smallness of the sum indicates the poverty of Dunbar,[2] but surely the poet should not have been in these alleged difficulties, for he had been drawing large sums regularly. The payment he did receive on the 14th May is stated to be 'in his pensioun', so that the pension had not lapsed, at least. The interval between 14th May and 8th August is quite short—too short for us to conclude that a radical change had taken place in Dunbar's position. If for some reason the extant records of the Treasurer had ended shortly before the 'Annue Pensiones' were compiled for the audit of 14th August 1512, no record would have survived of the pension payments to Dunbar of Martinmas 1511 and Whitsunday 1512, and the conclusion might have been drawn that the pension had ceased in 1511. Moreover, there are many instances in the Accounts of delay in payment of an instalment of a pension until after the close of the particular account to which it should strictly belong. The balance of Dunbar's pension due at Whitsuntide 1513 may have been paid to him in the autumn, or may have been payable but in fact unpaid because of the intervening catastrophe of Flodden. Or the drastic reduction in the figure may, on the other hand, have been final, and have had some connexion with the long-awaited benefice. But there is not sufficient evidence on which to judge, as no accounts of the Treasurer are extant for the period between 8th August 1513 and 25th June 1515. It is, however, perhaps significant that, of the beneficiaries listed in the 'Annue Pensiones' of 1511-12, the great majority either fared much worse in 1512-13 or got nothing at all in the way of pension, so that Dunbar may be considered lucky to

[1] MS. *Compot. Thesaur.*, 1512-13, f. 95. Referred to in the printed T.A., IV, p. 442.
[2] Mackay and Burnett, E.R., XIII, p. civ.

have received the £40 given him at Christmas 1512. The shadow of the approaching war is probably enough to account for the general decrease in King James's liberality in 1513.

Nominally at least, the pension was intended only to provide for Dunbar until he should be appointed to a church cure of £100 a year or more. What prospects were there of the benefice? As we have seen, he wrote much of the difficulties in his way. Benefices do not come the way of loyal followers, who have given long service to the King, but are given to flatterers and foreigners and multipliers. Sir John Kirkpakar collects benefices, and, though he has seven already, is determined to have eleven before even one shall go to a ballade-maker. Thus avaricious men increase their revenues while the burden of parish work falls on poor vicars. The ambitious cleric is not content with a bishopric but would climb to be a cardinal. Sir Bet-the-Kirk uses the parishes he controls as stakes at the gaming-table. Preference is given to Jok who once had to herd the stirks and 'muk the stabell'. Great parishes, kirks of St. Bernard and St. Bride, are given to the incapable, but Dunbar cannot obtain a kirk scantily covered with heather.

Yet there must have been many opportunities in the Church as then organised. The number of parish charges was certainly not so great as might be imagined. According to John Major, the one parish church sometimes had to serve for thirty villages, some of them as much as ten miles distant from the church, though divine service was conducted also by the household chaplains of the gentry. Major adds, however, that though the cures were few they were wealthy.[1] Under canon law the holding of a benefice with the cure of souls required residence, and therefore more than one such benefice was not to be held by the same person, but non-residence was very common in practice, with the consent of the archbishop or by papal dispensation, and the holding of benefices in plurality was rife. The favour of a lord or other landed gentleman was often enough to secure a charge for his nominee, but appointment to many benefices was largely arranged by royal influence, especially during the vacancy in a bishopric, and was a ready means of rewarding the King's clerks without cost to the exchequer.

Dunbar's reference to a kirk scantily covered with heather suggests that he would not have refused at that time even the humbler status of a vicar. The very size and wealth of a Scottish parish made

[1] Major, p. 30.

the parson disinclined, Major says, to do the work of the parish himself. It was customary to devolve the spiritual charge of the parish on a vicar, the parson or rector continuing to enjoy the whole stipend except for the provision which he made for the support of his vicar.[1] The vicar had the smaller share, and had to undertake the upkeep of the manse. But his standard of living was not so low as the meagre money allowance would, by itself, indicate. On his glebe he would be a farmer in a small way. The offerings which were customarily paid to a priest at the altar would add considerably to his income. Voluntary offerings were made at weddings, baptisms, confessions, and on many other occasions. On the day of the patron saint, at Christmas, and at Easter, an offering from every household in the parish was expected, and was scarcely voluntary any longer; nor was the corpse-present which was due on the death of a parishioner.[2] Once appointed, the vicar of a parish had permanent tenure of it.

The opportunities available for Dunbar in the Church were not limited to a parsonage or vicarage in a parish. The corporations of secular priests attached to the cathedrals and to the collegiate churches must have held out attractive prospects. Unlike the monastic houses, which were in remoter districts, the establishments of secular 'canons' were in the more important burghs and closely associated with town life. All the cathedrals except St. Andrews and Candida Casa were organised on these lines. Not being of the regular clergy, the canons had taken no 'religious' vows. They could hold private property, and each lived in his own house near the cathedral.[3] More numerous than the cathedrals were the collegiate churches, of which at the Reformation there were thirty-three, the majority dating from the fifteenth century. They included St. Giles, the Chapel Royal of Stirling, and Linlithgow. The collegiate churches followed in many respects the arrangements of the cathedrals. The chapter of canons formed a corporation under its provost, and held property in common, but each canon was also separately provided for from his 'prebend', the revenues of some parish church of which the canon was rector. St. Giles had sixteen of these prebendary canons. As in the case of other rectors of parishes, the canon placed his parish church or churches in the hands of a vicar, reserving for his own maintenance, however, the

[1] Dowden, *The Medieval Church in Scotland*, pp. 273, 60.
[2] ib., pp. 179, 181, 187. [3] ib., p. 58.

bulk of the revenues. The collegiate church and its prebends were under the control of the bishop of the diocese, but the pious laymen who founded canonries in great numbers sometimes reserved the right to present to both the prebend and the vicarage of the prebendal church. At St. Giles, presentation to the prebends lay with Edinburgh burgesses.[1] A considerable number of the churches in the land came to be in the hands of the collegiate corporations, though not on the scale achieved by the monasteries. Dowden estimates that by the early sixteenth century more than two-thirds of the parish churches were subject to the monasteries, Holyrood Abbey alone having twenty-seven parishes, and that, taking into account the parishes of the collegiate churches and of the cathedrals, probably three-fourths of the parish churches of the country were under regular or secular corporations.[2]

Restrictions had been placed upon the annexation of benefices by monasteries and cathedrals, but did not apply to collegiate churches, so that a prebend in a collegiate charge often consisted of the revenues of several parishes. Further, the same canon might hold a prebend in more than one collegiate church.[3] The canon himself was nominally resident, but even the dean had to reside for only six months of the year.[4] John Major states that 'the Scottish church possesses prebends many and fat; but such revenues are enjoyed "in absentia" just as they would be "in praesentia", which is a custom destitute of justice and of common sense.'[5] Since, however, he was supposed to reside, the canon had his own croft within the close, each house with its garden being separate.[6]

A prebend in a collegiate church would have maintained Dunbar in opulence, with dignity, leisure and comfort. If he could not reach such a 'sinecure', or could not reach it at one leap, he might still find a minor place as a 'vicar of the choir', for each canon had to provide a deputy so called, to officiate in the services of the collegiate church. The canon maintained his vicar of the choir with an allowance, which was often supplemented by the chaplaincy of one of the many endowed altars, or by a special endowment gifted for the purpose by a benefactor. The vicars of the choir outnumbered the canons who were in residence, and they had separate houses.[7]

When some of these more obvious opportunities for Dunbar in

[1] Dowden, pp. 60, 63, 108. [2] ib., p. 114. [3] ib., pp. 105, 75-76.
[4] ib., p. 75. [5] Major, p. 28. [6] Dowden, pp. 91-92. [7] ib., pp. 64-67.

the Church are reviewed, it is very difficult to believe that he could have failed in a prolonged and determined effort to obtain the benefice promised him for many years by the most influential patron in the land, King James himself. We have seen from *The Dream*[1] that he was offered a benefice on one occasion at least and refused it in hope of a better. It is hard to resist the conclusion that a main reason for his remaining so long without a church cure was the very amplitude of the pension he held in the meantime. Whether the pension of £80 a year, in 1510, was the result of his own importunity or was due to the wish of the King or of the Queen to keep Dunbar at court, its effect was to make preferment in the Church less urgent for him. It also made a benefice less likely, for, in terms of the Privy Seal grant, the benefice was to be of the value of £100 a year or more, and such churches were less numerous than those of £40, the figure stated in the original grant of pension in 1500. Dunbar's appointment to a benefice was, therefore, likely to be delayed indefinitely, if circumstances remained the same. But if some unexpected calamity were to happen—such as was approaching—and if the £80 pension were to vanish, the finding of a benefice would then become a matter of serious urgency, and Dunbar could scarcely fail to find it.

Meantime, then, Dunbar remained at court, enjoying what was to be a brief prosperity in the same circles in which he had keenly felt his former indigence. Two of his poems, perhaps written at this time, show that he was not without his enemies. In *How Sall I Governe Me?*[2] he protests against their uncharitable gossip. Whether his spirits are high or droop in sadness, an ill construction is placed upon his bearing. If he displays the magnanimity that comes of noble blood, he is said to be out of his mind. When he dresses smartly he is suspected of gallantries or pride, but if badly dressed it is whispered that he has fallen on evil courses. If he is seen too much at court, his friends are said to lack influence. When reward does come his way, slanderers surround him. Powerless to keep their tongues still, he can only do his best with God's grace and let them say what they will.

[1] *The Dream*, lines 101-105. Chapter XII.

[2] 'How sould I rewill me or in quhat wys.' B., f. 65b; MF., p. 323; R., f. 38. L. adopted as title the refrain in B., After line 25, MF. proceeds with 36-40, 26-35, and 41 to the end, thus securing a more logical arrangement. B. omits stanza 4. M. follows MF. mainly; but he does not indicate that he follows the order of stanzas of B., and that line 24 is omitted in MF.

The theme is much the same in *On Detraction*.[1] The manuscripts do not agree as to authorship, but Bannatyne ascribes the poem to Dunbar. Of the two versions in the Maitland manuscript, the first is anonymous and the second is stated to be the work of 'Stewarte'. The poem opens clumsily. On the previous night, musing in the garden under a tree, the poet heard a voice calling loudly that none could in those days escape disparagement. The rest of the poem is presumably a continuation by the same voice, but at the close there is no further reference to poet or garden. The complaint is that the reputation of neither King, lord, nor lady, is safe. The poet would gladly harass many of the critics, but such action would itself be misrepresented. He finds comfort in the wise sentiments expressed by good King James IV when in his youth, that man should act on high principles and pay no heed to critics. The poet himself will try to follow this advice and seek a place in heaven where he will be free from these attacks.

The close resemblances between this poem and *How Sall I Governe Me?* induced Sibbald[2] to print the latter as a continuation. Bannatyne may have ascribed both poems to Dunbar for the same reason. The metrical form is the same, and the theme is sufficiently like to make difficult the view that Dunbar wrote both poems. The historical precision of the line

> Gude James the Ferd, our nobill king

suggests a writer in the following reign. The identity of 'Stewarte' is unknown. Sir David Lindsay names, among the poets of the reign of James V, 'Stewarte' and 'Stewart of Lorne'.[3]

During these last years at the court of James IV when Dunbar's position seemed secure, it might have been expected that he would attempt a work on a larger scale than his usual short pieces. If he did make the attempt, the work has not survived. We have already seen

[1] 'Musing allone this hinder nicht.' B., f. 63b; MF., p. 168, and a second and often divergent version on p. 313. B. concludes with 'Finis q dumbar', MF.1 with 'finis', and MF.2 with 'Quod Stewarte'. Ramsay called the poem *On Detraction and Deming*. B. omits the ninth stanza, and MF.1 the sixth, the first line of which has been written and then deleted. In line 34, MF.1 has 'mouth', not 'mulls' (MF.2) as stated by M.

[2] Sibbald, II, p. 64.

[3] *The Testament and Complaynt of Our Souerane Lordis Papyngo*, S.T.S. edition, I, p. 57. B. assigns many poems to 'Stewart' and one poem to 'W. Stewart'. MF. attributes the last of these to 'Stewarte', and another poem to 'williame Stewart'.

that in 1508 he declared his intention of narrating at length the deeds of Lord Bernard Stewart of Aubigny, and of completing the work before Aubigny should return to France. Perhaps Aubigny's death a few weeks later made Dunbar desist. Probably the poet was too much interested in the busy court around him to emulate the larger and more scholarly conceptions of Gavin Douglas. Less than two months before Flodden, Douglas completed his impressive verse translation of the *Aeneid*, on the feast day of St. Mary Magdalene, 22nd July,[1] having taken eighteen months to the work, in which he engaged while immersed also in affairs of state and church. The literary and political ambitions of the younger poet are in marked contrast to the homely philosophy of his senior. A further contrast may be observed even in their attitudes to the language they used. In *The Goldyn Targe* Dunbar had written with pride of 'oure Inglisch'. Now, strongly Anglophile though he was later to be in politics, Douglas strove to avoid the 'sodroun' tongue and keep to 'our awin langage', though he did not hesitate to borrow from 'Latyne, Frensch, or Inglis' when he could thereby add variety or conciseness to his 'Scottis'.[2]

It is fitting to date in the last years of James IV a number of Dunbar's shorter poems in which he is no longer preoccupied with his own material position, and in which he gives the impression of speaking from mature experience. A few of them have still the court as background, but most are moral poems concerned with the lot of man and how he can best face it.

In *Rule of One's Self*[3] he gives advice to a youth on how to comport himself at court. Dunbar counsels him to have patience and to devote himself to his duties. Contentment will spare him much strife and enmity. He must use his eyes and ears but avoid the vanity of much speech. If he becomes a whisperer of rumours, none will trust him; and it will be safer not to allow scorn to be expressed even on his face. Let him beware to whom he discloses his thoughts, bearing in mind that by the turn of events a friend may become an enemy. Since his worth will be measured by the company he keeps, he must choose honourable men as his friends, and hold fast to God as unfailing support. He will find it perilous to

[1] Small's ed. of Douglas, IV, p. 231.

[2] ib., II, pp. 6-7, Introduction to the translation of the *Aeneid*.

[3] 'To dwell in court, my friend.' B., f. 68. In line 14, M. follows Dr. Ritchie's reading, 'vyle', but in the manuscript the word has been altered to 'vyld', with a longer final character. Hailes called the poem *Rewl of Anis Self*.

attempt by counsel or correction to guide the conduct of men of wilful nature. His wisdom will best be shown in control of himself. Dunbar's experience of court life caused him to draw up rules of conduct similar in some respects to those of Polonius. But the similarity is only superficial: there is the difference between caution and craft.

Advice by Dunbar to a young and enthusiastic friend who is in love, is given in *Ane Luvar Suld be Weill Advysit.*[1] It is worldly advice, concerned with the need for keeping up social appearances. The lover must be circumspect, for the slightest error in judgment will be reported in quarters where the lover would least wish to be disparaged. He must beware of misdemeanours, niggardliness, lying, pride, over-assurance, and speaking too freely of his love; in brief,

Be secreit, trew, incressing of your name.

But in the poem called *Of Love Earthly and Divine*,[2] Dunbar claims, as in *The Disputacioun Betuix the Nychtingale and the Merle*, that the love of God is the true love. It arises in its strength only when age comes in place of youth, and when the flames of Venus are dead. Now he begins to understand the folly of what he calls 'feynit luve', which differs completely from perfect love, so that no man who delights in the former can write adequately of the latter. Dunbar says that he has dwelt in love's court himself, but for one joy he could count fifteen anxieties. Now, on the other hand, his reward is not displeasure and disdain[3] but comfort. Where formerly he was jealous of another, to-day he would like all men to love where he loves. He was once ashamed to reveal his love or tell the lady's name, but now it is an honour to have his love of God known to all, and he cares not a bean for her two fair eyes.

[1] 'Be ye ane luvar . . .'. B., f. 212b. L. called the poem *Gude Counsale*. At the foot of the page of the MS., after 'ffinis', have been added the words 'ffinis etc. dumbar', in lighter ink and apparently by a different hand. But the addition may have been made only a little later than the transcription of the poem, and the ink immediately dried; the lack of support for the hand may have distorted the writing.

[2] 'Now cumis aige quhair yewth hes bene.' B., f. 284b. M. has omitted the two lines of the refrain with which the poem opens. L. (II, p. 363), followed by S. (p. 346), avers that the poem appears to have been also in the lost portion of the Asloan manuscript. He says the original table of contents of the MS. entitles poem xxv *The twa Luves, erdly and divyne*. But there is no such title in either the original or the later table of contents, poem xxv being *the disputacioun betuix the nychtingale and the merle*. Hailes called the poem *Of Luve Erdly and Divine*.

[3] Professor Bruce Dickins points out that 'denger' (lines 39, 56, and 62) means not 'influence' or 'dominion' but 'disdain' (*Mod. Lang. Review*, Oct. 1933, p. 507).

In a more mundane vein Dunbar wrote *Without Glaidnes Avalis No Tresure*,[1] which occurs in both the Bannatyne and Maitland manuscripts. The existence in addition of a version contemporary with Dunbar, in a *Minute Book of Seisins* in the Town Clerk's Office, Aberdeen, had escaped public notice until the writer came upon it; its text, and various particulars concerning it, may be found in an appendix.[2]

The poem opens with the words 'Be mery, man!' Worry shortens life and is to be avoided, whatever changes of fortune may have to be met. Humility before God should be cultivated; and we should borrow and lend freely with our neighbours, whose lot may be ours to-morrow. No benefit is to be expected from riches without a contented mind. Only what is spent is really enjoyed—food, drink, clothes; the remainder cannot be counted on, and in the end it is inherited by those who have contributed nothing to it. Ultimately an account must be rendered of our possessions before the judge of all men: if the sums involved are small, a true account is the more easily presented.

The manner in which the poem is set down in the Aberdeen records, alongside official entries, suggests strongly, as explained in the appendix, that the poem is contemporary with these entries. They are not in strictly chronological order, but in the neighbourhood of the poem are dated 1510 and 1511, the great majority being of October or November 1511. In May 1511 Dunbar had been in Aberdeen and written his description of the welcome given by the city to Queen Margaret. He could afford to be cheerful in money matters, as he could not in earlier years.

In line with this poem is another, *Thyne Awin Gude Spend quhill*

[1] 'Be mery, man, and tak nocht fer in mynd.' MS. *Minute Book of Seisins*, Vol. III, 1507-1513; B., f. 98; MF., p. 221. On the preceding page of B. is written

Hermes the philosopher
Be mirry and glaid honest and vertewous
For that suffisis to anger the Invyous.

In S.T.S., these lines are accordingly attached to the poem, with the title *Hermes the Philosopher*. M. says the poem is so entitled in B., but rejects the title and the two following lines as being merely the scribe's contribution since nothing of it appears in MF. There is, however, no justification in B. for attaching these three lines to the poem. Apart from them, f. 97b is blank, and the preceding f. 97 announces the opening of the third part of the collection, to consist of 'ballettis mirry and uther solatius consaittis'; the lines in question are preliminary to this third part and have no special reference to this poem by Dunbar. MF. reverses the order of the last three stanzas. M. follows B., but in line 33 it is B. that has 'werk', not MF.

[2] Appendix II.

thow hes Space.[1] Here again the poet advises the spending of earthly goods while opportunity remains. It is better in one's lifetime to be glad at Yule and Easter, for only what is spent can truly be called one's own.

In another poem the virtue of contentment is sung, *On Content*.[2] The covetous man, even if he has all the riches of 'Ynd', lives in effect in poverty. Dunbar recommends his brother-man to make good cheer with what is sent him and to thank God, defying a false world which causes those to repent most who serve it most. He and his fellows, who have small lordship in this life, should not repine.

Gif we not clym we tak no fall.

Among these poems of practical advice, *Best to be Blyth*[3] expresses equally an equable outlook. Often, Dunbar says, he muses on the changing world, and cultivates a cheerful disposition. What value has worldly gear in a life which lasts only the twinkling of an eye, in comparison with the life that is eternal? Had he himself allowed his heart to be heavy on account of an unkind world, he would have been dead long since.

He was to need all the cheerfulness he could muster. The shadow

[1] 'Man, sen thy lyfe is ay in weir.' B., f. 136b; MF., p. 225. MF. reverses the order of the second and third stanzas, with some advantage to the train of thought, and again of the ninth and tenth. The poem is anonymous in MF. M. in general follows B., but in line 8 'quhill' has been altered in B. to 'quhen', and the beginning of line 28 in B. with 'Man' need not, as stated by M., involve an unnecessary syllable; rather, since the MS. reads 'Man etc.', it leads to the inference that B. has here the same refrain as MF.

[2] 'Quho thinkis that he hes sufficence.' MF., p. 307; R., f. 5. The latter differs in so many lines from MF. that S. concludes that R. copied from a second version in the lost portion of MF. M. follows MF. in the main, but adopts preferable readings from R. This course would have been more satisfactory for lines 11-12 also: the reading of MF. is there inconsistent with the rest of the poem, particularly with line 14; the version in R., however, fits the context:

Quhairfoir thocht thow my brother deir
Not servit be with denteiss seir . . .

In line 18, MF. has 'sall sonast it', not 'sall sonast'. The title is Ramsay's.

[3] 'Full oft I mus and hes in thocht.' B., f. 98b, and a defaced fragment, in places differently worded, on f. 115b; MF., p. 337; R., f. 43. The fragment, B.2, ends with the word 'change' (line 9), and is scored through by five parallel vertical lines. An oblique line separates the fragment from the next poem in the MS., *One who is his Own Enemy*. B.1 concludes with 'etc.'. The 'q dunbar' which follows is in different ink but corresponding to that of the 'd' inserted in line 39 ('frawdfull'). MF. and R. omit lines 16-20. M. follows mainly the version of B.1, but does not mention the fragment, nor does he point out his reading from MF. in line 11; in line 21, M. has 'wardlis', whereas B.1 has 'warldis' (MF. 'wardlie'). Hailes supplied the title.

of approaching calamity threatened his whole world. Troubles with England, both at sea and on the unruly Border, had been continual even before the death of the cautious Henry VII, and his son was not likely to be so prudent. These disputes could have been solved, and both James and Henry VIII repeatedly expressed willingness to effect a settlement. But each was caught in the net of European alliances. The French menace to Italy had led to the Holy League of 1511, combining the Pope, Spain, the Empire, and England, in opposition to France. In these circumstances James was determined to stand by his league with France. The King of Scots made every effort, however, to break the deadlock. Though Henry's offers of compensation for injuries done were met by James with the firm demand that Henry should detach himself from the alliance against France, James at the same time tried to reconcile France with the Pope, so that the Holy League might be dissolved and with it the threat to France. Andrew Forman, Bishop of Moray, worked unceasingly towards this end, stressing in Rome the desire of James for peace in Christendom and a combined assault on the Turks, in which James was eager to use the considerable fleet he had built. Forman's efforts failed, the French were expelled from Italy in 1512, and Henry unsuccessfully attacked Guienne. In the autumn of the same year, hostile forces faced each other on the Scottish Border, but a serious outbreak was averted for the time. On both sides war was already considered to be inevitable, but as late as 24th May 1513 James made overtures to Henry, for there had been talk of a year's truce between England and France. On the 30th June, Henry crossed to Calais and invaded France. King James was thus driven to the only course which he regarded as consistent with his honour.[1]

Final preparations followed swiftly. The feudal array from all parts of the land was summoned to assemble in August on the Boroughmuir of Edinburgh. The King made a last pilgrimage to the shrine of St. Duthac at Tain, where he was on the 8th of August. With characteristic speed, James was in England on the 22nd. The banners of St. Andrew and St. Margaret were sent on after him, a man being commissioned to bring them 'in haist, that nycht that the Kingis Grace departit furth of Edinburgh'. Nor did the King wait for his artillery. It left on the 18th and 19th, drawn by teams of oxen. Carts carried the gunpowder, and the 'gun-stanis' were

[1] Hume Brown, I, pp. 264-267.

transported in carts, and in creels on the backs of horses.[1] Dunbar, at his age, is not likely to have accompanied the army. But with it went his hopes and fears.

[1] T.A., IV, pp. 519, 521; ib., Sir J. B. Paul, p. lxxix.

CHAPTER XVI

AFTER FLODDEN

FLODDEN was fought on the 9th September. On the following day, rumours of the disaster reached Edinburgh, and, in course of time, the melancholy tale of heroism became clearer. Both armies had fought on foot, the Scots with pike and the English with bill. Artillery had played little part. Of the four Scottish columns of closely packed pikemen, the extreme left had been victorious and quitted the field for plunder. The other three columns, their pikes ineffective on the rough hillside, had been broken up by the English bills, which with their axe-heads shore through the pikes. The Scots had made their last stand with their swords, to be overborne again by the bills with their longer reach. The gallant King, on foot like his men and at the head of the right-centre column, had fought to the last with sword in hand, and gone down only a few yards from where the Earl of Surrey was stationed.[1] Gradually the fearful roll of casualties became known in the city. The Scottish army had not been deficient in numbers, and the losses were nation-wide. They included thirteen earls, two bishops, two abbots, the Dean of Glasgow, and the Provost of Edinburgh.[2] What was not fully known by the citizens was pieced out by surmise and rumour. Tales of dreadful portents preceding the departure of the army were recorded, and equally morbid and mysterious accounts gained credence as to the fate of the excommunicated King James or of his body.

For months before Flodden, Edinburgh had been ravaged by the plague, which continued to trouble the unhappy city. The Provost and magistrates, when they left with the burgesses for the war, had left substitutes behind them. When the rumours of the defeat came in on 10th September, a proclamation to the citizens required them to have military equipment ready and to assemble on the ringing of the common bell, to defend the town against invaders. The pro-

[1] Dr. W. M. Mackenzie, *Flodden*, pp. 13, 15, 71, 84, 89-93.
[2] Mackay and Burnett, E.R., XIII, p. clxxxix.

clamation instructed women not to clamour and cry in the streets but to enter the churches and pray.[1] A standing watch was appointed, and large sums were raised to provide artillery and fortifications.[2] As stated in a previous chapter, the town had overgrown its old walls, which for convenience had been breached in many places. The Cowgate, beyond them, was by now to a great extent built up, and properties were spread over most of the rising ground to the south. To resist the expected invader the citizens were instructed to join up the dykes of these properties, to form a rough line not far from the marshy bank of the Burgh Loch which extended over the site of the present Meadows. No invaders appeared, but the project was soon taken up at public expense and the building of a wall received much attention up till 1520, though its perimeter was very long for defence if an attack had come.[3]

Henry VIII is said to have abstained from invasion because he was grieved at the news of Flodden, and for the sake of his sister and nephew.[4] The opportunity, moreover, afforded by an infant monarch under the guardianship of Henry's own sister, would make war seem unnecessary. In accordance with the will of the late King, Parliament, on the 21st September at Stirling, accepted the Queen-mother as regent and guardian of the prince who was there crowned as James V.[5] The Queen and the young King resided chiefly at Stirling Castle, which was carefully guarded, but they made occasional visits to Falkland.[6] Sir David Lindsay, as usher and 'kepar of the Kingis grace',[7] has left a vivid picture of the care and affection he lavished on the infant King.[8]

A poem perhaps written to the Queen-Mother, and perhaps by Dunbar, is that named by Laing *To the Queen Dowager*,[9] and appearing among the anonymous poems of the Bannatyne manuscript. There is no explicit mention of the Queen in the poem, which is consolatory in tone and written to a lady whose lord has been taken from her by death. Its phrasing is strongly reminiscent of Dunbar's poems and, still more, of the two poems—one anonymous and the

[1] *Extracts from Records of Burgh of Edinburgh*, I, p. 143.
[2] Wilson, p. 34. Arnot, p. 13.
[3] *Edinburgh*, 1329-1929, pp. 391-393.
[4] Pitscottie, p. 280. [5] Leslie, p. 148.
[6] T.A., V, p. 37; E.R., XIV, p. 8.
[7] Burnett and Mackay, E.R., XIV, p. cxlviii.
[8] *The Dreme* (S.T.S. ed. of Lindsay, I, p. 4).
[9] 'O lusty flour of yowth . . .'. P. 180 of M. See Appendix III, No. 3.

other possibly anonymous—definitely directed to the Queen, *Welcome to the Princess Margaret* and *Gladethe thoue Queyne of Scottis Regioun*, written respectively on the occasion of her arrival in Scotland and of an approaching birth, which have already been attributed to Dunbar in the course of this work. The stanza is, moreover, that of the latter of these, and also of several poems which are accepted as by Dunbar. Just as, years before, at her accession to the throne, she was described as

> Swet lusty lusum lady clere,

she is hailed now

> O lufsum lusty lady, wyse and trew.

Formerly, when she was about to be a mother, she was

> Fresche flour of youthe, new germyng to burgeoun,

and now the poet addresses her

> O lusty flour of yowth, benying and bricht.

Then she was

> One stalk yet grene, O ying and tendir flour,

and now

> Yung brekand blosum, yit on the stalkis grene.

Whereas, in his poem *Sweit rois of vertew and of gentilnes*, Dunbar had used, possibly with reference to Margaret, the phrase

> Delytsum lyllie of everie lustynes,

the lady now addressed is

> Delytsum lilly, lusty for to be sene.

On the death of King James in 1513, Margaret was still only twenty-four years of age, and was yet destined to marry twice. In such terms as those quoted, the poet reminds her of her youth and urges her to put away languor. She is to allow no dark cloud to obscure her from the sight of her followers, and no sable to hide her beauty. The poet commends himself in all humility to her, to whom he is and always will be a loyal servant till death, and for whose sake he will pen songs of comfort. She must not spoil her face with weeping even though Death has devoured her noble lord. Let her cast out care, be comforted, and have pity on her servant.

The Queen was not slow to comfort herself. Having given birth, on 30th April 1514, to a posthumous child of James IV, a prince who died in the following year, she married Douglas, the young Earl of Angus, on 9th August.

The power of the house of Douglas, a menace to the royal authority in the previous century, had often been exercised in league with England and in English interests. The privileged position now attained by Angus was little to the liking of other lords, and the effect was to aggravate the tendency to feudal anarchy which had begun to show itself as soon as the firm grasp of James IV was removed. Beaton, Archbishop of Glasgow and Chancellor of Scotland, who denounced the marriage, was seized by Angus at Perth and made to surrender his seal of office,[1] which was given to the uncle of Angus, the poet Gavin Douglas, who was already one of the Lords of Council, and who now rejected the command of the Council that he should restore the seal. In the autumn occurred the struggle for the archbishopric of St. Andrews between Gavin Douglas and Prior Hepburn, during which each party was in turn besieged in the castle, and which ended in the discomfiture of both and the appointment of Andrew Forman. Meanwhile, the Border was being devastated by English incursions.

A remedy for the dangers that threatened had been put forward by the French ambassadors in November 1513, when La Bastie had secured the agreement of Parliament to the French king's proposal that John, Duke of Albany and Admiral of France, should be sent from France to take over the government, keep order, and resist English penetration. Detained by Francis I, who decided that his departure might spoil impending French negotiations with England, Albany received a further summons a year later. Son of the outlawed brother of James III, and thus a cousin of James IV, Albany had spent his life at the French court, his mother being of the house of the counts of Auvergne. Should Margaret's two sons die young, as her other children had died, Albany would succeed to the throne of Scotland. Nothing was left undone by England at the court of Francis I to prevent Albany from setting out, but he arrived in Scotland on the 16th May 1515.[2]

The only poem by Dunbar which is definitely known to be later than Flodden is on the theme of Albany. The new governor spoke no English. He arrived in Edinburgh on the 26th and was received honourably by the Queen and the lords. For the occasion there were 'sindrie ferses and gude playis maide be the burgessis of the

[1] Leslie, II, p. 151. [2] E.R., XIV, p. 163.

toun to his honour and prayse'.[1] The Duke set about his task with determination. Already, in the previous year, the Council had decreed that the Queen-Mother, by her marriage with Angus, had forfeited her right of guardianship over the King. The Parliament of July 1515 made Albany regent and guardian of the King. The news reaching him that the Douglases were planning to remove the King from Stirling Castle to England, Albany proceeded to Stirling with an armed force. The Queen-Mother surrendered her charges to him, fleeing to England with her husband. Lord Home, for treason on the Border, was executed and his head placed on the Tolbooth.[2] In his place, as Warden of the Marches, Albany appointed his friend, the chivalrous La Bastie, who had fought in Aubigny's presence at the tourney in 1508. Gavin Douglas, the nominated Bishop of Dunkeld, was imprisoned for a time. Albany dealt equally firmly with Arran and the Hamiltons. He tried to make good the loss of guns at Flodden by establishing a new foundry at Edinburgh.[3] The demand of Henry VIII that Albany should be expelled from the country was rejected by Parliament, and the alliance with France was renewed instead. The Earl of Angus, leaving Margaret in England, made his peace with Albany, as did the Earl of Arran. It was with reluctance that Parliament agreed, at Albany's request, that he might return to France in the summer of 1517, and it was stipulated that he should not stay more than four months.[4] He left on the 6th June.[5] But he did not return until 1521.

The poem which provides the sole evidence that Dunbar survived the reign of James IV is named *Quhen the Governour Past in Fraunce*,[6] from the colophon in the Maitland manuscript, which ascribes the poem definitely to Dunbar. In the Reidpeth manuscript there is no colophon at all, not even a 'Finis' or 'Explicit'—an unusual circumstance. But since Reidpeth was simply transcribing the poems as he found them in the Maitland manuscript, the omission is no reason for doubting the authenticity of the poem or for upholding the suggestion[7] that the poem may have been ascribed to

[1] Leslie, II, p. 158. [2] ib., II, pp. 158-165.
[3] T.A., V, p. 67. [4] Leslie, II, p. 167.
[5] E.R., XIV, p. 292.
[6] 'Thow that in hevin, for our salvatioun.' M.F., p. 186; R., f. 28b. MF. concludes with 'Quod dunbar quhen the governour past in fraunce'. M. follows MF., but has altered 'thy' to 'this' in line 24 to conform with the refrain of the other stanzas.
[7] L., *Supplement*, p. 292.

Dunbar by mistake. Dunbar nowhere in the poem makes direct reference either to the Governor or to his departure, the only evidence of their connexion with the poem being the colophon added by Maitland. But the poet clearly refers to a period of time later than Flodden.

The poem is in the form of a prayer, and has on that account been named *Ane Orisoun*. Dunbar prays that the God who sent Gabriel with good tidings will have pity on the kingdom, which otherwise will be lost. Only a spark of heavenly wisdom, and the help of God's grace, can save Scotland from disaster. The poet prays that God will cease to take vengeance and will temper justice with mercy. Quiet has left the poor realm, which is divided within itself, and its people are infected with folly. God is entreated to give the people grace to make amends by contrition and penance.

In dating this poem, there is the difficulty that the Duke of Albany came to Scotland—and left it—not once but three times. After his departure in 1517, he remained in France until relations between England and France deteriorated sufficiently to induce Francis I to send Albany again, in 1521, and he left Scotland for the second time in October 1522. Returning from France a year later, he left finally in May 1524. Possible dates for Dunbar's poem, therefore, are June 1517, October of 1522, and May of 1524. But in the absence of any further evidence about Dunbar's life at this time it is safer to regard the date of the poem as June 1517, rather than to postpone it unnecessarily. For the same reason it is needless to pursue the political troubles of the time any further. Albany's influence was exerted on the side of public order, but also in French interests, and after each departure of Albany the English party among the barons revived, along with political anarchy. The Duke had scarcely gone in 1517 when his friend La Bastie, Warden of the Marches, set upon in a moss by the Wedderburns, was killed and his head attached by its long hair to the slayer's saddle bow.[1] The Queen-Mother was later to divorce her second husband and to marry a third. Gavin Douglas was to die, a proscribed exile in London, of the plague.

Leslie describes the social condition of Scotland after Flodden: 'The Realme now in sik distres, al drew to factiounis and pairties, sum to defend the quene, sum the nobilitie, al studiet to thair particular proffet, outher occupieng his nychtbours landis with

[1] Pitscottie, p. 301.

force, or his nychtbouris gudes wrangouslie, how ever he could.'[1] In the words of Sir David Lindsay,

> Oppressioun did so lowde his bugyll blaw
> That none durst ryde bot in to feir of weir.
> Ioke uponeland, that tyme, did mys his meir.[2]

Dunbar's poem, *Of Cuvetice*,[3] represents the whole nation as in decay. At court, generous conduct is now reputed a vice. Well-being has turned into wretchedness. Hawking, hunting, and horsemanship, have given place to cards and dice and, in general, to the amassing of illegitimate gains. In the countryside, honourable retainers have been dispersed, the laird keeping by him a single agent, who conducts his master's business to advance his own interests. The laird wears silk, but his tenants are in extreme poverty. Instead of well-filled granges and extensive stock, farmers possess only cats and mice. The burghs, both maritime and inland, have declined, where once was feasting on venison, wild fowl, wine and spices. Honest citizens, formerly clad in red and brown, are reduced to lousy rags. In this state of the world, says the poet, the man who performs deeds of charity and lives at peace is held to be a simpleton; he who can seize other men's farms, and exact payments from the poor, is considered a man of wisdom and action. The only remedy that the poet can offer is to cultivate a cheerful mind, estimating this world as not worth a cherry, and strive towards heaven where covetousness does not reign. The poem has more appropriate reference to the troubled state of Scotland after Flodden than to its comparatively ordered condition under the rule of James IV.

It is only by Maitland, and his transcriber Reidpeth, that Dunbar is named as the writer, for Bannatyne leaves the poem anonymous. In the last stanza the words

> Be mirry
> And sett not by this warld a chirry,

are exactly repeated in the last stanza of *One who is his Own Enemy*. It is curious that the latter poem is also anonymous in one of the

[1] Leslie, II, p. 155.

[2] *The Testament and Complaynt of our Souerane Lordis Papyngo*, lines 539-541 (S.T.S. ed. of Lindsay's poems, I, p. 72).

[3] 'Fredome, honour, and nobilnes.' B., f. 64b; MF., p. 6; R., f. 9. R. omits line 25 and lines 33-36. M. follows B.; he does not point out that 'heill' in line 29 is from MF., not from B., where the word is 'eill'.

manuscripts, this time Maitland's, though Bannatyne gives the poem as by Dunbar.

The authorship of *A General Satire*[1] is uncertain. It is ascribed to Dunbar in the Bannatyne manuscript, but to Sir James Inglis in that of Maitland.

Sir James Inglis appears first in the records as in receipt of a livery in 1511, and in 1512 was 'clerk of the Kingis closet' and 'chapellane to the Prince'.[2] He became Abbot of Culross. On 1st March 1530-1, he was murdered by Lord Tulliallan.[3] There was another Sir James Inglis, a chaplain in the Abbey of Cambuskenneth, whose duty in 1512-13 and in 1522-3 was to sing masses for the souls of James III and his queen,[4] and who, in 1533 and 1538, years after the death of the Abbot of Culross, was still so employed.[5] But Sir David Lindsay, not later than 1530 for Inglis is still alive, writes:

> Quho can say more than Schir James Inglis sayis
> In ballattis, farses, and in plesand playis?
> Bot Culross hes his pen maid impotent.[6]

The probability therefore is that the Inglis to whom *A General Satire* is ascribed in the Maitland manuscript was the Abbot of Culross, and also the man who took part as an actor in dramatic performances at court, receiving in 1511-12 money 'to be hyme and his collegis play cotis', and again in December 1526.[7]

The poem is a denunciation of the corruption and oppression which the writer sees around him in his dream. There are nobles out of number, but little concern is shown by them for the 'commoun weill', and hunger stalks the land. There are many traitors,

> And sic evill willaris to speik of king and quene.

Thieves, who are in great numbers, have the support of lords that share the spoils and only threaten retribution. Hunting over the growing crops does wrong to the cultivator. Tennis and other

1 'Devorit with dreme, devysing in my slummer.' B., p. 47, and a second version on f. 60; MF., p. 187. The lack of a title was made good by Ramsay: *A Generall Satyre*. The readings of B.1 are at times nearer to MF. than are those of B.2. The order of stanzas in MF. (given wrongly by S.) is more logical, having lines 46-55 following line 25, and reversing the order of the last three stanzas. M., who does not note the existence of B.1, has followed B.2 with some corrections which he does not indicate.

2 T.A., IV, pp. 250, 268, 441.

3 Pitcairn's *Criminal Trials*, I, p. 151, cited by Laing.

4 T.A., IV, p. 443; V, p. 199. 5 ib., VI, pp. 102, 447.

6 *The Testament and Complaynt of the Papyngo*, lines 40-42.

7 T.A., IV, pp. 321, 316.

games have their throngs of devotees. These denunciations, it may be observed, do not accord with the sentiments which are expressed as to the decay of sport in *Of Cuvetice*. Though there are

> Sa mony jugeis and lordis now maid of lait,

their administration is corrupt, and they oppress the poor on trivial excuses. Fashions in dress are too luxurious. Merchants are dishonest. Beggars prosper, harlots and clergy wear rich dresses, and the contagion of the 'glengoir' is widespread. The schools turn out asses and mules: few of the clergy preach and pray, and the land abounds in proud and dissolute prelates, abbots who are strangers to their abbeys.

As to the claims of Dunbar and Inglis to the poem, there can be no certainty. The arguments used are not convincing.[1] It is not clear why a brisker metre is needed for a poem by Dunbar, nor, in view of his metrical versatility, why he should be expected to have used this particular stanza elsewhere in his works. There is much inner and sectional rhyming in Dunbar's poems. It is true that his attitude was not generally antagonistic to the nobility, and that the expressions 'the commoun cawis' and 'commoun weill' are not to be found in his other poems and are suggestive of rather later times. But there are, as we have seen, poems by Dunbar in which he does enlarge upon the oppression suffered by the poor, and upon the corruption of the nobility, as in *Discretioun in Taking* and *In this Warld May Non Assure*. Dunbar's claim in *To the King: Complaint against Mure*, that he is not given to defamatory statements about lords, we have shown not to be wholly confirmed by an examination of his works. Moreover, Dunbar lived on into the anarchy that followed Flodden. It is perhaps noteworthy that a line of the Bannatyne version is distinctly reminiscent of a line of Dunbar.[2]

The mention of ill-disposed talk about King and Queen has been taken to indicate a date either between 1503 and 1513, or, in the next reign, between 1537 and 1542. If Sir James Inglis is the poet, the date would, on this hypothesis, be limited to 1503-1513, since his death took place in 1531. But Queen Margaret retained her title of Queen after Flodden. Again, the line which refers to newly

[1] M., p. 224.

[2] Line 33: 'Becawis thai spend the pelf thame betwene.' Cp. in *To the King: Off benefice, Schir*, line 5, 'Gif thame the pelffe to pairt amang thame'.

made judges and lords has been thought to refer to the foundation of the College of Justice in 1532, or to changes consequent on the enactment of 1503-4. But each successive Parliament appointed its Judicial Committee, 'dominos ad causas et querelas'. On the other hand, after Flodden many new appointments would have to be made, and the lawlessness of the time would give added force to the denunciations in the poem. Both date and authorship, however, must remain open questions.

The personal circumstances of Dunbar after Flodden are unknown. If the poem *To the Queen Dowager* is indeed by him, he appears to have been attached for some time to the Queen-Mother and her interests. On the other hand, if the poem *Quhen the Governour Past in Fraunce* belongs to 1517, Dunbar in that year regarded favourably the cause of the Duke of Albany, who had so firmly opposed the Queen's influence that she had fled to England. Perhaps the Queen's marriage with the Earl of Angus in August 1514, and her consequent identification for a time with the Douglases, caused the eclipse of Dunbar in so far as her favour was concerned. She had no longer the public funds at her disposal. Payments made to her from them in 1515 were for the period of her widowhood up to her contract of marriage, but were not paid for the period after her marriage with Angus.[1]

After Flodden, Dunbar does not appear in the Treasurers' Accounts in which formerly he appeared regularly. The accounts are not extant from 8th August 1513 to 25th June 1515, a date after Albany's arrival. They are also missing from September 1518 to June 1522, from April 1524 to August 1525, and from August 1527 to August 1529. But in the accounts that are extant there is no indication of Dunbar or of his pension. Of the courtiers whose names appear in the 'Annue Pensiones' of 1511-12, it has already been mentioned that the great majority either fared much worse in 1512-13 or received no pension at all. Reference to the accounts for the period from 25th June 1515 to 13th October 1516 shows that only in very rare cases are sums still being paid to the recipients of 1511-12. The probability therefore is that, just as Dunbar's receipts appear to have been affected by the general and drastic reductions in 1513 on the approach of war, they would disappear, like the receipts of almost all the others, as soon as the royal patron whose munificence had supplied them had fallen at Flodden.

[1] Burnett and Mackay, E.R., XIV, p. lx.

But what of the benefice so long sought importunately by Dunbar, and so long promised by James IV? This question has already been considered in the preceding chapter. The conclusion was reached that Dunbar could scarcely have failed to obtain a suitable benefice if the urgent need of it had remained, and the view was put forward that the chief reason why he apparently did not receive his benefice before the end of James IV's reign was the very size of the pension he enjoyed. Whether the sum of £80 a year was intended by the King to retain Dunbar at court or not, it would tend to have that effect. The promise of a benefice of £100 in lieu of the pension would make the finding of a suitable cure the more unlikely. In consequence, it would continue to be delayed, unless some unexpected disaster to the King removed the cherished pension. With Flodden, Dunbar's whole position must have been changed, and he would urgently seek the benefice promised. The Queen would have every incentive to provide him with it. The claims of a loyal servant of long standing could thus be met without further cost to the Treasury, which would be spared the continued payment of pension to him. But, in the new and straitened circumstances of the nation, he could not expect to hold his patrons to the earlier promise of a benefice of £100. So far as that precise figure is concerned, Dunbar's position would probably be that described by Robert Henryson:

> The man that will nocht quhen he may,
> Sall haif nocht quhen he wald.

Yet the opportunities offered by the Church, as already indicated, were such that Dunbar was little likely to fail in obtaining at least some benefice, and it would probably be something better than what he called 'ane kirk scant coverit with hadder'.[1] If the Queen failed him, he would have friends enough from the old days to help him. In 1516, the Duke of Albany, at the same time as he confirmed Forman as Archbishop of St. Andrews, distributed many other benefices, great and small. 'The noble men straue stiflie for the destributioun of smal benifices to thair freinds.'[2]

If we weigh all these circumstances, it is a justifiable presumption that Dunbar spent the last part of his life as a beneficed priest in the cure of souls. Even at an earlier period there are moods of weariness in his poems, when his lot at court oppresses him. Illness

[1] *To the King: On the World's Instability*, line 86. [2] Leslie, II, p. 162

and old age also show themselves. Even if Flodden had not brought down in ruins the social edifice to which he had habituated himself, the burden of years would in itself have counselled retreat. Flodden and its results would be decisive in their effects upon his spirit. He would wish to husband out life's taper, and a priestly charge, even if it was not a sinecure, would be the livelihood to which he would naturally turn. It is customary to regard his religious poems as the product of his last years. There is, in truth, no compelling reason why they should not be earlier poems, but the tradition is not without some cogency.

Most of these religious poems are concerned with recurring occasions in the Christian year, and several give the impression of being composed by a pastor whose mind is on his priestly ministrations.

One devotional work of a comprehensive character is *The Tabill of Confessioun*,[1] which outlines the delinquencies of body, mind and spirit that are to be borne in mind in the confessional if shrift is to be adequate. The colophon of the Maitland manuscript reads 'Heir endis ane confessioun generale compylit be maister williame dunbar', and that of the Howard manuscript 'Heir endis the tabill of confessioun compilit be M. William Dunber etc.' The words 'generale', 'compylit', and 'tabill', show the writer's attitude to his theme. Some of the phrases of the poem follow closely Lydgate's *Testament*.[2]

The penitent is represented as prostrate before the 'bludy figor dolorus' of Christ. The poet deals in turn with the misuse of the five senses, the seven deadly sins, the seven deeds of corporal mercy, the seven deeds of spiritual mercy, the seven sacraments, the ten commandments, the twelve articles of the creed, the four cardinal virtues, the seven commandments of the Church, the seven gifts of the Holy Ghost and the sins against it, and the seven petitions of the paternoster. These lead on to a less systematic enumeration of spiritual shortcomings that are to be laid bare before receiving the

[1] 'To the, O mercifull Salviour, Jesus.' B., p. 9, and a second version on f. 17b; MF., p. 199; Howard MS., f. 1. The title is from the last of these. B.1 and B.2 omit lines 81-88. In MF., lines 41-42 and 81-83 have been crossed out, and lines 43-48 and 84-88 have been omitted. M. states wrongly that lines 43-48 have been crossed out, perhaps meaning 41-42 which he does not mention. The Howard MS. places line 86 before 85, 140 after 142, and 149 after 150: it is the only complete version. M. follows B.2, supplying lines 81-88 from 'a collection in MS. in the British Museum', i.e. the Howard MS. He has made a considerable number of departures without indicating the fact. [2] P. H. Nichols, p. 219.

sacrament, not omitting the sins which the penitent has forgotten. The whole exposition is accompanied by a continual prayer for mercy. An interesting feature of the poem is the care taken by the post-Reformation scribes, Maitland and Bannatyne, to suppress, by deletion or omission, references to Roman rites of which the Reformers could not approve. In contrast with the unreformed text of the Howard manuscript, the Bannatyne and Maitland versions avoid mention of prayer for the souls of the dead, the seven sacraments, mass, penance, confirmation, extreme unction, payment of tithes and keeping of fasts.

Of the Nativity of Christ[1] is a hymn of gladness for Christmas morning. By a play upon words—a device rare in Dunbar—the new Sun surmounting Phoebus in the east is related to the Son of the Christmas introit, 'Et nobis Puer natus est'. His mother is the Rose Mary, flower of flowers. The heavenly bodies and powers, the elements, sinners, clergy, birds, and fishes, and quickening flowers, are all summoned to the harmony of thanksgiving. Familiar liturgical phrases are introduced or echoed from vespers and 'Te Deum', and in the last stanza from the angels' song of the missal —'Gloria in excelsis!'

The Maner of Passyng to Confessioun,[2] as it is called in the Howard manuscript, is written in Lent. It differs in character from *The Tabill*, being concerned more with the difficulties of actual ministration, and less with mystical categories and enumerations. Dunbar opens with the advice to fast and pray. No leech can heal a wound that has not been cleansed first, and God will not remit a sin that is concealed from the priest. Unless the penitent exposes his sins, one blind man will be leading another, and so both will be beguiled. The sinner should search in his mind most diligently for all relevant matter, and is recommended to conduct this self-examination before he comes to the priest at all. It is the duty of the priest to sit and listen, the responsibility of telling the sins being on the penitent, for none knows them better than he. It is not to be expected that the man who lets a whole year elapse, from Easter to Easter, without confessing, will not incur grave danger through forgetting many things. Finally, it is dangerous to postpone penitence until old age, and there is small merit in being

[1] 'Rorate celi desuper.' B., f. 27. Hailes supplied a title, *Of the Nativitie of Christe*.

[2] 'O synfull man, thir ar the fourty dayis.' Howard MS., f. 161. M. has not always followed strictly the spelling of the original.

troubled by sin at an age so advanced that one is incapable of wrongdoing.

Some of Dunbar's most ingenious rhyming and alliterative effects are lavished on *Ane Ballat of Our Lady*,[1] written perhaps for Ladyday. The Virgin is hailed as eternal empress of heaven, most royal rose, lily of paradise, gentle nightingale, bright precious stone, God's great suffragan. Extreme intricacy of form is wedded to most elaborate diction. Dr. Mackenzie remarks that many of the words are arbitrarily formed to suit the exigencies of the rhyming, and that others may be traced directly to the Latin hymns to the Virgin, from which Dunbar has borrowed many of his epithets. The poem glitters in its preciosity.

Another of his sacred poems, *Of the Passioun of Crist*,[2] tells of a vision experienced on Good Friday. While in the buildings of a friary, he entered an oratory and, reciting a paternoster, knelt to adore Christ and contemplate his sufferings for mankind. He paid his respects also to the Virgin, and suddenly fell asleep.

The vision which follows is a harrowing account of the Crucifixion and of the preliminary tortures endured by Jesus. The medieval mind derived much of its religious ecstasy from representations such as this. From his intense contemplation of the sufferings of Christ, St. Francis is said to have borne visibly the stigmata of his Master. The crucifixion and martyrdom pieces of the medieval painters show the same tendency to seek a communion by dwelling on agonising details presented to the senses, and the literature of the time has many analogous examples.[3] The dramatic 'mysteries' must also have afforded opportunities for this realism. The productions of an age are not to be divorced from the spirit which gave them life and significance. Pinkerton comments on this poem of Dunbar as 'a long poem on Christ's Passioun, as stupid as need

[1] 'Hale, sterne superne.' Asloan MS., f. 303. The poem is No. lxiii of that collection, and is given its title in the original table of contents. M. has not always retained the spelling of the manuscript.

[2] 'Amang thir freiris, within ane cloister.' Asloan MS., f. 290b; Howard MS., p. 168; MF., p. 203. The order of lines in Asloan is 1-32, 81-88, 41-95, thus omitting 33-40, repeating 81-88, and concluding with 95. In the Howard MS. the poem is complete except for the omission of lines 73-80 and 121-128, but leaf 171 (containing 33-72) has been misplaced and should follow leaf 168; line 100 is placed after 102. This is the only MS. in which the poem is anonymous. M. follows MF. but without always indicating departures. He makes no mention of the Howard MS. nor does he note the substitution (of lines 81-88 for 33-40) in Asloan.

[3] Examples may be seen in the Makculloch MS., poems III and XV.

be',[1] but to the scribe of the Howard manuscript it is 'Ane Devoit Remembrance of the passioun of Crist'.

When the poem has proceeded for two thirds of its length, the theme is given a new direction, passing from the description of Christ's sufferings to the poet's reflections as a procession of allegorical visitants address him in turn on the subject. Immediately before this change the poem is brought to a close in the Asloan manuscript, and at this point also the refrain of the poem is displaced by a new one. But the second part is genuinely a continuation, as shown by the agreement of the Howard and Maitland manuscripts. The opening lines and closing lines of the second part depend upon the first part, and the new refrain emphasises the turn in the thought, like the new rhyme in the sestet of a sonnet. Compassion, Contrition, Remembrance, and others, with appropriate gestures bid the poet mark well how Christ suffered, and Grace urges him to give a resting-place to the sufferer within three days—a reference to the approaching Easter sacrament. Contrition and Compassion then bestir themselves; the house is prepared by Conscience, Repentance and Penance, and is kept secure by Grace for the entry of Jesus. The poem concludes with the usual awakening: Christ's death causes the earth to tremble where the poet lies, and he wakens in perturbation, to write out immediately all that thus befell him on Good Friday before the Cross.

The spirited poem *Of the Resurrection of Christ*[2] is a hymn for the morning of Easter Sunday. The cruel dragon Lucifer has been confounded in battle by our champion Christ, the gates of hell are broken, and the triumphal cross is raised. Souls are redeemed from the trembling demons by the blood of Christ. Sacrificed like a lamb, he has risen like a lion. Aurora and Apollo have ascended in the sky and the night has gone. It is a poem of fierce joy.

The date of the poet's death is unknown. But Sir David Lindsay writes of him, in *The Testament and Complaynt of our Souerane Lordis Papyngo*, as deceased. An English translation of Lindsay's poem was printed in London in 1538, and one of the colophons of the print states that the poem was 'compyled by David Lyndesay of the mount and finysshed the xiiij day of Decembre in the yere of our lord 1530'.[3] Moreover, one passage of the poem comments on the

[1] Pinkerton, II, p. 456.

[2] 'Done is a battell on the dragon blak.' B., f. 35. Hailes called the poem *Of the Resurrection of Chryste*.

[3] S.T.S. ed. of Lindsay's poems, III, p. 64.

spectacular fall of Cardinal Wolsey,[1] which took place in the last weeks of 1529. The passage dealing with Dunbar links him with Walter Kennedy:

> Or quho can now the workis countrafait
> Of Kennedie with termes aureait,
> Or off Dunbar, quhilk language had at large,
> As may be sene in tyll his Goldin Targe?[2]

Lindsay proceeds to lament, in much more laudatory terms, Gavin Douglas, who died in September 1522.[3] Kennedy was at the point of death in 1505 when Dunbar wrote his *Lament: Quhen he wes Sek.* If Lindsay's order of naming the poets is the chronological order of their decease, Dunbar's death occurred before 1522.

[1] Lines 570-583.
[2] Lines 15-18.
[3] Polydore Vergil, *English History* (Camden Society), I, p. 105, quoted by Small, ed. of Douglas's poems, I, p. cxvii.

APPENDIX I

TEXTUAL SOURCES OF DUNBAR'S POEMS

1. Aberdeen Minute Book of Seisins, Vols. II and III

These unpublished manuscript registers are in the Town Clerk's Office, Aberdeen. The pages are not numbered. The entries in the volumes are not in strictly chronological order. Vol. II is wrongly described on its binding as covering the period 'From Jan. 1501/02 to 29th April 1504': the entries range from 1503 to 1507. In it, side by side on the same page, are *The Twa Cummers* of Dunbar and the unique copy of *Gladethe thoue Queyne of Scottis Regioun*, a poem apparently entered in 1506 or 1507 which the present writer has accepted as being probably by Dunbar (Chapter XII, and Appendix III, 2). Vol. III covers the period 1507 to 1513. In it, among entries dated 1510 and 1511, is the hitherto unnoticed copy of *Without Glaidnes Avalis No Tresure*, the text of which is given in Appendix II.

2. Chapman and Millar Prints

These are discussed in Chapter XIV. The bound volume of original prints is in the National Library. The S.T.S. edition, by G. Stevenson (Edin., 1918) is contained in the volume entitled *The Makculloch and the Gray MSS. together with the Chepman and Myllar Prints*. Mr. Beattie's photographed facsimile appeared in 1950.

3. Asloan MS.

The manuscript is in the possession of the Talbot de Malahide family in Dublin, but has been photographed page by page, and the photographs are in the National Library. Almost throughout, the manuscript is written in the one hand, that of John Asloan, who indicates his identity at various points. L. does not explain why he dates the manuscript in 1515 (L., I, p. x). On its outer cover it is described as 'MS. Temp. Jac. V'. A prose chronicle, *The Scottis Originale*, is included and is brought down 'Till oure soverane lord Iames the fyft that now Is'. A large part of the manuscript is missing, and the original table of contents shows that only a small proportion of the poems has survived. These include three poems by Dunbar, and a fragment of a fourth. One of the three is not elsewhere extant. The MS. has been edited for the S.T.S. by Sir W. A. Craigie (Edin., 1923-4).

4. Howard MS. (British Museum, Arundel MSS., No. 285)

This sixteenth century manuscript includes three poems by Dunbar, of which one is not elsewhere extant. It is a quarto collection of Scots poems and prose pieces, by various authors. The Earl of Arundel (1592-1646), one of the Howard family, was a zealous collector of MSS.

5. British Museum, Appendix to Royal MSS. No. 58

The manuscript is an English collection (with musical notes) of madrigals, motets, solos for lute and for spinet, and compositions for a chest of viols. It dates from the early sixteenth century. No. 8 is a solo for the spinet, *King Harry the VIIIth pavyn*. No. 21 is the anonymous *Welcome to the Princess Margaret*, which is accepted in Chapter IX as probably by Dunbar (Appendix III, 1); it is not extant elsewhere.

6. Bannatyne MS.

This collection of Scots poetry by various authors is in folio, in the National Library. The earlier part is generally regarded as a first draft, most of the poems in it being repeated, with variations, in the main body of the manuscript, and the 'Table of the haill Buik' does not take account of this preliminary draft. The poems of the main collection are systematically arranged to form five parts according to their themes. The draft has numbered pages but thereafter the numbering is by folios. The collection includes forty-six poems by Dunbar, of which three are duplicated and two in part duplicated, and another of his poems occurs in a duplicated fragment. Eight of his poems are found only in this collection, and two others do not occur elsewhere in complete form. There is also included the unique copy of the anonymous poem, *To the Queen Dowager* ('O lusty flour of yowth . . . '), which has been accepted in Chapter XVI as probably by Dunbar (Appendix III, 3). A later hand has indicated that the poems of the collection were transcribed 'be George Bannatyne in the tyme of his youth'. Bannatyne himself informs the reader at the close that it was 'written in tyme of pest' in the last three months of 1568, this being presumably the time when the compilation was completed. His sources were 'copeis awld, mankit, and mutillait'. Bannatyne's father, an Angus man, was a member of Edinburgh Town Council, a lawyer and Keeper of the Rolls, and depute to the justice clerk. George himself, after studying at St. Andrews, became an Edinburgh merchant, being admitted a gild brother in 1587 (Dr W. Tod Ritchie, Introd. to Vol. I of the S.T.S. edition of the MS.).

7. Maitland Folio MS.

Of the two Maitland manuscript volumes in the Pepysian Library, Magdalene College, Cambridge, only the Folio (No. 2553) includes poems by Dunbar. It includes works of various poets. There are sixty-one by Dunbar, of which six are duplicated, and of which another is partly duplicated; there is also a fragment of another of his poems. Five of his poems are not extant elsewhere, and two others do not appear in complete form elsewhere. Numbering is by pages, not leaves. A number of leaves have been bound in the wrong places, and some were already misplaced when Reidpeth made his copy in 1622. Two portions, now widely apart in the volume, are parts of an earlier collection which consisted of poems by Dunbar. Most of the poems have been written by the same scribe, but many other hands have participated. Though the leaves are mounted, the bottoms and tops of many pages are very much faded and worn. The manuscript was begun in or about the year 1570. Sir Richard Maitland of Lethington was then in old age. He had been Keeper of the Privy Seal and a Lord of Session (Sir W. A. Craigie, Introd. to Vol. II of the S.T.S. edition of the MS.).

8. Reidpeth MS.

This is a folio manuscript, Moore LL. v. 10 in the University Library, Cambridge. On the first fly-leaf is written 'A me Ioanne reidpeth septimo decembris inchoat 1622', and '1622 ffinis m . . . post', which may mean that it was completed in March of 1622-3. A quire is missing from the middle of the volume. The poems transcribed by John Reidpeth have been taken from MF., which at the time was less incomplete than it is now, though parts of it were already misplaced. Most of the poems are Dunbar's, but there are many by Maitland, and some by other poets. There are forty-seven by Dunbar, and three fragments of poems by him. Eight of the Dunbar poems have not survived except in this manuscript, and two others are not extant elsewhere in complete form. The eight unique copies have been printed by Sir W. A. Craigie in Vol. II of the S.T.S. edition of MF.

APPENDIX II

THE ABERDEEN COPY (1510-11) OF *WITHOUT GLAIDNES AVALIS NO TRESURE*

THE poem has been described in Chapter XV. The source of this new copy has been referred to in Appendix I, 1. The poem has been known hitherto from the texts of B. and MF., which ascribe the poem to Dunbar, but apparently the Aberdeen copy of the poem, contemporary with the poet, has escaped public notice. The present writer discovered it several years ago (as recorded in *The Times Literary Supplement* of 8th April 1939, p. 208) in Vol. III of the Aberdeen *Minute Book of Seisins*, in the Town Clerk's Office.

The poem is to be found a little more than half way through the book (the pages of which are not numbered), is anonymous, and has no title. On the right hand side of the first page of the poem, in the broad margin and opposite the first six lines, is an undated official entry, also of six lines, of a claim to certain articles by James Huchone the brother of George Tailor, and written in fainter ink. The irregularity of the indentations at the commencement of the lines of this entry, following closely the irregularity of line-endings of the poem, which is itself neatly and firmly set down as if no writing already on the page disturbed the scribe, shows that the poem was written first. Its claim to be contemporary with the other contents of the register is thus reinforced. The deeds are not entered in strictly chronological order. The poem occurs among entries dated 1510 and 1511: in the preceding five pages the entries are of October and November 1511, as are those of the following six pages, except that the first two pages after the poem bear the dates August 1510 and January 1510 respectively, and the third after the poem shows no date. The handwriting of this poem differs from the handwritings of the poems in Vol. II (see Appendix III, 2). That the poem has not entirely eluded notice is shown by the words 'Old Ballad ½ thro', written in ink in cursive characters, within the front cover of the volume, accompanied by 'Seen Oct./38' in the same hand and evidently referring to 1838, for other volumes of the register are thus marked with '1838' in the same handwriting.

The interest of this Aberdeen transcript lies in its adding one more to the small number of Dunbar's poems of which copies are known contemporary with the poet. There can be little doubt that the appearance of the poem among the Aberdeen records dated mainly in autumn, 1511, is connected with the poet's visit to the city in May of that year with Queen Margaret (Chapter XV). Both B. and MF. follow closely the general tenor of the Aberdeen text, differing from it rather in word, phrase, and spelling. It is in these respects much closer to B. than to MF., and follows the same order of stanzas as the former, whereas MF. reverses the last three. In the fourth stanza the Aberdeen scribe has omitted the penultimate line which, in B., reads: 'Tak thow example and spend with mirrines'. Likewise, 'nycht' is omitted in line 5.

The writer is indebted to Mr. J. C. Rennie, Town Clerk of Aberdeen, for permission to include the text, which is as follows:

Be mery man and tak nocht fer in mynd
The wavering of this wrechit vale of sorow
To god be hmmle and to thi frend be kyind
and with thi nichtbour glaidlie len and borow
his chance this It may be thine to morow
Be mery man for any aventure
for be wismen It has bene said afforow
Without glaidnes avalis no tresure.

Mak gude cheir of It god the sendis
for warldis wrak but weilfar nocht avalis
No thing is thine sauf onlie that thow spendis
The Remanent of all thow brukis with balis
Seik to solace quhen saidnis the assalis
Thy lyfe in dolour ma nocht lang indure
quharfor of confurt set up all thi salis
Without glaidnes avalis no tresure.

follow pete flie trubill and debait
With famous folkis hald thi company
Be cheritable and hmmle of estait
for warldis honour lestis bot ane cry
for truble in erd tak no malancoly
be rich in patiens gife thoue in gudis be pur
quha levis mery he levis michely
Without glaidnes avalis no tresur.

Thow seis the wrechis set with sorow and care
To gaddir gudis all thar liffis spaice
and quhen thar baggis ar full thar self ar bar
and of thar riches bot keping hes
quhill tothir to spend It that hes grace
quhilk of the wynning no labour hed na cur
Without glaidnes avalis no tresure.

Thocht all the wrak that evir hed levand wichit
War onlie Thine no mor thi pert dois fall
bot met and clacht and of the laif ane sicht
Yit to the iuge thow sall mak compt of all
ane Raknyng richt cummis of ane Regiment small
Be iust and Ioyus and do to none Iniur
and treuth sall mak the strang has walle
Without glaidnes avalis no tresure.

APPENDIX III

THREE POEMS ADDRESSED TO THE QUEEN, AND BELIEVED TO BE BY DUNBAR

1. *Welcome to the Princess Margaret*
2. '*Gladethe thoue Queyne of Scottis Regioun*'
3. *To the Queen Dowager*

Of this trilogy of poems addressed to the Queen—as bride, mother, and widow respectively—the first and third are anonymous in the manuscript but the anonymity of the second is less certain. All bear striking resemblances in phrasing to one another and to poems which are admitted to be by Dunbar (see the table below). They have therefore also been ascribed to Dunbar, and we accept them as probably his. Whether the occurrence of these parallel expressions is an indication that the poems are by Dunbar or, on the other hand, that some of all of the three are not by Dunbar, but by an imitator or imitators, must remain, however, uncertain.

1. *Welcome to the Princess Margaret*

The poem is in M., p. 178. For a description of this madrigal, see Chapter IX above, and footnote. For the British Museum MS., see Appendix I, 5. In the manuscript the words are written under the musical notes. Inside the large initial 'N' are sketched the features of a bearded man (see the facsimile in the appendix to Vol. I of S.T.S.). The very unconvincing suggestion has been made that the drawing may be a representation of the head of James IV or of Dunbar. The poem is anonymous and has no title. Laing unhesitatingly ascribed it to Dunbar.

2. '*Gladethe thoue Queyne of Scottis Regioun*'

Included in M., p. 179. The only source is the Aberdeen *Minute Book of Seisins*, Vol. II (see Appendix I, 1), towards the end of the book, the pages of which are not numbered. The S.T.S. editor of Dunbar states erroneously that the poem is in Vol. I. The editors have not seen the original, for though they state that the same volume contains also Dunbar's *The Twa Cummers*, they are not aware that the two poems are on the same page. The poem was first pointed out to Laing by John Riddell, advocate (L., *Supplement*, p. 303). Laing ascribed it to Dunbar.

The poem forms a column on the left side of the page, and *The Twa Cummers* is alongside it, forming a column on the right hand side. There is no other entry on the page. At first sight the handwriting of both poems appeared to be almost certainly the same (letter by the present writer to *The Times Literary Supplement*, 8th April 1939, p. 208), but further consideration suggests that each poem is in a different hand. *The Twa Cummers*, which is the shorter poem, is in slightly larger and more extended characters, its ink is a little darker, and certain letters (K, g, F, T, A) are formed differently. In the space to the right of the last three lines of the longer poem there is written—under the concluding line of *The Twa Cummers* and in such position that it would stand approximately upon the base-line of the last line of 'Gladethe thoue Queyne' if produced to the right—the ascription 'q dunbar'. This may, on the one hand, be taken to refer only to *The Twa Cummers* above it, or, on the other hand, as referring also to the poem opposite the conclusion of which it is written.

As to the date of entry, at the foot of the next page a short deed is entered in the same handwriting and ink as *The Twa Cummers*, but undated. Laing states correctly (*Supplement*, p. 303) that the deed following immediately upon the poems is dated 28th March 1506, and the one preceding the poems 25th October 1505. The entries in the volume are not, however, strictly chronological: dates on the preceding seven pages vary from 1505 to 1507, and on the succeeding six pages from 1504-5 to 1506. The poem, and the occasion for which it was written, are described in Chapter XII.

There are many differences in spelling between the text of M. and the original.

3. *To the Queen Dowager:* 'O lusty flour of yowth, benying and bricht'.

The poem appears in M., p. 180. The source is B., f. 238b. Anonymous and without title. Laing gave the poem the title, and attributed it to Dunbar. A description of it is given in Chapter XVI.

TABLE OF PARALLEL PHRASES

		POEMS OF DUNBAR	
Welcome to Margaret	*Gladethe thoue Queyne*	*The Queen in Aberdeen*	*To the Queen Dowager*
2. Princes most plesant and preclare.		65. O potent princes, pleasant and preclair.	
5. Younge tender plant of pulcritud.	2. Ying tendir plaunt of plesand pulcritude.	*The Thistle and the Rose* 166. Haill, plant of yowth.	
6. Descendyd of Imperyalle blude.	5. Our charbunkle chosin of hye Imperiale blud.		
9. Swet lusty lusum lady clere.			37. O lufsum lusty lady, wyse and trew.
13. Welcum the Rose bothe rede and whyte.	25. Roys red and quhit, resplendent of colour.	142. As the fresche Ros of cullour reid and quhyt.	
7. Freshe fragrant floure of fayre hede shene.	3. Fresche flour of youthe, new germyng to burgeon.		1. O lusty flour of yowth benying and bricht.
	4. Our perle of price, our princes fair and gud.	180. Our perle, our plesans and our paramour.	
	13. Mastres of nurtur and of nobilnes.	174. In bewty, nurtour, and every nobilnes.	
	27. One stalk yet grene, O ying and tendir flour.	*Sweit Rois of Vertew* 9. And halsum herbis upone stalkis grene.	4. Yung brekand blosum, yit on the stalkis grene.
		The Thistle and the Rose 167. Haill, blosome breking out of the blud royall.	
		Sweit Rois of Vertew 2. Delytsum lyllie of everie lustynes.	5. Delytsum lilly, lusty for to be sene.

APPENDIX IV

ANONYMOUS AND OTHER POEMS THAT HAVE BEEN THOUGHT TO BE BY DUNBAR

THE first three the author has accepted as probably by Dunbar. The fourth may be by Dunbar or by Sir James Inglis. The remainder the author has rejected.

I. ACCEPTED AS PROBABLY BY DUNBAR

1. *Welcome to the Princess Margaret.* 'Now fayre, fayrest off every fayre.' See Chapter IX, and Appendix III, 1.

2. '*Gladethe thoue Queyne of Scottis Regioun.*' See Chapter XII and Appendix III, 2.

3. *To the Queen Dowager.* 'O lusty flour of yowth, benying and bricht.' See Chapter XVI and Appendix III, 3.

II. BY DUNBAR OR BY SIR JAMES INGLIS

4. *A General Satire.* 'Devorit with dreme, devysing in my slummer.' See Chapter XVI.

III. REJECTED

5. *Responsio Regis.* 'Efter our wrettingis, thesaurer.' R., p. 1. There is no colophon, the title being apparently thought by the scribe to be sufficient to show that King James IV was the author. See Chapter XII.

6. *The Treatise of London.* 'London, thou art of tounes A per se.' M., p. 177. See Chapter VII. It is attributed in one MS. to Andrew Forman, in another it is anonymous, and in the remaining manuscript it is ascribed to 'a skote'.

7. *The Freiris of Berwik.* 'At Tweidis mowth thair standis a nobill toun.' M., p. 182. Sources: B., f. 348b; MF., p. 113. Anonymous in both MSS. Pinkerton (p. 65) describes it as 'supposit to be writtin be Dunbar'. In MF. the satire is against the Gray Friars, but B. reads 'blak' for 'gray' (lines 125, 466, 497) and 'monkis' for 'Minouris' (line 23).

8. *Kynd Kittok.* 'My Gudame wes a gay wif.' M., p. 169. Sources: B., f. 135b; CM., p. 192. In both, anonymous. Its style has been thought to be like Dunbar's, and each stanza has a tail-rhyme as in *For Donald Oure:*

Epetaphe. In CM. the poem occurs in the tenth part, which consists of four untitled pieces: (1) the concluding fragment of *The Tretis of the Tua Mariit Wemen and the Wedo*, ending with 'quod dumbar'; (2) *Lament: Quhen he wes Sek*, ending with 'quod Dunbar quhen he wes seik etc.'; (3) *Kynd Kittok*, ending 'Explicit etc.'; and (4) *The Tesment of Maister Andro Kennedy*, ending 'Explicit'. None of the four has a heading. It is true that *Kynd Kittok* is printed in connexion with some of Dunbar's pieces, but it is not true, as has been alleged, that the poems are printed in continuous form. In B., the poem follows *Thyne Awin Gude Spend quhill thow hes Space*, which ends 'q dumbar'. Dr. Mackenzie remarks that though, in each of the two sources, *Kynd Kittok* occurs in conjunction with Dunbar's work, neither has ascribed the poem to him.

9. *The Manere of the Crying of ane Playe*. 'Harry, Harry, hobbilschowe.' M., p. 170. Sources: Asloan MS., f. 240; B., f. 118b. In the Asloan MS. the poem is thus headed. The colophon of B. reads, 'Finis Of the droichis pairt of the play.' The Asloan version is incomplete, ending abruptly at the foot of a page, with line 165, the next leaf being lost and with it the name of the poet if it was known. Anonymous in B. Metrically, it closely resembles *Ane Ballat of the Fenyeit Freir of Tungland*. The style has been considered to be Dunbar's. The monologue is supposedly recited by a dwarf, and, in *The Flyting of Dunbar and Kennedie*, Kennedy ridicules Dunbar for his dwarfish stature (line 33). The dwarf says he never delighted to live where Erse was spoken: Dunbar, in *The Flyting* and in *The Dance of the Seven Deadly Sins*, is scornful of Gaelic speech. The dwarf refers to foreign lands, and Dunbar visited them.

10. *Counsel in Love*. 'Fane wald I luve, bot quhair abowt?' Included in L., II, p. 31. The source is B., f. 255, where the poem concludes with the words 'Finis q Clerk', of which 'Clerk' is in larger characters and in lighter ink as if quickly dried. A similar attribution to Clerk occurs at the close of *A Brash of Wooing* in B., a poem given to Dunbar by MF. and R. For this reason L. included *Counsel in Love* in his edition of Dunbar. It has been claimed that in its sentiments the poem resembles Dunbar's *The Disputacioun betuix the Nychtingale and the Merle*, *Of Love Earthly and Divine* and *Ane Luvar Suld be Weill Advysit*.

11. *Advice to Lovers*. 'Gif ye wald lufe and luvit be.' Included in L., II, p. 33. B., f. 230, anonymous. Laing prints it because it is in a metrical form used by Dunbar. A similarity of tone has been pointed to between this poem and Dunbar's *Ane Luvar Suld be Weill Advysit*.

12. *The Danger of Writing*. 'Faine wald I with all Diligence.' Included in L., II, p. 49. MF., p. 210. Laing includes the poem among poems attributed to Dunbar, because Pinkerton remarks that it is 'probably by Dunbar'.

13. *Ballat aganis Evill Wemen*. 'The beistlie lust . . . ' S.T.S. edition,

II, p. 266. Sources: B., f. 262; MF., p. 325; R., f. 39b. With this poem B. opens a new section entitled *Ballattis Aganis Evill Wemen*. In all the MSS. the poem is anonymous, MF. and R. ending with 'Explicit'. The version in B. is incomplete, as compared with that of the other MSS., and ends at line 35 but with the colophon 'Finis etc.'. In MF. and R., the poem is followed by Dunbar's *An Orison*, which is a separate poem and ascribed to Dunbar in each MS. The S.T.S. editor, however, on the grounds of similarity of style, puts the poems together as by Dunbar, though retaining the 'Explicit' between them. There is an exactly parallel case immediately following in R., 'Rycht fane wald I my quentance mak' (f. 40), ending 'explicit' and followed by Dunbar's *In this Warld May Non Assure*, the latter being indicated as his, but no claim has been made that the poem preceding it is also by Dunbar.

14. *Do for thyself quhill thou art Heir*. 'Doun by ane rever as I red.' Printed in L., II, p. 51. B., p. 32, and another version on f. 48b, both anonymous. In including the poem with others in the same metre as some by Dunbar, Laing remarks that 'although not actually by him, they may still serve, by comparison, to illustrate his compositions'.

15. *Jerusalem, Rejoyss for Joy*. Printed in L., II, p. 57. The source is B., f. 27b, where it is anonymous. Laing includes it for purposes of comparison. It is a Christmas hymn, following immediately upon Dunbar's *Of the Nativity of Christ* in the MS., the latter being given by B. to Dunbar. But B. groups poems by their themes, not by their authors.

16. *Now Glaideth every Liffis Creature*. Printed in L., II, p. 55. B., f. 27, anonymous. It is another Christmas hymn, is followed in B. by Dunbar's *Of the Nativity of Christ*, and is similarly ornate in style. L. prints it for purposes of comparison.

17. *Surrexit Dominus de Sepulchro*. Printed in L., II, p. 61, as by Dunbar. B., f. 34b. The poem precedes Dunbar's *Of the Resurrection of Christ* and is anonymous. In Dunbar's poem this opening line is used as refrain, but the words are from the matins for Easter.

18. *Ane Ballat of our Lady*. 'Ros Mary, most of vertewe virginale.' Included in M., p. 175. Sources: Asloan MS., f. 301; Makculloch MS., f. 183b; Forrest MS. (British Museum, Harley 1703), p. 79b. In none of the MSS. is the poem complete, and it is anonymous in all three except that the Forrest MS. ascribes the poem to 'A devoute Scotte, of love most entire'. It has been claimed as Dunbar's on the ground that, though its terms are not so exotic as those of Dunbar's *Ane Ballat of Our Lady*, the styles have much in common, and the stanza is one used by Dunbar.

19. *The Use of Court Richt Weill I Knaw*. (S.T.S. ed. of B., IV, p. 31.) B., f. 261b; MF., p. 170. Anonymous in both sources. In B., the poem follows immediately Dunbar's *The Fair Solicitors* and has a similar theme.

20. *Balade.* 'In all oure gardyn growis thare na flouris.' (S.T.S. ed. of CM, p. 156.) CM., third section, following *Sir Eglamour of Artois* on p. 88 with the heading *Balade.* At the foot of the page the poem breaks off unfinished, at line 19, two blank leaves following. No reason has been given for attributing the poem to Dunbar.

21. *To the Governor in France.* 'We Lordis hes chosin a chiftane mervellus.' Printed in M., p. 181. Anonymous in the source, B., f. 78b. The poem purports to be written by one of the Scots lords of the Duke of Albany. Lines 25-26 ('Covatyce ringis in to the spirituall state / Yarnand banifice the quhilk are now vacand') have been related to Dunbar's expectations of a benefice.

22. *The Sterne is Rissin of our Redemptioun.* (Printed in L., II, p. 59.) B., f. 30b, where it is anonymous. Laing includes it for comparison.

23. *Eird uppoun Eird Wonderfull is Wrocht.* (S.T.S. ed. of MF., I, p. 411.) MF., p. 338; R., f. 43. MF. assigns the poem to 'Marsar' but R. to Dunbar. Since R. transcribed MF., his authority is less where the two disagree. The poem derives from the English poem, dating from the early fourteenth century, of which there were many versions (Miss H. M. R. Murray, p. ix).

24. *Various Series of Poems of the Bannatyne MS.* As numbered in the S.T.S. edition of the MS., poems XXI-XLI have been thought to be a collection of devotional pieces by Dunbar; likewise a claim has been made for several other groups, LXVIII-LXXIX, CLXIX-CLXXXIV (except for CLXXVI, CLXXVIII, CLXXXIV), CXCII-CCI, and some of the poems in the sequence CCII-CCXX (J. T. T. Brown, *Scottish Hist. Review*, I, pp. 137-150).

APPENDIX V

THE SCOTS POETS OF THE *LAMENT: QUHEN HE WES SEK*

1. *Syr Hew of Eglintoun.* Line 53. Instead of 'The gude Syr Hew', MF. reads 'The Knycht ssir hew'. Of the Montgomeries of Eglinton in Ayrshire, none of the name of Hugh is on record who could have been deceased when Dunbar's poem was written. But the Montgomeries had obtained the barony of Eglinton through marriage with the daughter of Sir Hugh Eglinton of that ilk (*The Scots Peerage*, Sir J. B. Paul, III, p. 428). This Sir Hugh married a half-sister of Robert II and was Justiciary of Lothian in 1361, dying in 1377 (*Memorials of the Montgomeries, Earls of Eglinton*, I, p. 16). He took part in negotiations in London in 1358-9 as to the ransom of David II (Bain, IV, p. 8). There is no evidence, other than Dunbar's, that Syr Hew of Eglintoun was a poet, though attempts have been made to identify 'the gude Syr Hew' with Huchoun of the Auld Ryall (F. J. Amours, *Scottish Alliterative Poems*, Introd.). See also No. 10.

2. *Ettrik.* Line 54. The very existence of this poet is in doubt. B. begins the line with 'Ettrik', MF. with 'Etrik', but CM. with the words 'Et eik'. Laing points out that CM. habitually has 'et' for 'and', and therefore he strikes Ettrik out of the list of poets. Schipper is impressed by the agreement of the MSS., which do not, as does CM., use 'et' for 'and'. He regards this agreement as outweighing what seems to him to be a printer's error, and he thinks that 'Ettrik' might be an adjective describing 'Heryot', whose name is the next word in the line (S. ed., p. 288).

3. *Heryot.* Line 54. The MSS. call him 'Heriot'. He is unknown. See No. 2.

4. *Wyntoun.* Line 54. The author of *The Original Chronicle* describes himself as Andro of Wyntone, a canon-regular of St. Andrews and prior of Lochleven (ed. F. J. Amours for the S.T.S., II, p. 8). His long poetic chronicle of world history dates from shortly after 1420, at which time the writer was troubled by age. He resigned his priory in 1421-2(ib., I, p. xxx; II, p. xxxviii).

5. *Maister Johne Clerk.* Line 58. He and No. 6 are said to have been stopped by Death 'fra balat making and tragidie'. Perhaps only the 'balat making', therefore, applies particularly to Clerk. His identity is unknown, for so many persons bore the name. In *The Tesment of Maister Andro Kennedy*,

lines 81-89, Dunbar makes Andro leave his malison to 'Master Johne Clerk' for being the cause of Kennedy's death, and this Clerk has therefore been regarded as a physician (Chapter X). B. ascribes *A Brash of Wooing* to 'Clerk', though MF. and R. state that it is by Dunbar (Chapter V). B. attributes several other poems to 'Clerk'.

6. *James Afflek*. Line 58. He is so named in CM. and in B., but MF. gives the name as 'James Auchinlek'. The connexion of his name and that of 'Maister Johne Clerk' (No. 5) may intend 'tragidie' to have reference particularly to Afflek. His identity is unknown. The poem from the Selden MS., *The Quare of Jelusy*, edited by Laing in 1836, is stated by him to end with the words 'Explicit quod Auchin . . . ' (L., II, p. 357), but this reading of the words is contested (A. Lawson, *Scottish Hist. Review*, VIII, p. 325). Striking resemblances have been pointed out (Miss M. Gray, ib., VIII, p. 323) between lines from Dunbar's *The Goldyn Targe* and *The Thistle and the Rose*, on the one hand, and, on the other, lines from *The Quare of Jelusy* and from *Lancelot of the Laik* (ed. Miss Gray, for the S.T.S.), a poem which has been claimed (W. W. Skeat, *Scottish Hist. Review*, VIII, p. 1) to be by the same author as *The Quare*.

7. *Holland*. Line 61. He wrote *The Buke of the Howlat* (ed. F. J. Amours, in *Scottish Alliterative Poems*). This poem, an allegory, was composed at Darnaway in Moray, for Elizabeth Dunbar, the daughter of the Earl of Moray who in 1442 had married Archibald Douglas, the earldom thus passing to the Douglases. It was written between 1447 and 1455, and includes a eulogy on the Douglas family. The researches of Laing brought much information to light about the author (*Adversaria*, pp. 11-15). Richard Holland was secretary to Earl Archibald, and rector of Halkirk in Caithness and of Abbreochy in the province of Moray. After the downfall of the Douglases and the death of the Earl of Moray at Arkinholm in 1455, Holland was a canon of Kirkwall, and later vicar of the parish of Ronaldshay in Zetland. In 1479-80 a Richard Holland was in the service of Edward IV and of the exiled Douglases, and was sent to Scotland to intrigue against James III. He was excepted from the pardon granted by the Scots Parliament to a number of traitors in 1482 (F. J. Amours, op. cit., pp. xxiii-xxvi, 316).

8. *Barbour*. Line 61. *The Bruce*, by John Barbour, is dated 1375 by its author himself (ed. W. W. Skeat, for the S.T.S.). In 1357 Barbour was archdeacon of Aberdeen, and held that position till his death in 1395, holding as his prebend the tithes of the parish of Rayne in Garioch. He was one of the commissioners appointed in 1357 to arrange the payment of David II's ransom. In various years he obtained a safe-conduct from the English king to enable him to proceed to Oxford and to Paris to prosecute his studies. For his literary work he was awarded an annual pension by Robert II (ib., pp. xxix-xxxvi). *The Buik of Alexander*, a translation of two

French romances, has been attributed to Barbour by its editor, Dr. R. L. Graeme Ritchie.

9. *Schir Mungo Lokert of the Le.* Line 63. Dunbar regrets the passing of this poet with particular keenness. None of his works has survived. The Lockharts of the Lee were an ancient Lanarkshire family. On 27th February 1489 a knight of his name is recorded as deceased, 'umquhile Sir Mongo Lokart, knycht', his son and heir being 'Robert Lokart of the Leie' (*Acts of the Lords of Council in Civil Causes*, I, p. 128).

10. *Clerk of Tranent.* Line 65. He is thus named in CM., and also in B., but MF. reads 'The clerk of Tranent'. Dunbar adds that he 'maid the Anteris of Gawane' (in B. 'the awnteris of ser gawane'). Who he was, is unknown. Andrew Wyntoun, in his *Original Chronicle*, written shortly after 1420, speaks of a poem named *The Anteris of Gawane* as the work of 'Huchoun of the Auld Ryall' (ed. Amours, IV, p. 22). Attempts have therefore been made to identify Clerk of Tranent with Huchoun and Sir Hugh of Eglinton (No. 1), and to attribute to Clerk *The Knightly Tale of Golagras and Gawane* (ed. Amours, *Scottish Alliterative Poems*).

11. *Schir Gilbert Hay.* Line 67. He is so named in CM., but MF. reads 'Schir Gilbert Gray', and B. 'Ser gilbert gray'. Sir Gilbert Gray is unknown. The only surviving works of Sir Gilbert Hay are translations from the French, of which three, in prose, have been printed (*Gilbert Haye's Manuscript*, ed. J. H. Stevenson, for the S.T.S.). They deal respectively with the international law of arms, the institution of knighthood, and principles of government. A fourth is the long poetic translation, *The Buik of Alexander the Conqueror*. There are many Gilbert Hays in the records. The one in question, after spending twenty-four years in the service of the king of France, and rising to be Chamberlain to Charles VII, had returned to Scotland by 1456. At Roslin Castle, in that year, at the request of Lord Sinclair, he made one of his prose translations, *The Buke of the Law of Armys*, describing himself in its introduction as a knight, Master of Arts, and 'bachilere in decreis'. He also appears as a priest, in the same year. He seems to have been alive, though at an advanced age, in 1499, supervising the correction of a copy of his poem (ib., I, pp. xxvi-xxxii, 2).

12. *Blind Harry.* Line 69. John Major writes: 'There was one Henry, blind from his birth, who, in the time of my childhood, fabricated a whole book about William Wallace, and therein he wrote down in our native rimes—and this was a kind of composition in which he had much skill—all that passed current among the people of his day. . . . This Henry used to recite his tales in the households of the nobles, and thereby got the food and clothing that he deserved' (Major, p. 205). As George Buchanan studied in 1524 under Major at St. Andrews when Major was in extreme old age, Henry's work would date from about 1450-1460 (Moir, p. vii).

In the Treasurers' Accounts, payments are recorded to 'Blinde Hary' from 27th April 1490 to New Year's Day 1491-2 (T.A., I, pp. 133-184). The poem which has been ascribed to Major's Henry, *The Actis and Deidis of the Illustere and Vailyeand Campioun Schir William Wallace, Knicht of Ellerslie* (ed. Moir, for the S.T.S.), is plainly by a different man. It occurs in a manuscript dated 1488 and is anonymous. Its author states that it was based on a Latin history (ib., pp. 378, 376). Wyntoun (ed. Amours, V, p. 319) writes that 'Gret gestis' of the deeds of Wallace existed even in his time.

13. *Sandy Traill*. Line 69. He is unknown. Schipper mistook as an ascription to this poet the word 'thrall' at the conclusion of an opening line in B., 'No woundir is altho my hairt be thrall' (ed. S.T.S., III, p. 309).

14. *Patrik Johnestoun*. Line 71. His connexions were chiefly with Linlithgow and West Lothian, as shown by the records. For faithful service rendered and to be rendered to James III, Johnestoun was granted by the King in 1467 the lands of Kingsfield, and he was at the same time the official receiver of revenues from the Crown lands of West Lothian (E.R., VII, pp. 538, 534). In 1476 and 1477, payments were made to him for the dramatic entertainments which he organised at court—'pro certis joccis et ludis factis coram rege', and 'pro certis ludis et interludiis' (ib., VIII, pp. 333, 404, 512). That the interludes were in verse is possible from Dunbar's inclusion of Johnestoun among the poets. Under James IV, Johnestoun continued his productions, payments being made in the summer of 1488 and 1489 'to Patrik Johnson and the playaris of Lythgow, that playt to the King', and to him 'and his fallowis that playt a play to the King in Lythqow' (T.A., I, pp. 91, 118). He is referred to as deceased, in the records of 1495 (E.R., X, p. 495). In B., the poem called *The Thre Deid Pollis* is given to 'Patrik Iohinstoun' (S.T.S. ed. of B., II, pp. 142-144).

15. *Merseir*. Line 73. Dunbar adds that he 'did in luf so lifly write' (or, according to MF., ' . . . so lusty wryt') 'so schort, so quyk, of sentence hie'. His identity is unknown. Love-poems by Mersar appear in B., and MF. assigns to 'Marsar' the poem *Eyrd upone eird* which R. assigns to Dunbar (Appendix IV, No. 23).

16. *Roull of Aberdene*. Line 77. Of him and of No. 17, Dunbar writes 'Two bettir fallowis did no man se'. He is unknown.

17. *Roull of Corstorphin*. Line 78. See also No. 16. He is described as 'gentill'. Perhaps, therefore, he is the author of *The cursing of Sr. Iohine rowlis Upoun the steilaris of his fowlis*, which is attributed to 'Rowll' in B., and to 'roule' in MF. His identity is unknown, but the poem itself has been dated by Lord Hailes, p. 272, who points out that the Pope Alexander mentioned by the poet as reigning at the time must be Alexander VI, whose reign stretched from 1492 to 1503.

18. *Broun*. Line 81. This name appears only in B., ' . . . he [Death] hes laid broun'. Dr. Ritchie (S.T.S. ed. of B.) reads 'taie broun', for 'tane broun', and, as he states, the words are in different ink and may be a later addition. But the more likely reading is 'laid broun', for in the initial letter the sweep upwards to the loop is distinguishable. On the other hand, CM. reads ' . . . he [Death] hes done roune / With Maister Robert Henrisoun', and this 'done roune' is quite clearly borne out by the 'done rowne' of MF. 'Done roune' (i.e. 'held whispered conversation') is an idiom of Dunbar (cp. *The Dance of the Seven Deadly Sins*, line 112, 'he the correnoch had done schout', and also *The Devillis Inquest*, lines 24 and 49, 'rowndand' and 'rowndis'). The evidence of the texts is therefore conflicting. But there was certainly a poet of the name. B. contains two versions of a poem, the one attributed to 'Wa(lter) broun' and the other to 'Ssr wa(lter) broun' (Dr. Ritchie's edition, I, p. 58, and II, p. 127). He may be the 'Walterus Brown, pauper', who determined at St. Andrews University in 1475 and became master of arts in 1477 (Anderson, *Early Records*, pp. 57, 60).

19. *Maister Robert Henrisoun*. Line 82. He is so called in CM. In B. he is described as 'gud maister robert henrysoun', and MF. gives the surname as 'Hendersoun'. See Chapter V.

20. *Schir Johne the Ros*. Line 83. This poet was Dunbar's second in *The Flyting of Dunbar and Kennedie*. His identity is unknown. Laing's informant, J. Chalmers, thought that Ross was Sir John Ross of Montgreenan in Ayrshire, one of the Lords of Council (L., II, p. 420); he appears as 'John the Ross' in 1488 (T.A., I, p. 92), but was dead by June 1494 (E.R., X, p. 416); a successor of the same name appears in 1495 (*Acts of Lords of Council in Civil Cases*, I, p. 429). Another claimant is Sir John Ross of Halkhead, sheriff of West Lothian; Laing (II, p. 420) says, without giving any authority, that he died about 1506, but he was dead before 1502 (*Great Seal Register*, II, No. 2629); his successor, a grandson, was of the same name; both had the rank of baron, and both were companions of the King at cards and other amusements, the grandson as late as 11th March 1508 (T.A., IV, p. 105). Still another Ross appears in a partly illegible entry of 1498, 'giffin to Johne the Ros, otherwis . . . to mak his expens hame in Ros . . . ' (T.A., I, p. 389). Hailes thought that the 'Sir' probably indicated that the poet was a priest (Hailes, p. 273). His poems have not survived. An attempt has been made to show him to be the author of *The Wallace* and a reviser of Barbour's *The Bruce* (J. T. T. Brown, *The Wallace and the Bruce Restudied*).

21. *Stobo*. Line 86. Dunbar describes him as 'gud gentill Stobo'. In MF. this whole stanza is omitted. Dunbar says of him and of No. 22 that Death 'hes now tane' them, 'last of aw', and that 'all wichtis hes pete' on them. His name was John Reid, but he was regularly referred to as

Stobo. He was in the service of James II, James III, and James IV, in turn, and appears frequently in the public records. His work was that of royal secretary, charged with the writing of letters to Rome and to foreign parts generally. The pension awarded him for life in 1477-8 was to be paid out of the customs of Edinburgh to 'dilecto nostro familiari servitori et scribe Johanni Red nuncupato Stobo' (*Great Seal Register*, II, No. 1341). His work as a notary public ('Sir Johne Reid publik notar', *Acts of Lords Auditors of Causes and Complaints*, 1466-94, p. 93) in writing legal documents is sufficient to account for the reference to him in *The Flyting of Dunbar and Kennedie* (line 331). A priest, he was rector of Kirkcrist (*Great Seal Register*, II, No. 1810), 'Joh. Rede alias Stobo rectore de Kirkcriste'. In his secretarial work for the King he was closely associated with Walter Chapman: in 1497 there is record of a payment 'To Stobo and Watte Chepman, . . . for thare lawboris in lettrez writing the tyme the King past in Ingland' (T.A., I, p. 270). He accompanied James IV on pilgrimage to Tain in October 1504 (ib., II, p. 462). On 6th and 27th May 1505 he is noted as lying sick (ib., III, pp. 138, 142), and in July as deceased (E.R., XII, p. 372). His poems have not survived.

22. *Quintyne Schaw*. Line 85. See No. 21. Quintyne Schaw appears frequently from 1478-9 onwards in the records. A Quintin Schaw held lands at Dreghorn in Ayrshire, as shown by a charter of 1489, and was the son of Sir John Schaw of Haily (*Great Seal Register*, II, No. 1855). Laing, who relied in part upon notices of charters given him by J. W. Mackenzie, formed the opinion that this was the poet (L., II, p. 423). In 1501 he twice drew £10 from the Lord Treasurer, and in 1504 was in receipt of a yearly pension to that amount paid on 8th July (T.A., II, pp. 92, 93, 445). His death was therefore shortly afterwards, for it is reported as a recent event by Dunbar. A poem by Quyntene Schaw appears in MF. (S.T.S. ed., I, p. 385). There is no evidence to support the customary identification of Quintyne Schaw with the poet known as Quintene (see Chapter VI).

23. *Maister Walter Kennedy*. Line 89. B. describes him as 'Guid Maister Walter Kennedy'. Dr. Ritchie, in his edition, reads 'And' instead of 'Guid', but the capital letter is more like a 'G', and there is an extra pothook. In CM. and in MF. he is likewise 'Gud Maister Walter Kennedy'. He has been dealt with in the account of *The Flyting of Dunbar and Kennedie* in Chapter VI. Unlike the other poets in this list, Kennedy was not yet dead, though he 'In poynt of dede lyis veraly'. He may have recovered. His collected poetical works have been edited by Professor Schipper.

APPENDIX VI

PROBLEMS OF THE TEXTS OF *THE FLYTING OF DUNBAR AND KENNEDIE* AND *THE DEVILLIS INQUEST*

A. *The Flyting of Dunbar and Kennedie*

The manuscript sources are as follows: B., f. 147; MF., p. 53; R., f. 58. Also there is a fragment, lines 316 to the end, in CM.; line 316 is at the top of a page, the previous pages of the poem being lost, including the title-page. According to the original table of contents of the Asloan MS., the poem was contained in the lost portion of that collection. The title is from B. The texts of B. and CM. are straightforward, but there is a confused arrangement of stanzas in MF. and R. Sir W. A. Craigie points out in his edition of MF. (II, p. 69) that Maitland took the poem from an earlier copy which had four stanzas (i.e. 32 lines) to a page, and in which the second leaf (lines 65-128) and third leaf (lines 129-192) had been interchanged, so that Maitland copied these two groups of lines in the wrong order. Later the leaves of his own manuscript in turn became dis-arranged, so that the pages of *The Flyting*, which is entirely in what Professor Craigie calls 'handwriting A', are mixed with pages of other poems and other handwritings, whereas the correct sequence of *The Flyting* pages would be: pp. 53 (lines 1-35), 54 (lines 36-64, 129-136), 69 (lines 137-173), 70 (lines 174-192, 65-83), 71 (lines 84-120), 72 (lines 121-128, 193-222), 77-80 (lines 223-368), 59-63 (lines 369-552). When Reidpeth came to transcribe from MF., unthinkingly following its pagination, the confusion was undiminished, R. proceeding in the following order: lines 1-64, 129-136, 369-552, 137-192, 65-128, 193-368, the poem ending at line 368 with the colophon 'Finis coronat opus'. Opposite line 368, however, there is written in the right margin in very faded and worn cursive characters the injunction 'Ye must go bak quhair itt is writtin . . . '. The remainder of the sentence is obscure, but probably refers (in spite of the mistake in enumeration, 24 for 23) to a similar marginal note twenty-three stanzas back (i.e. opposite the continuation of the poem at line 369) to the effect that 'This verss is Kennedyis and contenewis with the 24 verss'.

M. prefers the text of CM., so far as it is extant, but takes lines 1-315 from B. This is wise: owing to fading and weathering, the reading of MF. is often obscure and has to be eked out from Reidpeth, who was in the habit of readily misconceiving the sense of his original. But M. does not follow B. strictly, deviating much more frequently than is indicated; M. has also converted B.'s final note to each section into an introductory heading, and, in doing so, omits the two appeals to the audience, 'Iuge in the nixt quha gat the war' (after line 48), and 'Iuge ye now heir quha gat the war' (at the end of the poem). In taking lines 316-552 from CM., M. makes some emendations, not all of which are necessary. In line 525 the transfer of the comma from before to after 'provit' has altered the sense, and 'sais' fits the context of line 318 better than 'sadis' (MF. reads 'sayis'). Professor Bruce Dickins (*Mod. Lang. Review*, Oct. 1933, p. 507) has pointed out that the alteration of 'tempise' (line 532) to 'temp[t]ise' is not required, and he cites 'tempand' in line 2 of *The Devillis Inquest* from B. The last two of these emendations have been adopted by M. from the S.T.S. ed. of CM. (ed. Stevenson).

In Chapter VI the reasons have been stated which led Laing to suspect that at least lines 497-512 had been misplaced and should have been in Kennedy's first reply. In the same chapter it has been shown that the apparent inconsistencies which aroused Laing's suspicions do not really exist.

Schipper, however, adopted Laing's view that the poems were inconsistent. Sir W. A. Craigie had not yet shown how the leaves of MF. had been misplaced. Schipper (1) misapprehended the sequence of stanzas as they were transcribed by Maitland, (2) wrongly assumed that Maitland and Reidpeth transcribed the stanzas in the same sequence, and (3) wrongly claimed that his objections applied in the same way to B. as to MF. and R. (S. ed., p. 146). Schipper therefore considered it necessary to place lines 405-406 in a section later than 77-80: but that is already the sequence in B., and in MF. when the leaves are correctly rearranged. An additional indication that Maitland knew that the last poem concluded with line 552 and that he closed it there may be observed in his colophon 'Quod Kennedy to dumbar' after that line, in addition to the 'Quod Kennedie to dumbar ut sequitur' with which he opens the final section of the poem at line 249; he provided no such final note for the other sections. Reidpeth, unaware that he is at the end, omits this colophon as a redundancy.

Schipper recast the whole series of poems to form six poems instead of four. He takes as basis the text of R. (and, as he thinks, MF.):

I. 1-24 by Dunbar (3 stanzas).
II. 25-48, by Kennedy (3 stanzas).
III. 49-64, 129-136, by Dunbar (3 stanzas).
IV. 369-552, by Kennedy (23 stanzas).
V. 137-192, 65-128, 193-248, by Dunbar (22 stanzas).
VI. 249-368, by Kennedy (15 stanzas).

Then, to adhere to 'artistic principles' and to smooth out apparent inconsistencies, he remodels the whole series, editing it in the following form:

I. 1-24, by Dunbar (3 stanzas).
II. 25-48, by Kennedy (3 stanzas).
III. 49-64, 129-136, by Dunbar (3 stanzas).
IV. 249-256, 321-360, 473-552, by Kennedy (16 stanzas).
V. 65-128, 137-248, by Dunbar, written from abroad (22 stanzas).
VI. 22 stanzas by Kennedy:
(*a*) 441-472, 377-392, 257-320, Dunbar being abroad.
(*b*) 393-440, 361-376, Dunbar being in Paris.

Baildon's edition adopts the text of Schipper.

It must be remarked on general grounds that not only do the versions of MF. and R., as analysed by Professor Craigie, provide no foundation for this reconstruction, but that B. also and CM. (so far as extant) are unmistakably opposed to it. CM. is a version contemporary with Dunbar, who may have had a hand in its editing. Schipper finds satisfaction in having reduced the inequality of length in the poems, but the reason why symmetry in this respect should be looked for is not clear. Examined in detail, his text is defective in many respects. There is a clear line of thought connecting lines 129-136 with 137 onwards, the theme being the misery of Kennedy as a beggar in Carrick and Galloway; S. breaks this thread by inserting 129-136 after 64. Dunbar's reference to 'Denseman on the rattis' (51) is more appropriate after his voyage past Denmark than before that voyage. Kennedy's defence of 'Irische' writing (345) is a reply to Dunbar's lengthy derogatory remarks on this subject in 105-112, rather than to line 49. Kennedy's first references (249-256) to the devil-ancestry of Dunbar are torn away from the more specific remarks which follow, and Kennedy's decision (323) not to prolong further his attack on Dunbar's ancestors is separated from the account of them which precedes and gives rise to that decision. It is true that in respect of the same theme Schipper succeeds in including 385-392 along with 257-320, but he has to leave 409-416 to another epistle, while the ordinary arrangement puts the whole of this episode into one section. The claim that, by making 129-136 succeed 64 to complete a separate poem, a reference to Quintyne has been appropriately introduced in answer to line 34, is pointless, for the answer to that line is already in Dunbar's reply (131). Again, Schipper says that his Section IV (by Kennedy) was written shortly before Dunbar's departure on his voyage, but this is contradicted by Dunbar himself in lines 89-90. The reconstruction is, moreover, deficient in its openings and endings. As compared with the openings of all sections of the authentic text, line 65 has an obvious weakness: and, in respect of this line, the inquiry whether Dunbar dares to flyte with Kennedy has surely no point at this late stage of the poem as reconstructed, though it has point in an early stanza of Dunbar's first attack. The metrical evidence is also noteworthy. In the generally accepted sequence, when once the opening shots have been exchanged, each poet delivers one, and only one, lengthy attack, each of which concludes with an extraordinarily elaborate volley of rhyming: though it is not accurate to say (M., p. 198) that Schipper misses this effect (for he does conclude a section with each of these two passages), the effect is largely lost, Schipper's final section ending weakly in this respect though not his sections IV and V.

To sum up, Schipper's reconstruction is open to the charge of arbitrary ingenuity, it is contrary to the versions of all three MSS. and of CM., and it betrays clearly that it is not the original form of *The Flyting*. It has been shown in Chapter VI that the difficulties of the authentic text, which Dr. Mackenzie has wisely adopted, are not insurmountable, and that reconstruction is unnecessary.

B. *The Devillis Inquest*

The poem itself has been described in Chapter VIII, and the sources are there detailed in a footnote. The poem is in B., MF., and R. The only coherent text is B. Successive editors have, however, condemned the three texts indiscriminately, and have thus been led to attempt synthetic versions for which there is no need.

MF., which is followed closely by R., has only 13 stanzas as compared with the 17 of B. The 'merchand' is dealt with quite differently in the two versions. Moreover, MF. has 5 stanzas which are not in B., and B. has 9 which are not in MF. The opening stanza of MF. differs from that of B., and records how the poet dreams he sees the Devil whispering at the ear of the 'commowne people'. Having defined the subject thus, though he has not mentioned the market-place as his scene, Maitland deals with the merchant, a series of craftsmen,—tailor, cobbler, baker, flesher, taverner,—the minstrel, the fishwives and hucksters, and sums up in stanza 10 with 'the rest of craftis'. But MF. continues unexpectedly, with the thief and then the courtier, and in a final stanza speaks of all estates, men and women, great and small, rich and poor, lay and clerical. These last three stanzas seem to be an afterthought, and they may be by a later hand than Dunbar's. But B. is not open to these objections. The introductory stanza of B. does not refer only to the 'commowne people' but to 'the peple' in 'the mercat'. Instead of tacking on the thief and courtier inconsequently, B. opens with the priest and courtier, following a sequence appropriate to his subject, as described in Chapter VIII. Similarly the thief in B. is properly placed among the hangers-on of the market, after the minstrel and dicer. In its last stanza, B. speaks of devils, instead of one devil as earlier in the poem, but the Devil has been described as being so ubiquitous that in final retrospect the use of the plural is reasonable enough. As an indication that B.'s stanzas on 'maltman', 'browstar', and 'smith' are spurious additions, Dr. Mackenzie (Appendix B of his edition) stresses the mere tagging on of the refrain in these cases. (Presumably he means to refer to the 'browstar' in this connexion when he mentions the 'bakstar', which occurs in all the MSS. and does not show the peculiarity of refrain which Dr. Mackenzie points out.) But Dunbar's vagaries make such an argument inconclusive, Of 54 poems by Dunbar with a refrain, 32 have the refrain with changes, but 22 without changes.

The evidence against B. as a sound text is therefore very slight. It remains to add that the editors have compiled their own composite texts, and that there has been some confusion as to the contents of the MSS. Laing follows B., inserting 'taverner' from MF. and R.—possibly to obtain the appropriate sequence of maltman, brewer and taverner; he concludes with the 'rest of craftis' from MF. and R., instead of the last stanza of B. In giving a list of stanzas peculiar to B., Laing omits those on the goldsmith, maltman, smith and dicer, and he wrongly includes the 'taverner' (which he himself points out in a later note is found only in MF. and R.), and the 'menstrall' and 'thief', both of which occur in all the MSS. The S.T.S. editor holds principally to B., but follows R. in inserting 'taverner' after 'fleschour', and 'rest of craftis' after 'fiche wyfis', and in including the two final stanzas of R. before finishing with the last stanza of B.; the insertions are indicated by square brackets. Schipper notes the curious fact that the S.T.S. editor in his footnotes has made no reference to MF. whatever, treating R. as if it were the only MS. other than B.: but it should be added that, in the appendix to the first volume of S.T.S., MF. is included among the sources of the poem. Schipper himself follows the same choice and sequence of stanzas as S.T.S., as far as the 'rest of craftis', with which he concludes. He wrongly states that he has taken 'browstar' from MF. (in which it does not occur), but in a later note he says correctly that it is in B. only. Dr. Mackenzie chooses MF. as basic source (he makes no mention of R.), following it in preference to B., but giving also, in italics, the stanzas found in B. only, with the exception of the 'merchand', which the editor records only in the notes, to avoid having two stanzas on this theme in his medley. The result is intended to show the 'probable sequence of re-handling'; the three final stanzas of MF. (not two, as he says in the appendix) are enclosed in square brackets to indicate that they are afterthoughts. There seems to be no reason for choosing the B. refrain for the 'Fleschour', and the 'you' of line 90 is presumably a printer's error.

BIBLIOGRAPHY

Works that are Referred to in the Text

1. Sources of the Poems

Aberdeen Minute Book of Seisins, Vols. II and III, in MS.
Chapman and Millar Prints.
Asloan MS.
Howard MS., Arundel No. 285, British Museum.
Appendix to Royal MSS., No. 58, British Museum.
Bannatyne MS.
Maitland Folio MS.
Reidpeth MS.
These have been detailed and described in Appendix I.

2. Public Records, in MS.

Compota Thesaurariorum Regum Scotorum, 1488-1492; 1500-1502; 1502-1504; 1504-1506; 1506-7; 1507-8; 1511-12; 1512-13. H.M. General Register House, Edinburgh.

Registrum Secreti Sigilli Regum Scotorum, Vol. II, 1498-1504. Vol. IV, 1508-1513. Register House.

Additional MSS., No. 7099, British Museum. *Transcripts from Accounts of Privy Purse Expenses of Henry VII.*

3. Other MSS.

Acta Facultatis Artium S. Andreae. St. Andrews University.

Annales Universitatis Glasguensis, Vol. I, 1451-1558. Vol. II, *Annales Collegii Facultatis Artium in Univ. Glas.*, 1451-1555. Glasgow University.

Livre des Conclusions de la Nation d'Allemagne, 1477-1492. Paris University Archives, No. 8.

Livre des Receveurs de la Nation d'Allemagne. H2588, Archives Nationales, Bibliothèque Nationale, Paris.

Livre des Conclusions de la Nation de Picardie, 1476-1483. Paris University Archives, No. 9.

Register of the Faculty of Theology, Paris University. MS. No. 5657A (Latin), Bibliothèque Nationale, Paris.

Cotton Vespasian C.xiv. British Museum.
Cotton Vitellius A.xvi. do.
Lansdowne MS., No. 762. do.

Forrest MS. (Harley, 1703) British Museum
Makculloch MS. (Laing MSS., No. 149). Edinburgh University Library.
MS. No. 394, Balliol College, Oxford.

4. EDITIONS OF DUNBAR'S WORKS

Baildon, H. B., *The Poems of William Dunbar*. Cambridge, 1907.
Laing, D., *The Poems of William Dunbar*, Vols. I and II. Edin., 1834. Supplement to Vol. I, 1865.
Mackenzie, Dr. W. Mackay, *The Poems of William Dunbar*. Edin., 1932.
Paterson, J., *The Life and Poems of William Dunbar*. Edin., 1860.
Schipper, J., *Poems of William Dunbar*. Vienna, 1894.
Small, J., *The Poems of William Dunbar*. S.T.S. Edin., 1884-1889. Vol. I, Memoir, by A. J. G. Mackay; Vol. II, Text, by J. Small; Vol. III, Notes and Glossary, by W. Gregor.

5. WORKS WHICH INCLUDE POEMS BY DUNBAR

Beattie, Wm., '*The Chepman and Myllar Prints*,' Edin., 1950.
Craigie, Sir W. A., *The Asloan MS*. S.T.S., Edin., 1923-4.
Craigie, Sir W. A., *The Maitland Folio MS*. S.T.S., Edin., 1919.
Ellis, G., *Specimens of Early English Poets*. London, 1801.
Hailes, Lord (Sir David Dalrymple), *Ancient Scottish Poems*. Edin., 1770.
Pinkerton, J., *Ancient Scotish Poems*. London, 1786.
Ramsay, Allan, *The Evergreen*. Edin., 1724.
Ritchie, Dr. W. Tod, *The Bannatyne MS*. S.T.S., Edin., 1928-1933.
Sibbald, J., *Chronicle of Scottish Poetry*. Edin., 1802.
Stevenson, G., *The Makculloch and the Gray MSS. together with the Chepman and Myllar Prints*. S.T.S., Edin., 1918.

6. STUDIES OF DUNBAR

Haliburton, H., *In Scottish Fields*. London, 1890.
Schipper, J., *William Dunbar: Sein Leben und seine Gedichte*. Berlin, 1884.
Smeaton, W. H. O., *Dunbar* (Famous Scots Series). Edin., 1898.
Taylor, Miss R. A., *Dunbar the Poet and his Period*. London, 1931.

7. OTHER LITERARY WORKS

Amours, F. J., *Scottish Alliterative Poems in Riming Stanzas*. S.T.S., Edin., 1897.
Amours, F. J., *The Original Chronicle of Andrew of Wyntoun*. S.T.S., Edin., 1914.
Atkinson, G., *Works of François Villon*. London, 1930.
Brown, J. T. T., *The 'Wallace' and the 'Bruce' Restudied*. Bonn, 1900.
Couch, Sir A. T. Quiller, *Studies in Literature*, Second Series. Cambridge, 1922.
Gibson, A., *New Light on Allan Ramsay*. Edin., 1927.
Gray, Miss M., *Lancelot of the Laik*. S.T.S., Edin., 1912.

Hamer, D., *The Works of Sir David Lindsay*. S.T.S., Edin., 1930-1934.
Irvine, D., *Lives of the Scottish Poets*. Edin., 1810.
Langhorne, J., *Poetical Works*, London, 1804.
Laing, D., *Adversaria*. Edin., 1867.
MacCracken, H. N., *The Minor Poems of John Lydgate*. E.E.T.S., London, 1934.
Mackenzie, Dr. A. M., *An Historical Survey of Scottish Literature to 1714*. London, 1933.
Moir, J., *The Actis and Deidis of the Illustre and Vailyeand Campioun Schir William Wallace, Knicht of Ellerslie*. S.T.S., Edin., 1889.
Murray, Miss H. M. R., *Erthe upon Erthe*. E.E.T.S., London, 1911.
Ritchie, Dr. R. L. G., *The Buik of Alexander*. S.T.S., Edin., 1921-1925.
Schipper, J., *The Poems of Walter Kennedy*. Vienna, 1902.
Shairp, J. C., *Sketches in History and Poetry*. Edin., 1887.
Skeat, W. W., *The Bruce: John Barbour*. S.T.S., Edin., 1894.
Small, J., *Poetical Works of Gavin Douglas*. Edin., 1874.
Smeaton, W. H. O., *Allan Ramsay* (Famous Scots Series). Edin., 1896.
Smith, Miss J. M., *The French Background of Middle Scots Literature*. Edin., 1934.
Stevenson, J. H., *Gilbert Haye's Manuscript*, 1456. S.T.S., Edin., 1901-1914.
Wood, H. Harvey, *Poems of Robert Henryson*. Edin., 1933.

8. Public Records

Accounts of the Lord High Treasurer of Scotland

Vol. I, 1473-1498, ed. T. Dickson. Edin., 1877.
II, 1500-1504, ed. Sir J. Balfour Paul. Edin., 1900.
III, 1506-1507 do. 1901.
IV, 1507-1513, do. 1902.
V, 1515-1531, do. 1903.
VI, 1531-1538, do. 1905.

Exchequer Rolls of Scotland

Vol. IV, 1406-1436, ed. G. Burnett. Edin., 1880.
V, 1437-1454 do. 1882.
VI, 1455-1460, do. 1883.
VII, 1460-1469, do. 1884.
VIII, 1470-1479 do. 1885.
X, 1488-1496, do. 1887.
XI, 1497-1501, do. 1888.
XII, 1502-1507, do. 1889.
XIII, 1508-1513, ed. G. Burnett and A. J. G. Mackay. Edin., 1891.
XIV, 1513-1522, ed. G. Burnett and A. J. G. Mackay. Edin., 1893.

Register of the Privy Seal of Scotland, Vol. I, 1488-1529, ed. M. Livingstone. Edin., 1908.

Register of the Great Seal of Scotland, Vol. I, 1306-1424, ed. J. M. Thomson. Revised Edition, Edin., 1912.

Register of the Great Seal of Scotland, Vol. II, 1424-1513, ed. Sir J. Balfour Paul. Edin., 1882.

Acts of the Lords Auditors of Causes and Complaints, 1466-1494, ed. T. Thomson. 1839.

Acts of the Lords of Council in Civil Causes, Vol. I, 1478-1495, ed. T. Thomson, 1839.

Acts of Parliaments of Scotland, Vol. II, 1424-1567, ed. T. Thomson. 1814.

Calendar of Documents relating to Scotland, Vol. IV, 1357-1509, ed. J. Bain. Edin., 1888.

Calendar of Spanish State Papers, 1485-1509, ed. G. A. Bergenroth. London, 1862.

Extracts from the Records of the Burgh of Edinburgh, Vol. I, ed. Sir J. D. Marwick. Edin., 1869.

Extracts from the Burgh Records of Aberdeen, 1398-1570, ed. J. Stuart. Spalding Club, Aberdeen, 1844.

9. OTHER HISTORICAL WORKS

Abelson, P., *The Seven Liberal Arts*. New York, 1906.

Adamson, J. W., *A Short History of Education*. Cambridge, 1919.

Anderson, J. M., *Early Records of the University of St. Andrews*. Edin., 1926.

Anderson, J. and Grant, F. J., *Protocol Book of Gavin Ros*, 1512-1532. Scottish Record Society. Edin., 1908.

Anstey, H., *Munimenta Academica Oxon.*, Vol. I. Rolls Series. London, 1868.

Arnot, H., *History of Edinburgh*. Edin., 1779.

L'Art de Vérifier les Dates. Paris, 1783.

Barbé, L. A., *In Byways of Scottish History*. London, 1912.

Bentley, S., *Excerpta Historica*. London, 1831.

Boase, C. W., *Register of the University of Oxford*. Oxford, 1885.

Brown, P. Hume, *History of Scotland*. Cambridge, 1911.

Bryce, W. M., *The Scottish Greyfriars*. Edin., 1909.

Buchanan, G., *History of Scotland*. Trans. J. Aikman. Glasgow, 1827.

Coissac, J.-B., *Les Universités d'Écosse*. Paris, 1915.

Conway, Miss A., *Henry VII's Relations with Scotland and Ireland*. Cambridge, 1932.

Coulton, G. G., *Five Centuries of Religion*. Cambridge, 1927.

Coulton, G. G., *Scottish Abbeys and Social Life*. Cambridge, 1933.

Dickson, R., *Introduction of the Art of Printing into Scotland*. Aberdeen, 1885.

Dowden, Bishop J., *The Bishops of Scotland before the Reformation*. Glasgow, 1912.

Dowden, Bishop J., *The Medieval Church in Scotland*. Glasgow, 1910.

Dunbar, Sir A. H., *Scottish Kings*. Edin., 1899.

Edinburgh, 1329-1929. Edin., 1929.

Fischer, T., *The Scots in Germany*. Edin., 1902.

Fraser, Sir W., *The Book of Carlaverock*. Edin., 1873.

Fraser, Sir W., *Memorials of the Montgomeries, Earls of Eglinton*. Edin., 1859.

Gairdner, J., *Letters and Papers of Richard III and Henry VII*. London, 1863.

Gairdner, J., *Memorials of King Henry VII*. London, 1858.

Hannay, R. K., *The College of Justice*. Edin., 1933.

Hannay, R. K., *Statutes of the Faculty of Arts*. St. Andrews University Publications, No. VII. St. Andrews, 1910.

Herkless, J. and Hannay, R. K., *The Archbishops of St. Andrews*. Edin., 1907.

Innes, C., *Munimenta Alme Universitatis Glasguensis*. The Maitland Club, Glasgow, 1854.

Innes, C., *Scotland in the Middle Ages*. Edin., 1860.

Jusserand, J. A. A. J., *English Wayfaring Life in the Middle Ages*. London, 1889.

Kerr, J., *Scottish Education*. Cambridge, 1913.

Leith, W. F., *Pre-Reformation Scholars in Scotland in the Sixteenth Century*. Glasgow, 1915.

Leland, J., *De Rebus Britannicis Collectanea*. London, 1774.

Leslie, Bishop J., *The Historie of Scotland*. Trans. J. Dalrymple, ed. E. G. Cody. S.T.S., Edin., 1888.

Little, A. G., *Studies in English Franciscan History*. Manchester, 1917.

Lyon, C. J., *History of St. Andrews*. Edin., 1843.

Macfarlane's Genealogical Collections. J. T. Clark. Scottish History Society, Edin., 1900.

Major, John, *History of Greater Britain*. Trans. and ed. A. Constable. Memoir by A. J. G. Mackay. Scottish History Society, Edin., 1892.

Melville, E. W. M. Balfour, *James I, King of Scots*. London, 1936.

Menary, Dr. G., *Life and Letters of Duncan Forbes of Culloden*. London, 1936.

Michel, F., *Les Écossais en France: les Français en Écosse*. London, 1862.

Mill, Miss A. J., *Medieval Plays in Scotland*. St. Andrews University Publications, No. XXIV. Edin., 1927.

Owst, G. R., *Preaching in Medieval England*. Cambridge, 1926.

Paterson, J., *History of the County of Ayr*. Ayr, 1847.

Paul, Sir J. Balfour, *The Scots Peerage*. Edin., 1904-1914.

Pitcairn, R., *Ancient Criminal Trials in Scotland*, 1488-1624. The Maitland Club, Edin., 1833.

Pitcairn, R., *Historical and Genealogical Account of the Principal Families of the Name of Kennedy*. The Bannatyne Club, Edin., 1830.

Pitscottie, R. Lindesay of, *The Historie and Cronicles of Scotland*. Edited A. J. G. Mackay. S.T.S., Edin., 1899.

Rait, R. S., *History of Scotland*. London, 1914.

Rashdall, H., *Universities of Europe in the Middle Ages*. Edited F. M. Powicke and Emden. Oxford, 1936.

Reports of the High Court of Justiciary in Scotland, Vol. I. Edin., 1895.

Robertson, D. and Wood, Miss M., *Castle and Town*. Edin., 1928.

Samaran, C. and Moé, A. van, *Auctarium Chartularii Universitatis Parisiensis*, Vol. III. Paris, 1935.

Simpson, Dr. W. D., *University of Aberdeen Quatercentenary of the Death of Hector Boece*. Aberdeen, 1937.

Scotichronicon. Fordun, J. and Bower, W. Trans. F. J. H. Skene. Edited W. F. Skene. Edin., 1872.

Smeaton, W. H. O., *The Story of Edinburgh*. London, 1905.

Terry, Prof. C. S., *A History of Scotland*. Cambridge, 1920.

Wilson, D., *Memorials of Edinburgh in the Olden Time*. Edin., 1848.

10. PERIODICALS

Edinburgh Bibliographical Society Publications, Vol. I (E. G. Duff, 'Notes on a Leaf of an Early Scottish Donatus'), 1896.

Modern Languages Review, October 1933 (Review by Prof. Bruce Dickins of Dr. W. M. Mackenzie's *The Poems of William Dunbar*.

Publications of the Modern Languages Association of America, Vol. XLVI, 1931 (P. H. Nichols, 'William Dunbar as a Scottish Lydgatian').

Saga-Book of the Viking Society, Vol. XII, 1945 (A. S. C. Ross, 'Jólaköttur, Yuillis Yald, and Similar Expressions').

The Scottish Antiquary, or Northern Notes and Queries, Vol. XIII, October 1898 (Review of W. H. O. Smeaton's *Dunbar*).

Scottish Historical Review

Vol. I, Jan. 1904 (J. T. T. Brown, 'The Bannatyne Manuscript').

Vol. III, July 1906 (Translation, by Sir H. Maxwell, of the *Scalacronica* of Sir T. Gray).

Vol. IV, Oct. 1906 ('Tilting in Tudor Times').

Vol. VIII (J. M. Anderson, 'The Beginnings of St. Andrews University, 1410-1418'; Miss M. Gray, 'Vidas Achinlek, Chevalier'; W. W. Skeat, 'The Author of *Lancelot of the Laik*'; A. Lawson, Note on Miss Gray's Article).

Vol. XVII (Sir J. Balfour Paul, 'Clerical Life in Scotland in the Sixteenth Century').

Scottish Notes and Queries, Third Series, Vol. IX, 1931 (T. Innes, 'Two Countesses of Moray').

Times Literary Supplement

21st Feb. and 10th July 1924 (Professor Bruce Dickins, 'Contributions to the Interpretation of Middle Scots Texts', and 'Middle Scots Texts'.)

14th Dec. 1935 (Professor Dickins, 'The Flyting of Dunbar and Kennedie').

8th April 1939 (J. W. Baxter, 'William Dunbar').

INDEX TO THE POEMS

GENERAL INDEX